LOGISTICS HORIZONTAL COLLABORATION

AN AGENT-BASED SIMULATION APPROACH
TO MODEL COLLABORATION DYNAMICS

物流横向协作体系

一种基于多智能体建模法的

仿真研究

朱杰 著

重庆大学出版社

内容简介

产能利用低、交货周期长、成本高、规模不足是物流和供应链运营之间存在的主要矛盾。企业间进行物流横向合作与协同是当今世界应对物流竞争与挑战的一种创新方法。这种合作协同式物流在实践中迅速发展，然而其对参与伙伴和供应链网络的影响却被低估。本专著基于案例研究并采用与多智能体仿真相结合的方法，研究探索物流横向协作的关键要素、模式与过程，并从微观到宏观层面量化分析企业行为与合作网络对物流系统的影响。研究结果表明，在物流横向协作背景下，各类合作与信息共享在多个维度产生了更好的收益。本专著为实践者和学者提供了关于如何开展供应链项目合作或研究的见解与参考。

图书在版编目（CIP）数据

物流横向协作体系: 一种基于多智能体建模法的
仿真研究: 英文 / 朱杰著. --重庆: 重庆大学出版社，
2021.10
ISBN 978-7-5689-2893-9

Ⅰ.①物... Ⅱ.①朱... Ⅲ.①物流－系统建模－英文
Ⅳ.①F253.9

中国版本图书馆CIP数据核字（2021）第147847号

物流横向协作体系：一种基于多智能体建模法的仿真研究
Wuliu Hengxiang Xiezuo Tixi: Yizhong Jiyu Duozhinengti Jianmofa De Fangzhen Yanjiu
朱 杰 著

责任编辑：牟 妮　　　　　　版式设计：牟 妮
责任校对：王 倩　　　　　　责任印制：赵 晟

*

重庆大学出版社出版发行
出版人：饶帮华
社址：重庆市沙坪坝区大学城西路21号
邮编：401331
电话：（023）88617190　88617185（中小学）
传真：（023）88617186　88617166
网址：http://www.cqup.com.cn
邮箱：fxk@cqup.com.cn（营销中心）
全国新华书店经销
重庆升光电力印务有限公司印刷

*

开本：720mm×1020mm　1/16　印张：17.25　字数：440千
2021年10月第1版　2021年10月第1次印刷
ISBN 978-7-5689-2893-9　定价：96.00元

CONTENTS

LIST OF
ILLUSTRATIONS

- TABLES -

- FIGURES -

INTRODUCTION
TO THE THESIS

Underutilized capacity, long shipping lead time, high costs and lack of sufficient scale are showcases of logistics inefficiencies that have troubled many supply chain operations. Logistics horizontal collaboration (LHC) is believed to be an innovative approach to tackle the increasing logistics challenges. This kind of collaborative logistics is quickly gaining momentum in practice but relevant contributions in literature are scarcely seen. So far it remains unclear how LHC could be structured and operated given the limited understanding of the various characteristics and forms of LHC between companies. Furthermore, the explicit impact of LHC on the participating partners, as well as on the supply chain system is understudied. Very few studies have explored the process of collaboration and how it links to performance behaviours.

Case studies and agent-based simulation are employed in this thesis to study the research gaps identified above. Case studies are initially conducted to examine the key elements which can support the design of LHC, and to make a classification of models for collaboration. These are followed by agent-based simulation to model a typical collaboration process and work out what benefits would emerge if participating in horizontal collaboration and how the collaboration can produce the impacts on the supply chain operations for individuals and the system as a whole.

The case studies suggest that "collaboration structures" "collaboration objectives" "collaboration intensity", and "collaboration modes" are the four key elements critical to the design of a LHC project. Each element represents an important aspect of the collaboration and exhibits different characteristics and forms. Based on these key elements, several typologies are derived which together provide a comprehensive view to explain the different types of LHC in practice. The simulation modelling demonstrates that LHC can significantly benefit the logistics efficiency in terms of capacity utilization and customer service in the sense of order fill-rate, and such beneficial effects are consistently observed in different supply chain environments. In particular, LHC can produce better logistics performance in a relationship-based supply chain network where downstream customers can support upstream shippers with more stable and predictable demands. On the other hand, information sharing in the collaboration, for the most part, does not facilitate the higher collaboration gains for partners. Specifically, sharing either the demand or supply information in the horizontal collaboration is not helpful in increasing collaboration gains. Hence there is a difference for the value of information sharing in the context of horizontal collaboration as opposed to vertical collaboration, the latter of which is often justified as providing more beneficial gains. The research findings provide insights for practitioners and scholars about how to develop a type of collaboration project or study, as well as enabling a better understanding of the dynamic collaboration effects.

Zhu Jie

June 2021

CHAPTER 1
INTRODUCTION

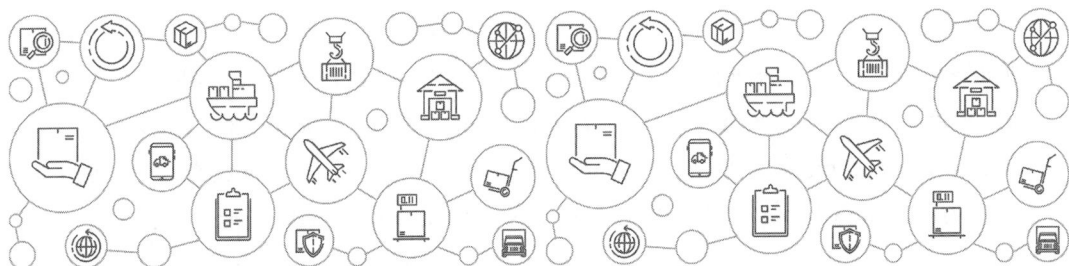

1.1 Background

Since the 1990s, the rapid development in information technology and the fast pace of globalization have brought a great change to the marketplace and business operations. Under such circumstances, the business operations have become more complicated. The business companies must view their operations from a totally new perspective — to operate from a broader view in terms of time and space. Supply chain management is developed from such a point of view which advocates that companies should act as a network that is based upon the concepts of collaboration and process integration (Sabath, 1998). This is because in today's global environment it is "supply chains that compete rather than companies" (Christopher, 2011).

Among the various supply chain activities, logistics is a key function since it acts as a physical link that connects the companies in the supply chain, enabling the flow of materials and resource (Coyle et al. 2003, Naim et al. 2006), making it a key integral part of the overall supply chain management (Ellram, 1991). In the execution of supply chain management, managing the logistics effectively is vital to enable the smooth running of a supply chain system because the failures in the logistics service would affect the business performance, either directly or indirectly, through sales, costs and quality of service. Thus, in an era of fast changing marketplaces and fierce competitions, mitigating the inefficiencies and risks in logistics can directly benefit the company's business operations and contribute to the achievement of a sustainable competitive advantage.

Entering into the 21st century, world economy growth has slowed down sharply and is battling with severe depression following the global financial crisis starting from 2008. In the meantime the pressure of market competition is increasing significantly at a global scale, particularly for commodities and services. In this situation, more companies are now trying to identify new ways and better ways to decrease operating costs in order to sustain their profitability and healthy development. They have increasingly realized the importance of effective supply chain management to their global business, and logistics as a key part of this. This in turn has elevated the need to improve key logistics activities such as warehousing, transportation and distribution. These activities are directly associated with the services needed to deliver products to customers, and the associated costs. It is, therefore, now becoming critical that companies start to re-think and re-build their logistics processes for the purpose of cost saving and better delivery performance for customers.

Unfortunately, nowadays a great many companies are being troubled by the logistics inefficiencies, reflected by issues such as an underutilized transportation capacity, a long shipping lead time, a high cost and a lack of sufficient scale (Cruijssen et al. 2010, Palmer et al. 2012). In today's marketplace, companies often consider two logistics strategies for operating their supply chains (Abdur Razzaque and Chen Sheng, 1998).

(1) Outsourcing logistics — the dominant approach adopted by many industries and firms who want to concentrate on their core competency (Africk and Markeset, 1996, Foster, 1994) .

(2) Self-building (in-house) logistics — adopted by traditional vertical integration companies, or companies that increasingly believe they can build the logistics as a core competency (e.g. Amazon, JD.com)

There are intrinsic disadvantages in following either of these models, however. The first model (outsourcing) often results in a high cost with poor stability, predictability and flexibility in logistics service operations due to the shipper's lack of direct control over logistics. The shipper's logistics performance is greatly affected by, and subject to, the capability of the outsourced logistics service providers (LSPs), and this represents a significant risk to the shipper's ability to fulfil customer demand. The second model (self-building) requires a huge initial investment and entails significant challenges regarding how to plan a better demand supply matching between the logistics capacity being first positioned in the market and the actual demand volume that can be attracted to fill this capacity. If large, sufficient, stable and structural freight flow cannot be maintained, significant operating costs must be borne without creating any value which negatively affects the overall business performance. In addition, most companies sell a great variety of products with countless configurations, the demand for which is extremely difficult, or impossible, to anticipate reliably, thereby creating a great risk that the pre-positioned capacity will be either under-utilized or over-stretched.

Operational inefficiencies seem to be a common problem in either the outsourcing or self-building logistics. One of the biggest root causes can be attributed to the fragmentation in both the demand and supply resources (Cruijssen et al. 2010). Most companies nowadays (shippers or logistics service providers) are highly dependent upon their own logistics networks and capacity if they are to fulfil the demand from their customers (Palmer et al. 2012). Due to the reactive and asset heavy nature of logistics and transport businesses, operations efficiency is vulnerable to the fast changing demand if the capacity utilization is completely planned for and subject to the company's own demand sources. Frequent capacity underutilization, on the one hand, or shortages, on the other, can become a critical issue when the demand is not stable, structural and predictable (Zhu et al. 2014). The unpredictability and structural inefficiencies have been a long-standing problem in the logistics marketplace, since it generally lacks an effective approach to connecting the existing available, but fragmented, logistics resources and networks for more productive use. Consequently, the logistics industry is undergoing a fundamental change in its operations style to counterattack the logistics inefficiencies as well as the deficiencies found in the current ways of managing logistics. One innovative logistics concept that has recently emerged is Logistics Horizontal Collaboration (LHC), which aims to bring together the compatible companies and parallel supply chains to share logistics capacity and capabilities in order to significantly improve the efficiency, flexibility and stability for running logistics.

1.2 The New Logistics Model—Horizontal Collaboration

In the past few years, logistics horizontal collaboration (LHC) has been gaining attention as a new business concept that can help to make the logistics sector more efficient, effective and sustainable. Horizontal collaboration in logistics is defined as active collaboration between two or more firms that operate at the same level of the supply chain and perform comparable logistics functions (Cruijssen et al. 2007a).

An important distinction from traditional supplier-to-customer logistics collaboration is that horizontal collaboration encourages coordination and integration across rather than along the supply chains (as shown in Figure 1.1). This collaboration could be organized between suppliers upstream, or between customers downstream, who might belong to different supply chains but who are willing to form partnerships to share part of their logistics resources, such as transportation and warehousing. Under this logistics paradigm, a fragmented demand in logistics system can be effectively orchestrated to enable large, stable and structural freight flow, while a dispersed supply, such as transport capacity, can be additionally deployed at the cross-supply chain network level where its overall utilization rate can go up significantly, leading to greater cost savings.

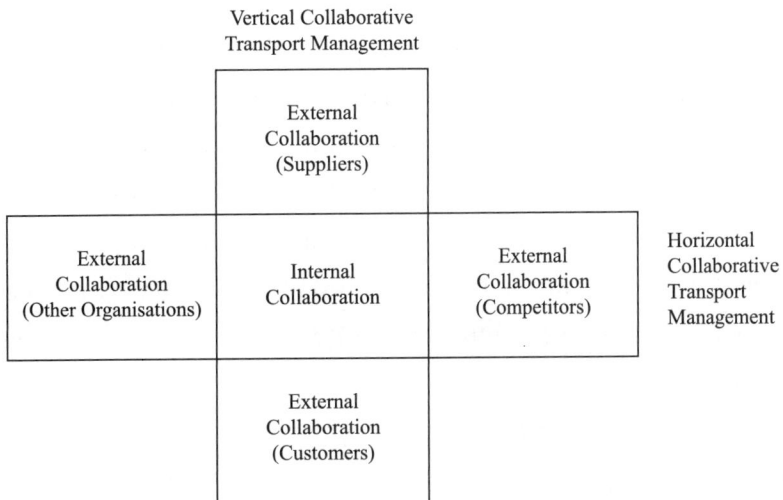

Vertical Collaborative
Transport Management

	External Collaboration (Suppliers)	
External Collaboration (Other Organisations)	Internal Collaboration	External Collaboration (Competitors)
	External Collaboration (Customers)	

Horizontal Collaborative Transport Management

Figure 1.1 Differences between vertical and horizontal collaboration in logistics and transport (Mason et al. 2007)

One notable form of LHC is the collaborative distribution of goods between compatible shippers. In traditional vertical logistics collaboration, major interactions are between shippers and customers with the priority to coordinate the logistics process so that relevant shipments could be delivered on-time. In such situations, the logistics distributions from the various shippers to the various customers are independent and separate. From the network perspective, there are considerable overlaps of the transport networks and goods are moved in parallel supply chains, which is very inefficient. Alternatively, horizontal logistics collaboration encourages shippers across these parallel supply chains to work more closely and proactively to plan and consolidate their goods in more synchronized ways, hence increasing the load utilization and cutting down the cost before shipments are delivered to the next stage of the supply chain.

Horizontal collaboration is in a sense an effective supplementation to supply chain logistics vertical collaboration to enable better optimization over the entirety of the logistics processes in the supply chain network. It can be expected that by collaborating horizontally, considerable improvements can be achieved in terms of asset utilization, the total logistics cost and the carbon footprint, while also, in many cases, improving the service level towards customers. Horizontal collaboration has until now, however, not been widely practised in the logistics marketplace, since its unfamiliar and complex nature has made it difficult to be implemented broadly (Palmer et al. 2012). Consequently, there is a strong need for both practitioners and researchers to contribute more relevant research in this area, so that better understandings can be developed regarding the forms and characteristics of such new collaboration model in logistics, eventually facilitating more successful implementations and thus contributing to a future improvement in the logistics industry.

1.3 Motivation

The motivation for this research is entirely driven by the practical issues and concerns I experienced in the logistics industry. Before 2012 I worked in an American PC manufacturing company based in China, and was responsible for architecting logistics projects and systems. It was at that time when I was deeply impressed by the complexity to manage logistics, and how difficult it is to maintain the logistics operations efficiency, the importance of which the company strongly emphasized and is striving for excellence.

Unfortunately, logistics was often found to be the biggest constraint for this company, along with its extended supply chain, reflected by the high cost, long order delivery time, frequent capacity shortages or low utilization, unpredictability in demand and unstable service, etc. These logistics issues significantly hampered the other operations in the supply chain and prevented the company from retaining leadership in what was a hyper-competitive marketplace.

More specifically, I was able to observe very low utilization and delays in the daily logistics operations. This directly incurred high shipping costs for the company itself and poor delivery service for customers. The main reason for this low utilization was a lack of sufficient scale. For example, in order to maintain the delivery frequency and lead time commitment for customers, the company had to ship out orders every day regardless of whether the trucks, containers or airplane space were being efficiently used. Furthermore, transportation solutions such as rail often required a minimum volume threshold to provide the service. This led to difficulties in attracting sufficient volume in a very short time window and hence delayed the transportation. High order volatility and the unbalanced ordering pace and size from customers were also among the root causes for low utilization and delays. Logistics capacity needed to be planned in advance according to a forecast, but high demand variations led to the adoption of a conservative and high buffer strategy, with slack capacity being retained in order to cope with uncertainty. Capacity in the logistics marketplace, however, is unlike inventory that can be carried over: it is only usable for a specific time and if it is not used it perishes, causing frequent waste and low utilization. On the other hand, unbalanced order waves can pressurize the supply of capacity. Customers tended to release big orders, often at the end of the order receiving cycle, creating extreme challenges in preparing capacity in both production and logistics. In these circumstances supply shortages were also inevitable, causing shipment delays.

These problems are deeply rooted in the current supply chain and logistics configurations and show that using the traditional and internal optimization methods are difficult and unlikely to lead to significant improvements. By analysing the freight flow network, however it was found that many other manufacturers' outbound logistics networks were in parallel and were highly overlapped. These manufactures were all centrally clustered in one part of China producing and shipping orders to the same regions or the same customers. Many of them were also in collaborative relationships in supply and manufacturing (the so called "vertically clustered supply chain"). The question arising, therefore, is that if they can be clustered for manufacturing and supply, why can they not be clustered to promote collaborative outbound logistics? In fact, many opportunities for collaboration in logistics that could fundamentally change the way the current logistics system behaves have been identified. Prior to I left this sector, however, practical implementation of new paradigms were only just beginning with a few trials in which I was involved. From the success of these trials, however, it was evident that this new style of logistics management had much potential and it was this realization that encouraged the decision to undertake further study of this newer kind of collaborative logistics system.

From a broader perspective, the research also seeks to make a small contribution to the development of the logistics industry in China. As can be seen from Figure 1.2, when comparing the logistics cost in relation to the GDP of China, USA and Japan (the three largest economies), it is noticeable to see that China spends more than double the amount on logistics to support its GDP growth. The high cost percentage (near 1/5 GDP) strongly indicates the low levels of efficiency in the current logistics operations within the various industries constituting the Chinese economy. The problems of energy wastage, traffic congestion, and environmental pollution are becoming a serious and terrible fact in China, despite, or perhaps because of, its rapid growth. Poorly implemented logistics have contributed greatly to the growing severity of these issues, and this needs to be addressed urgently. Realistically, the Chinese economy has to change its growth pattern from extensive to intensive, increasing quality rather than quantity, as is always stressed by the state government. This requires logistics as the key player in the economic activities to become more intensive rather than extensive type of development. The concept of logistics horizontal collaboration strongly fits with this strategic goal since it is much emphasized on maximizing the utilization of resources in the current system without or reduces the need for adding new supplies/resources. The Chinese Ministry of Commerce made a clear official statement in early 2013 to encourage research and practice in collaborative and synchronized distribution, which is a major type of horizontal collaboration in logistics and freight transport, for the purposes of cost reduction and efficiency improvement.

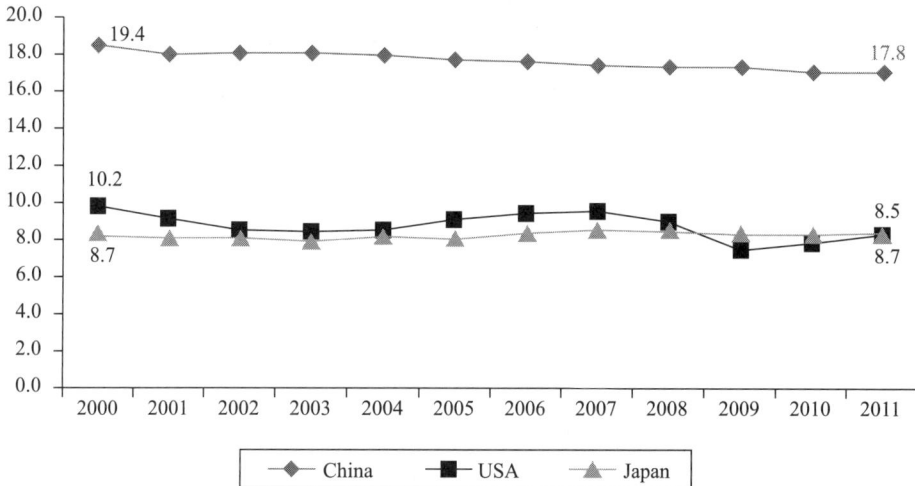

Figure 1.2 Logistics cost comparison between China, USA, Japan (in GDP percentage)
(Source: China Logistics Information Centre)

In the meantime the rapid development of some industries in China has imposed significantly greater challenges for logistics. One typical example is the E-commerce industry. The pace of the development of E-commerce has become explosive since 2010 and it is now among the largest, as well as the most advanced, online marketplaces in the world. With the hyper-growing population of customers shopping online every day, logistics infrastructure and delivery services have become a terrible constraint. People often have to wait for their orders to be delivered for more than one week, forcing the industry players to begin huge investment in E-commerce logistics. The dramatic growth in E-commerce businesses has led to an equally dramatic increase in the number of logistics companies offering delivery services, but most of these are SMEs with just one or two trucks/vans. The high degree of fragmentation is the current situation for E-commerce logistics. This has resulted in severe competition based on low prices, which has in turn caused the E-commerce logistics to have very low profits, inefficient and poor service performance among E-commerce logistics providers. To fundamentally change this situation requires fundamentally different thinking. Logistics companies, particularly small companies, need to be more collaborative rather than competitive to consolidate their supply power so that they can explore better the economy of scale in their operations to save costs, and to consolidate their distinguishing capabilities to offer customers much better service. Thus because of the high number of small logistics companies and the high level of fragmentation, logistics horizontal collaboration has a great potential to explore and bring the potentialities of these logistics SMEs into full play.

Furthermore, the recent communication with industry professionals has indicated that the developments of E-commerce marketplace in China have triggered a number of new trends that could profoundly affect the logistics styles, which include:

● Order immediacy (E-commerce logistics is now putting an unprecedented emphasis on delivery speed. Big companies are challenging to achieve delivery within 24 hours, or less).

● Omnichannel retailing (creating more channels for marketing, order receiving and logistics delivery paths and modes. This leads to smaller and fragmented orders, and further complexity to connect logistics to the various sales channels. Horizontal collaboration can be helpful for sellers to aggregate and deliver these small batch orders in economical and flexible ways).

● Online to offline integration (O2O). (Online retailers are developing strategic horizontal partnership with offline retailers to position inventory of goods nearest to customers, and explore alternative ways for sending and receiving parcels. A notable partnership example is seen between Walmart and JD.com).

● Cutting out the middle man and reducing the total logistics cost. Goods of origin shippers (factories/farms...) conduct multi-batch-small-volume deliveries directly to the community-based retailing outlets, rather than shipping to central and regional warehouses for order fulfilment. (To shift to such delivery pattern, it requires intensive horizontal collaboration between shippers for trunk, urban and last mile transport to ensure cost efficiency and service requirements).

● Asset light E-commerce sellers seek industry wide alliances to build open and shared logistics systems (e.g. Cainiao Network).

● Asset heavy E-commerce sellers with strong self-building logistics (who also declared themselves as "logistics companies") have begun to open their transport assets and network for social use, and with equal terms (e.g. JD.com).

- Business crossover has become prevalent. E-commerce companies are investing massively in building up their own logistics system nationwide, while traditional logistics providers are also building up their own E-commerce, taking full advantage of their robust logistics system. All have the target to enhance the customer shopping experience, a great part of which is tied to the service quality in logistics.

- New and non-traditional entrants (typically technology and internet companies) have started to challenge the traditional logistics styles. They have brought many new technologies into the marketplace (e.g. cloud computing/Internet of Things/drones/driverless cars), business models (e.g. crowdsourcing/sharing economy/social E-commerce), and mind-sets (e.g. Internet Thinking, User Focus, Iterative Thinking, Craftsmen Spirit, Minimalism).

These new trends have brought many new changes and challenges for the management of logistics operations, but on the other hand they have also served to stimulate new thinking and innovations to transform the traditional approaches to logistics. Logistics horizontal collaboration represents a particularly promising aspect of these new opportunities.

1.4 The Research Agenda

A review of the literature on horizontal collaboration in logistics and freight transport (see Chapter 2) reveals that there is a problem concerning how this horizontal collaboration should be structured and organized. Many of the previous studies have focused on the factors that are driving or prohibiting LHC, but fewer of them have studied the dynamic practice of LHC. There is also a fundamental lack of understanding in the literature regarding the distinguishing characteristics and forms of LHC between companies, especially when LHC is embedded into the wider supply chain context. Also, a lot of attention has been paid to studying the concept of horizontal collaboration itself, but the explicit impact of horizontal collaboration on the participating partners, as well as the supply chain system, remains understudied. Very few studies have explored the process of collaboration and how it links to performance behaviours.

The research agenda for this study is therefore to (1) examine the key elements which can support the design of LHC, and make a classification of models for collaboration; (2) model the collaboration process and work out what benefits would emerge from participating in horizontal collaboration and how this collaboration can produce impacts on supply chain operations for individuals and the system as a whole.

1.5 Expected Contribution of the Research

This study aims to contribute to the field of logistics horizontal collaboration in two main ways. First it aims systematically to explore and classify the different forms of collaboration by conducting a typological analysis. This can provide a study framework for a better understanding of the distinguishing features among the alternative types of collaboration, and how the collaboration can be structured and operated. Hence it will contribute to knowledge in the design phase of horizontal collaboration for logistics and transport.

The explicit modelling of the collaborative process and the effect on the participating partners and the supply chain system has rarely been attempted. This study, therefore, will also aim to contribute to the development of knowledge concerning how to model the various forms of collaboration in action and to examine the effect of this collaboration on supply chain performance. This helps to improve the knowledge in the operations phase of horizontal collaboration for logistics and transport.

This study is also expected to demonstrate that simulation modelling, specifically agent-based simulation, is a useful tool to analyse and explain the behaviour patterns of a supply chain logistics system, by explicitly defining and modelling the individuals of the system. This is where the empirical approach cannot make the definitive measurement and predictions.

1.6 Structure of the Thesis

Chapter 1 introduces the study background and points out some key issues and constraints that impede the healthy development of the logistics industry. It then introduces logistics horizontal collaboration (LHC) as the key focus of this study, and as a means of providing innovative thinking and measures to cope with the challenges of managing contemporary logistics and improving operations performance. Driven by the current gaps in knowledge, the objectives for this study are set out and the significance of the study is highlighted. This is then followed by an estimation of contributions and an outline of the thesis structure.

In Chapter 2, the study focuses on examining the existing literature in respect to LHC with the objective of developing knowledge on the state-of-art development in LHC, thereby laying a research basis for this study. Based on these gaps in the literature, research questions are developed to shape this study towards a particular area of interests and to situate this study among others. From the methodological point of departure, the use of agent-based modelling in the supply chain context is also reviewed.

Chapter 3 clarifies the methodologies applied during the present study. It first justifies the case study design, and explains the different data collection methods employed and the means used to analyse the data and synthesize findings. Second, it introduces the agent-based simulation to be applied after the case study, and demonstrates the purpose and value of applying it for the study of some particular issues that cannot be effectively addressed by other means. The links between the case study and the simulation are clarified and the step-by-step process of building the simulation model is described.

Chapter 4 studies LHC from a qualitative perspective. In this Chapter, the key objective is to examine the main elements that support the development of an LHC project, and to make a classification of models for collaboration based on the dynamic characteristics described by the key elements. An empirical case research is carried out following the data collection and the research process described in the research design in Chapter 3.

Chapter 5 studies LHC from the modelling perspective. It aims to quantify the benefits and effects of participating in LHC. It begins with an illustration of the development of a simulation model, which permits the findings drawn from the case studies and the literature review to be taken into account. It then presents the simulation results for the different experimental settings. The results are first analysed within each model setting to find out the key insights. Then the results of all settings are cross-compared to identify any further insights.

Chapter 6 discusses the main findings from the various parts of studies. The research questions are revisited and answered. The implications of the research, its contributions and limitations are discussed for practical and academic evaluation. The directions of potential future studies are also discussed.

Chapter 7 provides the concluding remarks to close the thesis.

CHAPTER 2
LITERATURE REVIEW

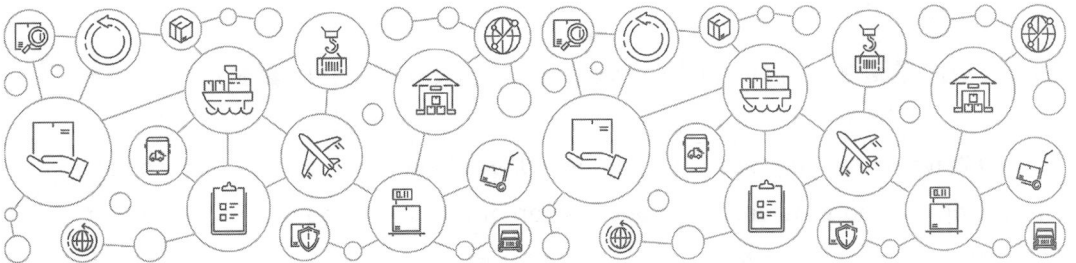

2.1 Introduction

The aim of this chapter is to review the relevant literature so as to lay a foundation for the subsequent research design and research work. To place the study into the context of the existing knowledge, two research fields of the literature are surveyed.

In Section 2.2, the study investigates the literature focusing on the collaboration of logistics in supply chain management. In the first place, the study provides a brief discussion of the conventional logistics collaboration that is vertical in nature, and illustrates the key concepts/approaches for logistics collaboration in the vertical supply chain context. Secondly, the existing literature regarding LHC is thoroughly reviewed and discussed. This contributes to the identification of the research gaps in the current body of knowledge in this area and helps to inform the formulation of the research questions in this study.

In Section 2.3, the research questions are developed based on the gaps identified in the current literature regarding LHC and the methodological needs to conduct the study.

In Section 2.4, the study examines how the agent-based simulation (ABS) approach has been used for modelling supply chain problems, in order to obtain useful insights with regards to how the ABS model could be designed in this study, and to specify the conditions and limitations of using this approach to model the supply chain issues.

Finally, Section 2.5 concludes the chapter.

2.2 The Collaboration of Logistics in Supply Chain Management

Collaboration in logistics is said to be achieved when two or more companies, including the logistics service providers, enter into a strategic partnership and exchange or share resources with the goal of making decisions and undertaking logistics-related activities that will generate benefits that they cannot (or only partially) generate individually. The level of collaboration can range from information exchange, joint planning, joint execution, to strategic alliance (Audy et al. 2010).

There are a variety of collaborative activities in the supply chain, including logistics collaboration, which can be grouped into two main categories according to their structure: vertical and horizontal (Simatupang and Sridharan, 2002). Vertical collaboration takes place between partners (typically suppliers and customers) located at different levels of the supply chain, while horizontal collaboration refers to partnership between two or more unrelated or competing organizations that operate at the same level of the supply chain (Barratt, 2004).

2.2.1 Vertical Collaboration in Logistics

Vertical collaboration has long been the dominant focus in logistics operations largely due to the prevalence of the supply chain management concept since 1990s. Supply chain management often requires tight and seamless integrations between different independent parties along the vertical chains for the purpose of better demand and supply matching to drive down cost and increase quality and service. This mainly focuses on the coordinated flow of materials and information throughout the whole chain, using joint decision-making processes and the management of relationships between partners to achieve success (Christopher, 1992; Mangan et al. 2008). The need to improve supply chain integration places increasing pressure on the logistics operations, which act as the physical links that connect the fixed points in the supply chain (Coyle et al. 2003), and hence is a key integral process in contributing to the overall goal of successful supply chain management (Ellram, 1991). Morash and Clinton (1997) note that effective supply chain integrations often stress the importance of time compression, which will result in more frequent logistics deliveries so as to cut down the stock holding at each channel echelon, as well as faster transit time that helps to shrink the pipeline inventory hence saving costs and increasing responsiveness. In the meantime, many supply chains are moving towards the adoption of a just-in-time concept (Ohno, 1988; Womack et al. 2007), and this also brings out more significant challenges in terms of managing the logistics activities both effectively and efficiently. These challenges and incentives arising from the supply chain management largely stimulate the need to organize the logistics operations towards more collaborative approaches, involving both upstream and downstream players working together to plan and execute the logistics flows better across the supply chain echelons. Thus, logistics vertical collaboration has often been considered to be the key area for investigation and development, both by practitioners and researchers.

There is extensive academic research on the aspects of vertical logistics collaborations in supply chains. For instance, Stefansson (2006) and Knemeyer et al. (2003) investigate the different types of 3PLs *(third party logistics — a provider of outsourced logistics services that encompass anything that involves management of the way resources are moved to the areas where they are required <Africk and Markeset, 1996, Foster, 1994>)* and the relations with supply chain partners to facilitate better organized logistics flows across the supply chain. Meanwhile, Tate (1996), Moore (1998) and Lambert et al. (1999) discuss the critical success factors for logistics partnerships, such as information sharing, fairness, trust, etc.; Stank et al. (2003) measure the collaborative logistics performance, such as supplier operational effectiveness, costs, customer satisfaction and loyalty, etc., resulting from such collaborative partnerships. There are also a large number of studies on the specific types of logistics vertical collaboration models between manufacturers and retailers. (e.g. Waller, et al. 1999; Slikker, et al. 2005; Tyan, et al. 2003; Esper and Williams, 2003, etc.) Among these works, two of the classic collaboration models have been widely researched and practiced: Vendor-Managed Inventory (VMI) and Collaborative Planning, Forecasting and Replenishment (CPFR). A brief illustration of these is given below to offer a taste of the typical kinds of issues that vertical logistics collaboration deals with.

Vendor-managed inventory (VMI) is a collaborative logistics replenishment model that is widely utilized in IT and the retailing industry. In this model, the downstream customers of the products (normally retailers) share the point of sales data (POS) directly with the product suppliers, instead of supplying inaccurate forecasts, while suppliers often fully take over control of the responsibility for the planning, replenishment and management of their customer's product inventory, usually at the customer's warehouse, although the ownership is still kept by suppliers until the final consumption is pulled through by customers. By operating in this way, significant benefits can be reaped such as increased shelf availability for customers, and reduced inventory costs resulting from better demand-supply matching (Chopra and Meindl, 2007, Salzarulo, 2006). Disney and Towill (2003) demonstrate at an operational level how the adoption of a collaborative vendor-managed inventory strategy can also have a beneficial effect on transport optimization and on increased flexibility.

In the USA, the widely adopted Collaborative Planning, Forecasting and Replenishment (CPFR) model in supply chain management has also been extended to have a logistics and transport dimension. Initially, the CPFR model mainly stressed the importance of the accuracy of the forecast (demands, orders, and sales), which can be improved by having upstream suppliers and downstream customers working more closely (VICS, 2004). Later, however, it was extended to incorporate logistics and transport planning, leading to the development of the "Collaborative Transportation Management" (CTM) model. Sutherland (2003) defines CTM as "a holistic process that brings together supply chain partners and logistics service providers to drive inefficiencies out of the transport planning and execution process". In particular, CTM is responsible for the conversion of "order forecasts" that are deployed through CPFR into "shipment forecasts". Karolefsky (2001) adds that CTM constitutes "the missing link" of supply chain collaboration. It means that the "order forecasts" stated by CPFR cannot be fulfilled without the effective development of "logistics forecasts". More importantly, CTM includes not only the concept of building strong relations between sellers and buyers, but also includes logistics service providers (Esper and Williams, 2003).

While many aspects of vertical collaboration in the supply chain have been considered, much less attention has been devoted to horizontal logistics collaboration. The next section therefore gives a thorough examination of the state of art development in this new area.

2.2.2 Horizontal Collaboration in Logistics

According to Cruijssen (2006, 2007b), logistics horizontal collaboration (LHC) refers to the active collaboration between two or more firms that operate at the same level of the supply chain and perform comparable logistics functions. It is noticeable that in the logistics and transport marketplace, generally LSPs consider horizontal collaboration to be an interesting approach to reduce costs, improve services, or protect market positions, among other things (Cruijssen et al. 2007a). Mason et al. (2007) point out that logistics and transport provision often has to be reactive to a fluctuating demand, and if the relevant assets can be additionally deployed on parallel supply chains, their utilization rate goes up by spreading the fixed costs of the assets among more activities, thus producing a more attractive business proposition. There is therefore considerable opportunity for research into horizontally collaborative solutions in the field of logistics.

While vertical logistics collaborations have already been covered by an abundant body of literature, research on horizontal collaboration in logistics is still in its infancy (Cruijssen et al. 2007a; Schulz and Blecken, 2010).

To identify the most relevant contributions of LHC, a search was performed among the key international journal data bases (Business Source Premier (EBSCO), ProQuest , ABI, Emerald, Web of Science (WOS), Science Direct, Google Scho lar), looking for the term *horizontal collaboration/cooperation/partnership/alliance AND logistics/freight/transport(ation)/delivery/distribution within titles*, key-words and the abstract of the paper. The following sub-sections will discuss the relevant literature in broadly chronological order. The major research focus and contributions will be illustrated.

2.2.2.1 Early Concepts and Cases Studies

LHC was first addressed by Caputo and Mininno (1996), who suggested that, apart from close collaboration between partners along the vertical supply chain, more effort should be devoted to collaboration at the horizontal level of the supply chain, and that considerable gains could be reaped if all related logistics activities could be initially optimized before they were transferred to the next level of the supply chain. In fact, it is argued that horizontal collaboration between institutions located at the same level of the supply chain is one of the important preconditions for setting up a more efficient vertical integration programme in the supply chain. Particularly, various potential policies for coordinated activities of horizontal collaboration between shippers or distributors are proposed, such as cross-sharing warehouses, standardization of packaging, part numbers, joint distribution, and purchasing. There were no real cases of implementation of these strategies in the 1990s, however, indicating that the majority of the practitioners and researchers at this time were unaware of this innovative business concept.

Entering into the 21st century, some researchers began to take notice of this innovative idea for operating logistics, with a few studies of some initial practices based on this new collaboration concept. Both Bahrami (2002a) and Hageback et al. (2004) undertook case studies to examine the cost savings from the economies of scale that can be explored from a particular collaboration strategy called "collaborative transportation" that aims to effectively merge partners' respective distribution activities with the purpose of increasing transport asset utilization, shipping frequency and reduce costs. Both studies identified the positive results realized by implementing such collaboration in their logistics operations and advise that such real life horizontal collaboration practice can bring significant cost reductions ranging from 2.4% to 9.8% and to over one-third depending on how it is organized and scaled up.

Later on, more case studies of the different kinds of collaboration practices in the industry were illustrated by Mason et al. (2007). Examples such as coordinated pallet distribution and collaborative commission of logistics IT services are proven to generate unique value beyond the traditional practice. Their case study emphasized the point that the newly innovative business models built on the concept of horizontal collaboration have the potential to further optimize logistics operations and enhance value solutions, thereby challenging many traditional methods for managing logistics.

2.2.2.2 Opportunities and Impediments

Since 2007, a growing awareness of the LHC concept and practice has attracted more studies. Among these, a great portion has specially focused on investigating the opportunities provided by and impediments facing LHC. With respect to the benefits of horizontal collaboration in logistics, the idea that cost reduction is one of the most relevant benefits is widely accepted, while the perceptions of the barriers to conducting LHC tend to vary given the specific operational scenarios.

Firstly, from the theoretical perspective, Cruijssen et al. (2007b) conducted an extensive literature review of the collaboration associated opportunities, impediments, and facilitators, drawing on general management and organizational theories, which provide some important implications for LHC. The major opportunities concluded for LHC can be categorized as (1) cost and productivity; (2) customer service; and (3) market position. For impediments, (1) partner selection; (2) determining and dividing gains; (3) negotiation position; and (4) information and communication technology (ICT) are the four main areas that can hamper LHC. In addition, major facilitators for horizontal partnership are identified as (1) information sharing; (2) incentive alignment; (3) relationship management; and (4) information technology.

To validate the literature review above, Cruijssen et al. (2007a) contributed a large-scale empirical survey on the opportunities and impediments for LHC and confirmed that most of the benefits and impediments drawn from the general literature are also well supported by LSPs. In particular, more than half of their surveyed LSP companies considered that by collaborating horizontally a company's productivity on its core activities will have high potential to increase, hence reducing costs. The core activities in the context of LSPs can refer to similar (or overlapping) business such as sharing of truck capacity to decrease empty mileage, better usage of storage facilities and increased load factors. Interestingly, it was also found that customers do not expect LSPs to collaborate horizontally, since this might potentially jeopardize their own negotiation position in respect to individual LSPs as well as the vertical coordination process along the supply chain. Collaboration between LSPs is only encouraged when downstream customers could enjoy significant cost reductions. Therefore, horizontal collaboration in the context of LSPs is mainly a means for LSPs to increase their own productivity and cost efficiency, rather than as a reaction to requests from the demand side. The most significant barriers for LSPs, meanwhile, are identified as partner selection and fair allocation of shared workload and cost savings. The former indicates the lack of a structural approach for developing horizontal collaboration, while the latter reveals the issue of an imbalance in collaboration gains and bargaining power between partners.

The thorough studies contributed by Cruijssen et al. (2007a), (2007b) have apparently facilitated further work to explore the opportunities and impediments in respect to LHC. Several studies of these are discussed next.

Schulz and Blecken (2010) found that there is a difference in weighting the collaborative benefits between the commercial and public sectors. In the public sector, greater importance is assigned to lead-time reductions and quality improvement, in contrast with the unremitting focus on cost reduction in the commercial sector. In terms of the barriers, a different ranking is also identified. The most troubling issues in the public sector are about cultural differences, mutual mistrust, lack of transparency, inadequate resources, and treating logistics as a core competence and hence rejecting collaboration. Industry and market characteristics are therefore quite important contextual factors that can influence the focus of collaboration. Another important finding suggested that smaller sized organizations, in particular, can benefit more from the horizontal collaboration by gaining access to logistics services that would otherwise be impossible for them to access.

The benefits and barriers related to LHC have also been addressed by Hingley et al. (2011), who investigated the role of fourth-party logistics (4PL) to coordinate partners and optimize benefits ("A 4PL is an integrator that assembles the resources, capabilities, and technology of its own organization and other organizations to design, build and run comprehensive supply chain solutions" — Foster (1999). Key findings indicated a number of benefits that would improve the current logistics operations such as cost reduction, the potential for increased asset utilization, and the facilitation of a more environmentally friendly approach to distribution management. The study found, however, that only suppliers and LSPs are interested in participating in collaboration managed by 4PL, with retailers being very unwilling to support 4PL and LHC. There tend to be several underlying reasons for this: first, it was found that most retailers nowadays are large enough in size and scale through previous mergers and acquisitions and that they may, therefore, have arrived at a point of horizontal saturation with a general lack of motivation to participate LHC. Second, retailers' predominant emphasis on sustaining the service level and protecting sensitive and confidential data makes them largely unwilling to collaborate and share physical distribution management with other retailers. Third, horizontal collaboration between upstream suppliers and between LSPs may negatively impact the service performance for retailers such as on-time delivery. In such a scenario, retaining supply chain control and secrecy means more to retailers than the cost efficiencies realized through horizontal collaboration and 4PL. This is in line with Cruijssen et al. (2007a), who pointed out that horizontal collaboration is mainly a means for LSPs to increase their own productivity and cost efficiency, rather than as a reaction to requests from the demand side. As a result, retailers as gatekeepers and channel leaders are motivated more to safeguard their own interests.

It is therefore hard for suppliers and LSPs to realize the synergic benefits from horizontal collaboration without seriously taking into account the retailer's dominant power in the supply chain. An important question for future study is therefore how the collaboration practice at the supply chain horizontal level could be organized in ways that least endanger the vertical supply chain coordination and performance.

Cruijssen et al. (2010) further found that the current logistics market structure in Belgium is highly fragmented, which leads to significantly low efficiency for LSPs. LHC as a promising strategy can help to improve this overall efficiency. In addition, it noticed that LHC is more frequently considered by LSPs as a "defensive" strategy aimed at increasing operating efficiency and protecting market share, rather than an "offensive" strategy to enter new markets or actively attract additional clients in present markets. Furthermore, the study findings indicated that there should be a minimum degree of efficiency and scale required for the partners so as to allow more effectively coordinated activities to reap benefits and overcome impediments.

Determining and dividing costs and gains is one significant barrier that threatens horizontal collaboration, but the current literature directly addressing this issue is scarce, as mentioned by Cruijssen et al. (2007a). To fill this gap, Krajewska et al. (2008) developed a model to study how to distribute costs and profits among freight carriers in a horizontal partnership. In their model, game theory was used as an approach to costs and profits sharing. Likewise, Audy et al. (2011) studied a cost-savings sharing approach that can provide satisfactory and meaningful allocation between partners. On the basis of the Equal Profits Method and Alternative Cost Avoided Method, they have proposed a new method with some modifications that support a stable and profitable coalition. A case study using this method was conducted in the furniture industry and the potential cost-savings were analysed.

Another model was developed by Cruijssen et al. (2007c) who used a vehicle routing model to investigate the potential cost savings that can be attained through one basic form of horizontal collaboration — joint route planning. Sensitivity analyses were conducted based on seven operations characteristics (the number of partners, orders per partner, the average order size, the standard deviation of order size, the time window width, the size of distribution areas, market shares) to evaluate the effect on cost reduction. The results indicated that the joint route planning is most beneficial in situations where there are a large number of partners of a uniform and not too large size. Furthermore, the cost reduction will increase if order sizes are small compared to a standard truck's capacity, time windows are narrow, and inter-customer distances are large.

2.2.2.3 Governance Mechanism

Governance is a fundamental management aspect that influences how companies engage and interact within the collaborative relationships. Due to the complexity arising from these bilateral or multilateral collaborative relationships, conflicts and issues of commitment are highly likely to affect the effectiveness of collaboration. Implementing the appropriate governance mechanism is therefore critical to the success of LHC. With a focus on collaboration among LSPs, Wallenburg and Raue (2011) investigated how the different nature of conflicts might affect the outcomes of LHC and concluded that social governance (relationship management/personal interactions) is perceived as a better choice than formal governance (contractual/written agreement) in dealing with conflict resolution issues in LHC.

Continuing this work, Schmoltzi and Wallenburg (2012) further investigated the specific effects that formal and social governance mechanisms have on collaboration commitment and effectiveness and how collaboration complexity will shape such effects. It was found that both formal and social governance mechanisms have a substantial positive effect on performance. Formal control becomes particularly important when organizational complexity grows, while issues and frictions caused by strategic complexity increase the relevance of both formal and social control for collaboration success.

2.2.2.4 Development Framework

Establishing horizontal collaborative partnerships is not an easy matter and involves a number of considerations before implementation. Hence, recent studies have considered the frameworks for analysing and implementing LHC.

It takes time and resources to establish, maintain and develop horizontal collaboration between firms. Therefore, checking the compatibility of the two companies in advance is very important. Naesens et al. (2009) developed a strategic decision support framework that allows companies to mutually evaluate their strategic fit for resource pooling in inventories. They have identified 58 performance attributes which can be used as the measuring base and developed an analytic hierarchy process (AHP) to rate these indicators which provide a more comprehensive decision support about whether collaboration is possible.

Verstrepen et al. (2009) proposed a stage-wise approach to develop LSP collaboration. They discussed a conceptual development framework consisting of four subsequent phases for developing an LHC project. Each phase involves different tasks, ranging from strategic positioning to moderation, that describe an entire life cycle for the development and implementation of a collaboration project.

Palmer et al. (2012) explained a development framework for horizontal collaboration consisting of three stages characterized by "exploration", "assimilation" and "exploitation". This represents a continuous relational learning process in which partners explore together the potential improvements in their operations, with each then assimilating internally the changes they have to make to enable the collaboration, exploiting these efficiently together again and sharing fairly the outcomes of the collaboration.

Moutaoukil et al. (2012) proposed a collaboration framework based on three levels of collaboration: strategic, tactical and operational. The first level is corresponding to the engagement process involving strategic activities like the selection of partners and definition of management rules. The second level is related to the management of interdependencies which deals with planning and coordination issues between partners. The third level is concerned with the effective implementation of operations that ensures the execution of relevant plans and specifications.

Audy et al. (2012) described a general framework for developing and managing efficient logistics collaborations between firms, which can be used in the context of horizontal collaborative logistics. This framework firstly explains the main stages for building an inter-firm relationship, namely the objectives to reach, the organization of the collaboration to implement, and the partners to select. Then it describes how to manage collaborations in terms of responsibilities, leadership, and benefits sharing. In addition, some coordination mechanisms are proposed to support information sharing, the planning and execution of logistics activities, and benefit sharing, which could help managers to design their collaboration schemes.

Pomponi et al. (2013) suggested that firms need to accumulate a relevant experience in horizontal collaboration in order to increase their mutual trust. They hence proposed a conceptual framework that identifies three incremental steps in the collaboration development. Each stage is characterised by a specific combination of aims and shared assets. At the operational level, companies collaborate mainly for operations-related performance such as cost reduction and quicker response, which involves the shared use of data and fleet. When entering into the tactical level, companies might collaborate on more complex logistics problems like multimodal transport and start to share their own facilities and warehouse. When the partnership becomes strategic, collaboration will be centred on innovation and joint investment, through sharing market power and expertise.

Pomponi et al. (2015) proposed a trust-based evolutionary framework for LHC. The framework assumes the trust and extent of collaboration as the main dimensions along which subsequent steps of horizontal collaborations are developed. Collaboration development is incremental and has three stages (i.e. operational, tactical and strategic). The different collaboration intensity is mainly influenced by the level of trust developed between partners over time. Initially, due to the limited trust, the collaboration needs some form of contractual boundary (i.e. agreement-driven trust). As partners get to know one another, the shared knowledge will enhance mutual understanding and expectations (i.e. knowledge-driven trust). Eventually, when partners know each other's wants and requirements and acts in ways that exceed each other's expectations, the collaboration fosters itself (i.e. collaboration-driven trust).

Generally speaking, past studies mainly used three approaches to analyse and propose the LHC development frameworks. The first approach suggested that the development of a LHC project is an incremental process that would therefore need a stage-wise approach to ensure proper activities (e.g. partner selection, performance control) are conducted at each critical phase. The second approach considered the collaboration development based on the planning and decision levels. The collaboration activity should be designed according to whether it meets the strategic, tactical, or operational goals. The third approach considered the level of trust as the key measurement to develop collaboration. Trust levels hence affect the extent of collaboration.

2.2.2.5 Classification of Collaboration Models

Whilst the literature on LHC is in its infancy, lots of the previous studies have focused on explaining the benefits, barriers and development process of LHC. In contrast, fewer studies attempted to investigate and classify the different types of LHC models in the practice. Two of the authors attempted to provide the typology analysis of horizontal collaboration models that might be applied in the various areas of logistics and transport operations.

Cruijssen (2006) described thirteen LSP collaboration models such as freight sharing, group purchasing, co-branding and knowledge centre, based on which they developed a tentative typology that incorporates four dimensions in order to characterize the proposed models: (1) operational scope (operational, tactical, strategic); (2) competitive relationship (presence/absence); (3) combined assets (e.g. facilities/expertise/market power); (4) objectives (e.g. cutting cost/growth/innovation).

Leitner et al. (2011) proposed a conceptual framework to classify the possible types of LHC according to two collaboration dimensions: the level of collaboration intensity that goes from no collaboration to intense collaboration relationship, and correspondingly the potential of business consolidation in terms of the different logistic activities, which varies from absence of collaboration (individual transport planning and optimization) to high collaborative approach (coordination between logistics and production).

These typologies are simplistic and non-systematic however, due to a number of limitations. First, most LHC models are described very briefly. For instance, it is not clear about the logistics players involved, the specific resources and information shared, and the design of the collaborative process. Such information is critical and needs more concrete and insightful discussion. In addition, the relevant typologies of LHC models are merely the conceptual discussion with no support of a formal research process and data analysis. More rigorous and systematic investigations are required. Furthermore, some proposed LHC models are not strongly related to the key logistics and transport operations (e.g. knowledge centre, co-branding). Efforts are further needed to investigate into the logistics and transport sectors for proper LHC practice.

2.3 Research Questions

The topic of collaboration in logistics has been thoroughly studied and widely discussed by both scholars and practitioners. Among the possible forms of collaboration, horizontal collaboration is still a neglected area and the related literature is still in its infancy. The review of the available literature has indicated that the current studies of LHC mainly centre on the following issues.

- Factors that are driving or prohibiting LHC
- Development framework
- Case study of a specific practice
- Governance mechanism

First of all, many earlier studies have discussed the benefits and barriers of implementing LHC. This is perhaps a routine logic to start with a research on a new business concept. Given the limited understandings of LHC, one appropriate way to start is by exploring the related opportunities and the associated challenges of implementing this new collaboration concept. Hence, a lot of discussions were made to reveal the benefits and barriers of LHC, in terms of either the theoretical or empirical context.

On the other hand, many recent studies have focused on proposing the development framework for LHC. These frameworks suggested that collaboration development can be an incremental process or based upon the level of planning and trust. However, most of these frameworks are very generally presented and conceptually-driven, and lack of empirical evidence to support their development and application. For instance, frameworks proposed in (Pomponi et al. 2013, Pomponi et al. 2015) and (Moutaoukil et al. 2012) were formulated based on the literature review.

There are also a number of case studies conducted. However, these studies focused on specific forms of collaboration (e.g. joint transportation) or investigated a particular industry sector (e.g. the furniture industry), which did not provide a comprehensive analysis of the possible alternative collaboration in practice.

Several other studies also investigated the social issues such as how trust or conflicts can affect the collaboration, and studied the relevant governance mechanisms to deal with them. These contributions are primarily theoretical which might not support the practical development of the LHC project, however.

In summary, through the surveying of the existing contributions the study has been able to identify two important gaps in the current body of knowledge regarding LHC.

First of all, past studies of LHC have predominant focuses on the driving/ prohibiting factors and the development frameworks. There are some common limitations among these contributions:

 • Many studies tended to analyse LHC primarily from the theoretical standpoint and a lot of discussions were conceptual based on the literature without the empirical evidence to support.

 • Some studies have proposed elements and factors to analyse LHC, but miss to explain their relevance to the LHC development and practice from an operational perspective. For instance, the elements such as trust (Pomponi et al. 2015), conflicts (Wallenburg and Raue, 2011), and commitments (Schmoltzi and Wallenburg, 2012) are very general aspects of issues in inter-organizational management. These issues are, however, not the central aspects of logistics and transport operations.

• There is limited investigation on the forms and strategies of LHC. Although some studies have mentioned the related LHC concepts and strategies, their discussions are not systematic and are often simplistic as aforementioned. Further in-depth examinations cannot be found. This reveals the limited understanding on the operational management of LHC in current contributions.

Consequently, it can be argued that in current literature rare studies seriously explore the different types of LHC in practice. Seldom the studies have analysed LHC based on the operational perspective. "How to design and run the LHC?" This is a very key and practical question which is still not clear enough in the current contributions. Therefore, a more thorough investigation is required into the different types of LHC in the practical world. Such study will help systematically classify and illustrate the various forms and properties of collaboration, and consequently contribute to the better design and implementation of LHC in concrete terms.

Also, prior research in the field of LHC has generally adopted empirical methods and tended to analyse horizontal collaboration from the qualitative perspective, such as culture, opportunities and impediments. In contrast, there is little research that systematically and rigorously examines the impact of horizontal collaboration on participants' supply chain operations, such as capacity utilization and order fulfilment. Many questions remain to be answered. For example, will companies fulfil customer orders better if they join an LHC network? Will participating in horizontal collaboration have a positive or negative impact on the participants' logistics cost and service level? Will it be beneficial to participate in horizontal collaboration? How significant the benefits are? Will the benefits of joining horizontal collaboration be different for different participants? Hence, there are problems in quantifying the actual effects of horizontal collaboration in the logistics supply system which constitutes a major barrier for the further development of this body of knowledge. In order to assess the impact of collaboration and to understand better horizontal collaboration in action over time, the explicit modelling and representation of the collaboration partners and their behaviours is required.

Hence, to fill the two important research gaps in respect to LHC identified above, three specific research questions have been developed:

(1) What are the key elements to be considered for developing logistics horizontal collaboration?

(2) How can logistics horizontal collaboration networks be classified?

(3) How will partners behave and interact in the logistics collaborative network and how might this have an effect on the individuals, as well as the logistics system as a whole?

2.4 The Application of Agent-based Modelling in Supply Chain Management

Supply chain management is concerned with the management and integration of the various organizations involved in the upstream and downstream of the supply chain for enabling the better flow of products, services, finances and information from the primary sources to the final customers (Christopher, 1992, Chopra and Meindl, 2007). Because the supply chain system often involves a large network of organizations and a broad scope of activities to manage, making decisions in this complex environment can be very challenging, and there is therefore a need for appropriate methodologies to support this decision making.

Enabled by the recent advances in computing power, simulation modelling is increasingly becoming a viable approach to assist decision-makers to analyse the complex issues in supply chains. Simulation is an experimental approach used to mimic real-world systems that, unlike real-world systems, can then be experimented upon without being confronted with real-world consequences (Pidd, 2006, Peck, 2004, Winsberg, 2003). The use of simulation modelling as a tool for researching supply chain theories and evaluating supply chain strategies has attracted growing attention. Various simulation techniques have been used to model a wide spectrum of supply chain issues at strategic, operational and tactical levels. In this context, one recently popular simulation modelling technique is Agent-Based Simulation (ABS). ABS is particularly well suited for modelling the behaviour of complex systems over time, and is thus potentially applicable to complex and dynamically developing supply chain systems.

Since a key focus of this research is to study the dynamic behaviours and effects of LHC, a simulation modelling approach needs to be employed for the effective analysis. This study considers Agent-Based Simulation (ABS) as a suitable modelling approach to explore the process of collaboration and how it links to performance behaviours. From the methodological point of departure, a review of the key characteristics and use of ABS modelling would be useful to inform the model design for studying LHC.

Given the fact that the prior research in the field of LHC has mainly been empirical and qualitative methods, there wasn't in the past a real case of ABS research identified in this area. This part of the literature review therefore, extends to a broader scope to explore the ABS application in the wider supply chain management (SCM) context.

In the supply chain modelling literature, the ABS approach has been highlighted as an increasingly suitable method to model supply chain problems and its application has grown rapidly in recent years. The section hence explores the features and advantages of ABS, and how ABS has been applied to study issues in the SCM context. The rest of this section is structured as follows. Section 2.4.1 provides a brief review of the main features of the present supply chain modelling and simulation methods. In Section 2.4.2, the paradigm of ABS for modelling the supply chain is analysed and compared to other key supply chain simulation techniques. Section 2.4.3 explores how ABS has been applied to model some of the key issues in supply chain management.

2.4.1 Methods of Modelling Supply

The literature on supply chain modelling is vast and covers many approaches. Broadly speaking, current modelling methods can be grouped into two mainstream families: analytical modelling and simulation modelling (Gokhale and Trivedi, 1998).

Analytical (or mathematical programming) modelling methods call for the solution of a mathematical problem using various algorithms and equations. Many Operational Research-based (OR) models belong to this family, including methods such as linear/ mixed integer programming, queueing theory, game theory and network optimization models (Poler et al. 2013, Ravindran, 2008). On the other hand, simulation modelling methods are developed to mimic the behaviours of the various elements in a supply chain system over time in order to study and predict the outcomes from sample histories by running a simulation program (Altiok and Melamed, 2010).

It is argued by some authors that using analytical (or mathematical) modelling methods to model the supply chain could be less efficient because mathematical models are usually difficult to construct for realistic cases and can only tackle small-scale problems (Thierry et al. 2010, Ahn and Lee, 2004). In contrast, simulation modelling methods tend to be more flexible for exploring the behaviours and performance of the large-scale situations that can exist in a typical supply chain system. A number of authors argue that there are several advantages of applying simulation over analytical modelling approaches when seeking to model the supply chain (Lee and Kim, 2008, Gokhale and Trivedi, 1998, Thierry et al. 2010, Chan and Chan, 2010, Nikolopoulou and Ierapetritou, 2012b, Altiok and Melamed, 2010). The advantages are:

- Analytical models rely strongly on assumptions that tend to be over-simplified. It is challenging to construct a model using mathematical programming when dealing with many variables (the so-called "curse of dimensionality"). Mathematical models are therefore usually limited to solving small-scale problems in the supply chain. Simulation models on the other hand, can capture and model many elements and variables. The assumptions for the modelling can be relaxed or made more realistic. The advantage of simulation over analytical modelling lies in the fact that very large numbers of detailed behaviours in the supply chain can be captured allowing the supply chain to be modelled from a broader perspective.

- Analytical methods seek optimized and exact solutions from the modelling, which requires the problems to be formulated in a static and deterministic way, which is difficult to apply when facing a complex and stochastic environment. In contrast, simulation methods seek good but approximate solutions. The ability to carry out "what-if" configurations provides additional flexibility to identify a "best" configuration, which further strengthens the adoption of this approach.

• As opposed to the analytical models, which are built on abstract mathematical expressions, simulation models often use representations that are closer to reality. Many simulation tools support the graphical visualization of the system behaviours through animation, which helps the modeller and model users to observe the temporal evolution of the model's state and statistics in the course of a run. Such features facilitate a better understanding of the modelled system.

Overall, when the finer level of detail and broader model boundary are important, the advantages of simulation models outstrip those of analytical models. Simulation modelling is therefore argued to be a more effective approach for modelling supply chain systems that are usually large-scale and complex in nature.

2.4.2 ABS Vs Other Simulation Approaches in Supply Chain

Supply chain system modelling is challenging due to the broad scope of issues and complex interactions between supply chain organizations. In recent years ABS has been increasingly recognized to be suitable for modelling supply chain problems due to its ability to model the complexity of the supply chain system. Before ABS, two classic simulation approaches were widely used for supply chain modelling, namely Discrete-Event Simulation (DES) and System Dynamics (SD).

This section compares the key characteristics of these three approaches for modelling the supply chain system in order to distinguish ABS from the classical supply chain simulation approaches, highlighting the advantages of the former.

2.4.2.1 Discrete Event Simulation

DES models suggest that real-world systems and processes are represented by a set of distinct events (Altiok and Melamed, 2010). From a technical standpoint, DES views a system as a network of activities and queues where state changes occur at discrete points of time (Brailsford and Hilton, 2001). In DES, objects and people are modelled individually and can be referred to under the generic term of "entities". Figure 2.1 demonstrates a classic DES approach to modelling the design of a supply chain. In this Figure, raw material entities enter the circuit board manufacturing process and are transformed into circuit board entities. Next, the circuit board entities enter the next supply chain tier, i.e. the Surface-Mount Technology (SMT) manufacturing process. Finally, the entities leave SMT as the final product entities.

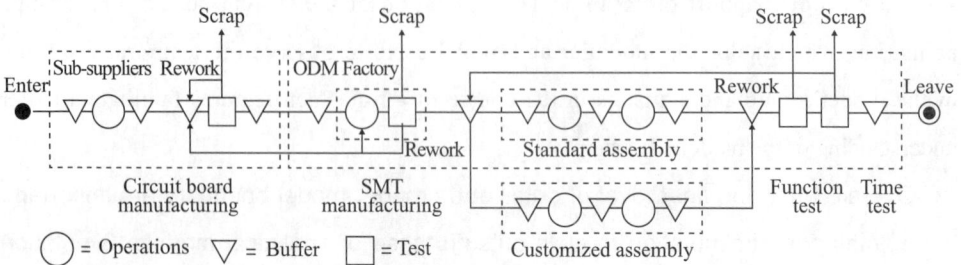

Figure 2.1 Example of a discrete event simulation model of a supply chain design

In the literature, it is generally argued that the DES approach is more suitable for modelling Supply Chain Management (SCM) issues at the operational level (Lane, 2000, Sweetser, 1999, Taylor and Lane, 1998), since it is more focused on the process of the supply chain activities and an individual entity's journey through the modelled supply chain. Hence, DES models are most popular for modelling supply chain problems such as network configurations, inventory control policies, manufacturing planning and scheduling related to the queuing problems. From DES perspective, the elements that describe the structure of the supply chain (events, activities and processes) are considered as passive "objects" that are pre-defined by the modeller. Chatfield et al. (2007) and Siebers et al. (2010) argue that using DES to model a supply chain usually implies a network perspective and focuses on representing the supply chain's topology and infrastructure, while generally discounting the control and decision processes that occur within each supply chain player.

2.4.2.2 System Dynamics

SD has its roots in Jay W. Forrester's Industrial Dynamics (Forrester, 1961), which is a simulation approach that investigates the effect of information feedback and delays on the dynamic behaviours of a system. In the context of supply chain systems, the dynamics existing between firms in supply chains can cause errors, inaccuracies and volatility, hence creating huge uncertainties, which increase for operations further upstream in the supply chain (Slack et al. 2006). SD simulation is therefore a means of inferring the time evolutionary dynamics endogenously created by such system structures (Lane, 1997).

SD models represent a system as a set of stocks and flows (Brailsford and Hilton, 2001, Pidd, 2006). Figure 2.2 shows an example of an SD model that captures the relationship between two stocks: retailer inventory and supplier orders. The retailer inventory increases with incoming shipments from its supplier and decreases with sales. Likewise, the supplier orders increase with incoming orders from the retailer and decrease with production which will then be shipped to the retailer.

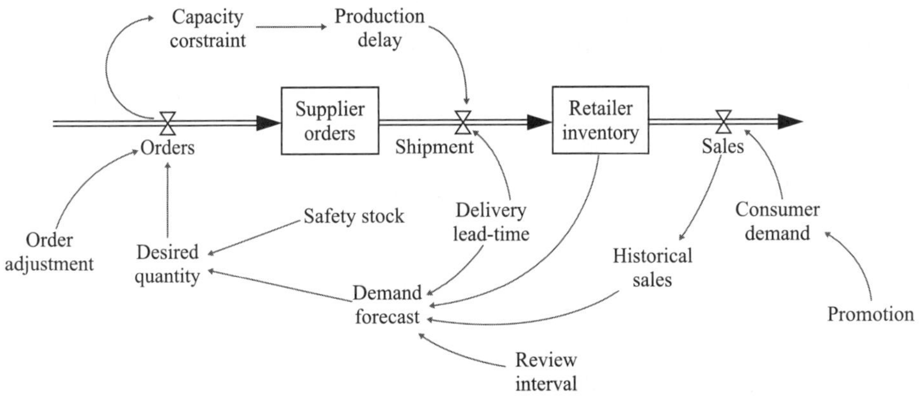

Figure 2.2 Example of a system dynamics model of a supply chain design

In contrast to DES models, in SD models, the individual entities are not specifically modelled, but are instead collectively represented as a continuous quantity in a stock. Movement to or from a stock is represented by a flow, which is defined to be the rate of change of a stock. Another difference from DES is the management of time, in that the state changes are continuously monitored over time in SD models (the time is usually advanced by small discrete steps of equal length) (Angerhofer and Angelides, 2000, Akkermans and Dellaert, 2005). In addition, SD models are generally deterministic and variables usually represent average values (Pidd, 2006).

Due to the fact that SD models are usually built with a "distant" perspective, it has been claimed that SD is more suited to modelling the supply chain problems at a strategic level (Lane, 2000, Sweetser, 1999, Taylor and Lane, 1998). For instance, the typical supply chain problems that are frequently modelled using SD are supply chain integration and the bullwhip effect. The SD model approach has several advantages in respect to modelling the supply chain (Angerhofer and Angelides, 2000, Tako and Robinson, 2012). First, it cares about the structure of the system, which enables the modeller to take a holistic view of the supply chain system, integrating many sub-systems. Second, the use of causal loop diagrams helps to capture a dynamic view of the cause and effect relationships between policies and decisions among the supply chain organizations. Third, building SD models requires less detailed data than DES models. On the other hand, the SD approach requires the modeller to represent the supply chain as a set of closed-form equations, which are inflexible when it comes to constructing the desired form of model. Also, the models do not represent supply chain processes that contain multiple stages, since the behaviours of individual supply chain participants are not explicitly modelled (Chatfield et al. 2007). SD, therefore, is not as effective as DES in modelling the operational issues in the supply chain, although it can be used for the early/intermediate stages of analysis and decision making when less detailed models or results are required.

2.4.2.3 Agent based Simulation

ABS has been increasingly used for studying supply chain issues since it caters for the disadvantages inherent in the DES (discounting the control and decision process of individuals) and SD approaches (systems only profiled at the aggregated level). The ABS modelling paradigm focuses on modelling the individuals in the (supply chain) system, known as "Agents" who can represent people, machines or companies. Agents have autonomous behaviours, often described by simple rules, and interact with other agents, who in turn influence their own decisions and behaviours. The global (system-level) behaviours then emerge as a result of these myriad interactions of agents and their individual behaviours (Eppstein et al. 2011, Niazi and Hussain, 2011, Macal and North, 2010). Since ABS centres on the individual characteristics and behaviours, it provides an effective way to study a system by explicitly modelling every unique individual of that system. A typical agent structure is illustrated in Figure 3. Agents interact with other agents in the supply chain network (e.g. place an order or fulfil an order). Based on the knowledge gained from the interaction, agents may change their attributes (e.g. inventory levels) and update their beliefs or behaviours (e.g. supplier selection rules).

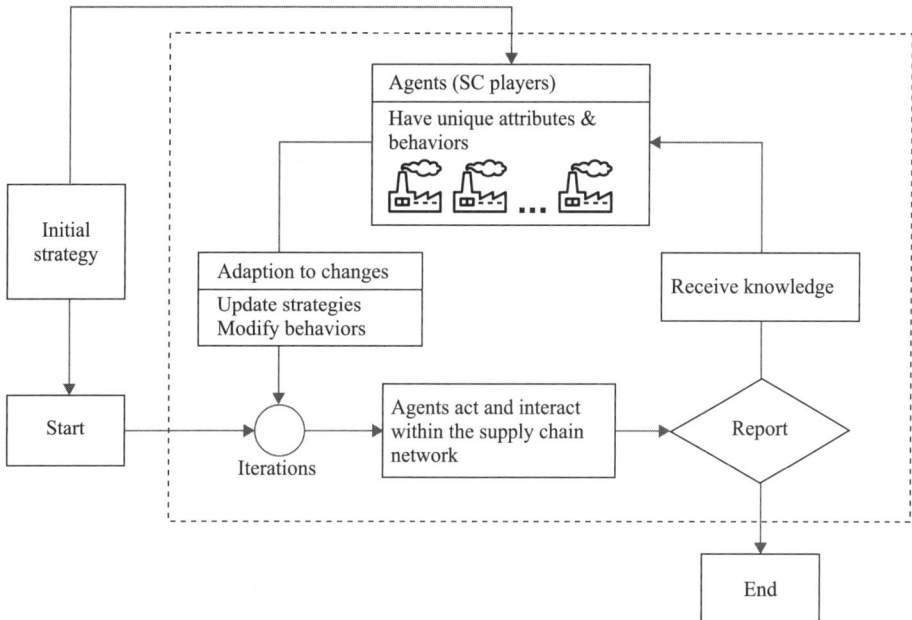

Figure 2.3 Example of an agent-based model of a supply chain design

ABS has some specific features that have allowed it to be increasingly recognized as an alternative approach to modelling supply chain issues. First, the supply chain system is a complex system consisting of many individual organizations with different objectives and action strategies. It is easier to model these heterogeneous agents in ABS than in DES (due to the passive/few interactions between objects) and impossible in SD (since this assumes a homogeneous collection of individuals). In ABS, heterogeneity can be defined both for the agent characteristics and his decision/action rules. Second, learning and adaptive capability can be modelled for the individual agents. Such proactivity in responding to the changing environment is difficult to represent in DES models because of their fixed structure and process, but this is an important aspect in modelling the supply chain, where an explicit representation of human/organizational decision making is required in order to examine the system behaviours effectively. SD models can be used to model learning and adaptive capability at the population level but not at the individual level.

Consequently, ABS is an ideal approach for developing a model that requires the explicit analysis and representation of individual behaviours (such as inventory decisions on the part of every supply chain player), and it can also be used to examine the linkages between those micro agent details and the macro system behaviours (such as system costs and the bullwhip effect). From this viewpoint, employing ABS would help the modeller to obtain greater flexibility in terms of addressing both the macro and micro supply chain problems at the same time in the same model. Supply chain issues that can be effectively modelled by SD but not by DES (e.g. coordinated decision making) as well as those that are more suitable for DES than SD (e.g. manufacturing scheduling/the queuing problem) can both be integrated within an ABS model to form a hybrid model (Eldabi et al. 2016). In summary, ABS complements DES and SD as a simulation approach in supply chain modelling.

2.4.3 Review Method

This paper seeks to provide a review of the ABS methods used in supply chain applications. The study is based on a review of the published papers that describe the modelling of supply chain issues. The research process for this review followed the procedures explained further below.

2.4.3.1 Databases and Keywords

In order to identify the scientific literature that describes the use of ABS to study supply chain problems, a search was performed in the well-known journal databases (Business Source Premier (EBSCO), ProQuest , ABI, Emerald, Web of Science (WOS), Science Direct, IEEE Xplore, and ACM digital), looking for a combination of terms "agent-based simulation/modelling/model" and "supply chain" within paper titles, keywords and abstracts. The search considered only digital works written in English up to March 2015. Both academic journal papers and conference papers were included. Other publications such as books, trade papers, technical reports or newsletters were excluded. The search presented over 300 papers.

2.4.3.2 Screening Process

To ensure the identification of papers addressing the defined topic, a screening process was carried out. First, duplicate papers found from the different databases were removed, reducing the number of papers down to 116. Second, a quick scan of the abstracts of these 116 papers was conducted to filter out irrelevant papers, as well as papers with only the abstract available in each search engine. Following this scanning check a total of 91 papers were retained.

After the paper list had been retrieved, the full papers were downloaded. Since there could still be some irrelevant papers, an additional screening process was conducted. First, those papers that only described the conceptual model of ABS without any actual model implementation and experiments were excluded from the review list. The study aims to investigate how ABS is used to model supply chain issues hence the included articles must feature a complete ABS model. Second, those articles adopting the terminology "multi-agent system (MAS)" were examined carefully to distinguish the multi-agent system engineering problems from simulation studies using multiple agents. The latter is included because it is essentially the same as ABS. Finally, papers in which the keyword "supply chain" appeared in their titles or abstracts but which were not in fact focusing on supply chain problems were not considered. By applying these screening criteria, a final total of 73 relevant ABS papers was confirmed and used for the review analysis.

The literature shows that ABS has been used to study many types of supply chain problems. Table 2.1 shows the fields that ABS modelling has been applied to (the detailed breakdown can be found in the appendix). It is noteworthy to see among the list of supply chain issues that the most frequently modelled are related to the fields of supply chain collaboration, inventory management, risk/uncertainty management and supplier selection. This "big four" accounts for 77% of the total number of ABS applications and are therefore the main supply chain application fields using ABS.

Table 2.1 Agent-based modelling application fields in relation to supply chains

Application Field	Number of Papers
Supply Chain Collaboration	19
Inventory Planning and Management	15
Risk and Uncertainty Management	12
Supplier Selection	10
Supply Chain Competition	5
Pricing Strategy	3
Resource Allocation	2
Production Policy	2
Contract Scheme	2
Regulation Policy	1
Organization Governance	1
Buyer-Supplier Relationship	1

2.4.4 The Use of ABS to Model Key Supply Chain Problems

The following sections aim to provide a more detailed review of ABS applications within the four fields in order to understand the different ways in which the ABS approach has been applied and what results have been achieved.

2.4.4.1 Supply Chain Collaboration

The fundamentals of SCM are about creating a partnership to facilitate communication and collaboration between individual firms in the supply chain network. ABS seems to be particularly useful to model supply chain collaboration given that the ABS paradigm centres on individual behaviours and interactions, which enables the collaboration model to be profiled at a greater level of detail compared to other simulation methods. It also offers greater flexibility to model a wider range of different types of collaboration strategies. The literature shows that the collaboration within the supply chain in general can be modelled in two different forms: (1) collaboration based on sharing information; (2) collaboration based on sharing physical capacity and profits. The following subsections discuss the relevant applications in more detail.

2.4.4.1.1 Sharing Information

Information sharing is regarded as a major form of collaboration in the literature. A supply chain is a complex network that involves a lot of local decisions and activities. As a result, none of the members in a supply chain can have a full picture of the networked operations, and consequently, face uncertainty when trading with each other in the network. This issue creates incentives for member parties (or agents) to pursue information sharing through collaboration in order for them to gain greater visibility of how others perform and thus better align their operations when they trade and collaborate. This shared information can be used by different supply chain agents to make wiser or more appropriate decisions when they operate as a part of a bigger supply chain network consisting of complex inter-organizational connections.

The literature revealed that information sharing in a supply chain context can be modelled in two main ways: sharing demand information and sharing supply information.

Sharing demand information between supply chain partners was found to be the most common. This includes specific demand information such as sales/order forecasts, point-of-sales (POS) data, and customer inventory depletion information. The following part presents some typical ABS works in order to illustrate how each type of demand information is shared and modelled, and what the effects are.

Caridi et al. (2005) studied the Collaborative Planning Forecasting and Replenishment (CPFR) process between a manufacturer and a retailer who are willing to collaborate in the exchange of sales and order forecasts. Three distinctive CPFR models were implemented, representing different levels of collaboration. The first model represents the conventional approach to CPFR, in which the retailer shares their order forecasts with manufacturers, whereas the manufacturers share their sales forecasts with retailers. Both then work together to try to narrow down the gap in their demand forecasts. The second (advanced) model enables trading agents a further collaboration ability to relax operational constraints for forecasting according to a priority list where the ranking for the relaxation of constraints is recorded. Within the third (learning) model, agents are more intelligent than in the previous ones, due to their ability to learn from the past, which allows them to collaborate to reset criteria threshold values (KPIs) for forecasting based on historical data that would indicate the product life cycle and market trend. Through modelling and comparison, it was concluded that CPFR strategies, coupled with dynamic constraints relaxation (i.e. the advanced model) and with criteria/rules updated through historical data analysis (i.e. the learning model), achieved greater benefits than the conventional CPFR in terms of total costs, inventory level, stock-out level and sales.

Xu and Zhu (2013) analysed the influence of demand information sharing in a retailer-dominant supply chain. Their model investigated four settings: (1) no information sharing; (2) information sharing between retailer and manufacturer; (3) information sharing between retailer and supplier; and (4) all the members of supply chain being involved in the information sharing. The simulation results showed that the total cost of the supply chain was the highest in the case of no information sharing. When demand information is accessed by all supply chain members, the total cost of the supply chain can be kept to a minimum. The result also suggests that sharing demand information has a much stronger value for the upstream players.

Bhattacharyya and Zhang (2010) examined the effect of demand information sharing between sellers and buyers in an E-commerce supply chain (B2B E-hub). Five different demand information sharing strategies were compared: (1) no information sharing; (2) sharing aggregated hub demand (AHD) information; (3) sharing aggregated end demand (AED) information; (4) sharing aggregated buyer inventory position (ABI) information; (5) a hybrid approach that combined AED and ABI. The simulation results showed that sharing both AHD and AED is beneficial to the sellers in terms of cost. This is mainly due to the lower inventory level and lower stock out penalty costs. While a lower inventory level results from a higher frequency of ordering, the same benefit is achieved with a lower order frequency (hence lower ordering cost) in ABI. This suggests that sharing the buyers' inventory consumption information as the demand signal is more valuable than directly sharing the aggregated demand information. In addition, more does not necessarily mean better. Sharing more than one type of demand information together might not always be more beneficial as it might complicate the agent decision making in response to the demand changes.

Lin et al. (2002) examined the effects of demand information sharing on supply chain performance in electronic commerce. Three levels of information sharing were implemented in the model: order information, inventory information, and demand information. The findings indicated that sharing demand information achieved the lowest total cost, the highest order fulfilment rate, and the shortest order cycle time, whereas sharing order information leads to the lowest order fulfilment rate and the longest cycle time. When sharing buyers' inventory depletion information, buyers tended to trade with a specific supplier for a longer period of time. When sharing order or demand information, however, buyers tended to switch suppliers more frequently. This demonstrated that sharing inventory information is a workable alternative when the cost of switching is relatively high.

Lau et al. (2004) investigated the impact of different levels of demand information sharing on supply chain performance under the various supply chain structures. Four levels of information sharing strategy were implemented, characterized by which supply chain echelons are engaged in the information sharing and the information type, such as sharing only the order information or sharing the mean and variance of demand with a purpose to hide the actual demand and cost structure. The results showed that no single level of information sharing dominates the others from the perspective of individual companies. However, the value of sharing demand information between downstream echelons is more significant in terms of supply chain operating costs than that of sharing information between upstream echelons, regardless of supply chain structures.

Chatfield et al. (2004) examined the effect of sharing demand forecast information. This information is used to predict the demand in lead-time and inventory parameters updating, which can affect the order streams, inventory levels and stock-outs. With no information sharing, each supply chain node generates its own forecast based on their local information. The forecast is then used to generate the parameters for purchasing and supply. When information is shared, the nodes in the supply chain are aware of the current customer demand. This awareness informs their forecasts and allows them to fine-tune their planning parameters. The results showed that the sharing of downstream information decreased the demand variance amplification significantly for upstream players. This is because the end-customer's demand order stream has a variance less than or equal to the variance of the orders coming from the downstream partner. This customer information smoothens the fluctuations in the planned inventory level so that the resulting order stream has a lower variance. Information sharing also protects a supply chain against "cascading failures" (stock-outs), especially for a supply chain system with more echelons.

In contrast to sharing demand information, sharing the supply related information downstream to customers was considered only infrequently. The types of supply information that can be shared include capacity, inventory, backlog and lead-time. The following part introduces three available ABS works which modelled these kinds of information sharing.

Chan and Chan (2004) studied the retailer-supplier collaboration problem in terms of the quantity and delivery date flexibility needed to cope with the demand dynamics. Instead of setting a fixed delivery date, a bigger delivery window was allowed to ensure a more proactive collaboration between retailers and suppliers. Quantity flexibility, on the other hand, ensures that retailers can choose to receive a lower order quantity if their cycle demand was not as strong as predicted. Within the range of delivery dates, retailers and suppliers would enter into a collaboration process in which suppliers will repetitively check/share their latest inventory production status with retailers, who will then take this information from the supply side and decide if they want to ask their suppliers to arrange the order delivery earlier or later according to their own inventory depletion progress. Through the modelling, and comparison with the conventional order fulfilment approaches, where no inventory information sharing and flexible coordination are allowed, the collaboration model significantly reduced the total system cost and increased the order fill-rate (service level). Moreover, the proposed collaboration was not only able to reduce the total system cost/increase fill-rate, but the impact of increasing demand uncertainty was also suppressed. That means the marginal cost against uncertainty was reduced significantly.

Sawaya (2006) analysed the effects on supply chain performance of sharing suppliers' lead-time forecasts with customers. Specifically, the supplier prepares an estimate of the internal queue time based on the current finished goods inventory position, current orders and backorders, the expected capacity in the future and the mean demand it expects in the future. Then the supplier gives customers their best guess of when orders it receives the next day will be shipped from the factory. This estimate is used by the customer in their calculations to determine their demand orders during lead-time in place of an estimate of the lead-time from observed orders and received shipments. The results suggested that, for the most part, the value of suppliers sharing shipment lead-time forecasts for future orders with their customers is not strong. Sharing lead-time information can have a net negative effect on the system and on the manufacturing organization since it appeared that this might create a mechanism that forces the supplier to keep greater inventory. When the variability of the lead-times is high and the demand volume is high, the sharing of lead-time information has greater benefits, however. This is even more pronounced when the capacity is variable and known somewhat in advance of the day on which the actual capacity is realized, which indicated that if the precision of the lead-time forecast is high enough, and then the benefits could be well worthwhile.

Ibrahim and Deghedi (2012) studied how the sharing of factory disruption information can help minimize the evolution of risk downstream in the supply chain and improve both the whole chain's and each member's performance. The model introduced factory breakdown as a source of supply disruption that can severely delay order delivery. When the factory does not notify the downstream elements of the supply chain of the breakdown problem, the downstream players only realize this problem when no shipment is received, and thus switch to another factory. In this scenario, all the entire downstream players will suffer from delayed shipments and the accumulation of backorders. When the factory immediately alerts them of the breakdown, however, the players throughout the whole chain can act swiftly to adjust their orders. The results showed a significant reduction in the cost of the supply chain and each of its agents due to the sharing of breakdown information. In addition, the analysis found that the significance of sharing breakdown information became greater with when the disruption frequency increased. Despite the possible confidentiality of the disruption problem to the factory agent, the results showed that the factory would benefit most in terms of cost reduction, if the breakdown information is shared.

Overall, the current ABS literature has shown that modelling the sharing of demand-related information upstream in the supply chain is more common than sharing supply related information to downstream supply chain organizations. This is perhaps driven by the conventional approach for managing the supply chain which is largely based upon demand forecasting and inventory planning. This indicates that the primary focus of modelling of information sharing is to make the demand associated data much more transparent and thus to give it more of a role in controlling the supply to match closely with demand (i.e. increasing forecast accuracy, reducing the bullwhip effect/excess inventory). Using ABS to model the sharing of supply information and using this to control and match the demand closer to the supply is only infrequently considered. In addition, comparing and combining the two types of information sharing represents an interesting implementation for ABS. There is certainly plenty of room for further studies in this regard.

2.4.4.1.2 Sharing Capacity and Profits

Collaboration based on sharing physical capacity and profits are of high practical value and are often seen in many real collaborations in the supply chain. The literature review identified several ABS works that model these kinds of collaborations.

Albino et al. (2007) analysed the benefits of supply chain collaboration in industrial districts (ID). Collaboration was modelled in the form of sharing production capacity between similar firms (horizontal collaboration) at two supply chain stages (suppliers and buyers). The collaboration between suppliers seeks to balance the utilization of production capacity between suppliers, meaning that suppliers proportionally share the excess demand according to their available capacity thus ensuring their co-existence in the long term. The collaboration between buyers, meanwhile, emphasizes the minimizing of the unsatisfied customer demand, meaning that unsatisfied orders tend to be allocated to the buyer agent with a higher level of available production capacity. Several demand scenarios and organizational structures were configured to represent the different ID supply chain environments for collaboration. The results showed that collaboration in production has a substantial positive effect on the ID performances in terms of efficiency and flexibility. Further, when the collaboration in

IDs is characterized by the presence of leader firms, there is a greater improvement in efficiency at the expense of losing flexibility as the demand variability increases.

Xie and Chen (2005) studied the horizontal collaboration among retailers in the supply chain. This collaboration was among retailers who pursue the partnership for higher profits. The collaboration was modelled as full collaboration, i.e. when several retailers collaborate, they form a coalition and act as a single large retailer and they take a uniform price, and share their inventories, costs and profits. Under this configuration, all the retailers inside a coalition are highly coordinated. They all try to maximize the coalition's total profit; yet different coalitions and outside retailers are purely competitive. The results revealed that the size of the collaboration network, and several other factors, can affect the stability of the coalition structure. When more participants are involved in the network, there are more incentives for partners to break from the existing partnerships. The collaboration also has prominent external effects, which makes it more beneficial for outside retailers.

Giannoccaro and Pontrandolfo (2009) studied a collaboration mechanism based on revenue sharing negotiation in the supply chain. The model assumed that the negotiation process between retailers and distributors is affected by three main variables, namely: the agent's propensity to negotiate, the propensity to threaten to abandon the negotiation, and the propensity to collaborate. The simulation results showed that the best supply chain profits were obtained when the contractual power for both supply chain agents is low, regardless of the degree of collaboration. In such a case, both actors have a high propensity to negotiate and a low propensity to threaten to abandon the negotiation, and the negotiation therefore tends to end more frequently with an agreement. A high degree of collaboration for both supply chain agents also assures high supply chain profits, regardless of the contractual power. Thus, the best scenario is characterized by low contractual power and high collaboration for both agents. Further, it was found that the asymmetric distribution of contractual power between the actors reduces the chance of the adoption of revenue sharing.

From the above, ABS has shown a good ability to model various forms of supply chain collaboration. This is because ABS focuses on modelling the interactions and exchanges between agents which can incorporate the different sorts of shared materials.

2.4.4.2 Inventory Planning and Management

The issues related to inventory management are found to be modelled intensively using simulation including ABS (Tako and Robinson, 2012). This literature review confirms this. For example, Zhang and Bhattacharyya (2010) examined and compared the inventory management and performance in the traditional and E-commerce supply chains. A typical order-up-to (OUT) inventory replenishment policy was implemented in the model for all supply chain agents to follow. The results identified that all agents tend to keep more inventories and backlog lose fewer orders in the e-marketplace than in traditional supply chains. The effects on upstream distributors and manufacturers are more profound than those on downstream retailers. Similarly, Dong et al. (2012) developed a model based on two continuous inventory replenishment strategies, the (R, S) and (Q, R) policies, to analyse the inventory replenishment performance in a three-stage supply chain. They found that under the (R, S) policy the service level (order fill-rate) is better, and the shortage costs are lower, but the inventory holding costs are slightly higher than those under the (Q, R) policy. Overall, the (R, S) policy is better than the (Q, R) policy as an inventory planning and control method. In another example, Moyaux et al. (2004) compared three ordering policies and their effectiveness in terms of reducing inventory variations and back order costs.

In addition to more traditional supply chain inventory models that focus on stable operational processes, the new features given by ABS simulation enable the modeller to configure the agent with a learning capability, allowing them to learn from past experiences so as to make better inventory decisions. For instance, Jiang and Sheng (2009) constructed an inventory model to investigate the dynamic inventory control issues under the non-stationary customer demand where the use of traditional time- or event-trigger inventory policies were not accurate. Case-based reinforcement learning was applied and was proved experimentally to be effective in this situation. Similar benefits can also be found in a study by Kim et al. (2008). They developed an action-reward learning-based inventory control model for a two-stage serial supply chain with the non-stationary customer demand. Two learning strategies (centralized and decentralized learning) were implemented for comparison with the inventory control method with no learning. The results showed that the two learning models outperformed the inventory model without the learning control in terms of average inventory cost. In another application, Kim (2009) studied the effects of trust accumulation between supply chain trading agents. The learning capability was allocated to the agents, who could then use this to analyse the historical performance of their counterparts and hence increase or decrease their trust level towards each of them, thereby affecting the order and supply decisions. The simulation results revealed that agents' decisions on forecasting, ordering and supply based on the trust relationship can contribute to an apparent reduction in the variability of inventory levels. This result can be explained by the fact that mutual learning and trust development based on past experiences of trading diminishes an agent's uncertainty about the trustworthiness of his trading partners and thereby tends to stabilize inventory levels.

2.4.4.3 Risk and Uncertainty Management

ABS is also employed to study the supply chain risks and uncertainty. Supply chain risks can refer to those unexpected and disruptive events that can cause instability and increased costs in operations. Due to the numerous interacting factors that contribute to increased vulnerability and uncertainty in supply chains, traditional methods might be inadequate for the management of supply chain risks and uncertainty. ABS represents a recent development in supply chain modelling which can address the dynamic behaviours of risk/uncertainty issues and which has been regarded as highly appropriate for studying risk/uncertainty management.

The ABS modelling of supply chain risks can be carried out in three different but not mutually exclusive aspects, namely the identification and creation of various types of risk events, risk management, and performance measures of the risk impact and coping strategies. For instance, Sirivunnabood and Kumara (2009) modelled a supply chain network under supplier risks, in which four types of risks were imitated, including rare and short, rare but long, frequent but short, and frequent and long risks.

In addition, two risk mitigation strategies (having a redundant supplier and reserving more inventories) were applied to compare the performance. The results highlighted that both approaches are effective but are subject to different risk conditions. In another work, Ehlen et al. (2014) studied how a particular chemical supply chain could potentially behave during and after disruptive events, and how the operation of the supply chain could be affected by the disruptions in terms of scope and duration. The results of this model were used to inform homeland security policymakers about how to prepare better for, prevent, and mitigate losses to the U.S. chemical sector.

Most ABS work to study the supply chain uncertainty has focused on the demand uncertainty and have proposed various approaches for improving the management of the uncertainty, such as the model described in Datta and Christopher (2011). They modelled the effectiveness of several proposed mechanisms for reducing the demand uncertainty in a make-to-stock supply chain. The results indicated that a centralised information structure without widespread distribution of information and coordination is not effective in managing the uncertainty within supply chain networks. In another example, Hing Kai and Chan (2006) proposed a mechanism with an early order completion contract in order to improve the supply chain costs and the order fill rate under the impact of the demand uncertainty. Various levels of the demand errors and variations were modelled throughout the modelling process to evaluate the effects of the proposed mechanisms on supply chain performance.

2.4.4.4 Supplier Selection

ABS is often used to study the supplier selection problem in a supply chain, given that procurement is one the three main functions of SCM (the other two are manufacturing and logistics). Procurement is crucially important to SCM because about 50—70% of the costs of a final product are paid to suppliers, which means that those suppliers are responsible for more than half of the overall value-added activities in a typical supply chain. It is therefore worthwhile to make careful decisions when selecting suppliers to guarantee both the quality and quantity required for the supplier activities. ABS can be one effective decision support tool to model the various scenarios and mechanisms for supplier selection, given that it can capture the micro complexity associated with one unique agent's learning and evaluation process.

Yu and Wong (2015) built a negotiation model to evaluate a supplier selection process that involves a bundle of products with synergy effects. They showed that the purchasing company and suppliers can reach agreements on the details of products simultaneously and thus exploit the synergy effect between products.

Fu-ren et al. (2005) studied trust as a criterion for supplier selection in a complex three-tier supply network. Within their model, manufacturers can select suppliers based on the perceived degree of trust in their partners and on their current quotations. The ratio of these two factors to one another modulates the supplier selection decision, which may also affect the subsequent supply chain performance. The results found that the proposed trust mechanism helped to reduce the average cycle time and increase the in-time order-fulfilment rate in certain market environments but at the expense of increased material costs. Furthermore, a higher trust or propensity to trust leads to a higher in-time order-fulfilment rate. Conducting supplier selection using the trust mechanism is therefore better than using the only quote price and due date.

Liu et al. (2014) presented a multi-criteria decision-making approach to support the selection of appropriate suppliers. Two important evaluation elements for supplier selection related to trust and reputation were considered and a decision model for supplier selection was developed based on these elements to evaluate the performance. The simulation experiments demonstrated that the proposed trust and reputation model can effectively filter unfair rating scores to evaluate the trustworthiness of suppliers. In addition, due to the proposed multi-criteria decision-making method, customers would select the most suitable supplier rather than the best supplier in the supply chain.

Schieritz and Grobler (2003) studied how the different order fulfilment strategies and supplier attractiveness affect supplier selection and the supply chain structure. Downstream agents rely on a performance evaluation mechanism based on system dynamics to measure and record the supplier's delivery performance, and upstream agents adopt either a FIFO strategy or a relationship-based strategy to fulfil orders. The results showed that when using the FIFO strategy, every possible link between the customer and supplier agents is realized and suppliers are switched frequently. On the contrary, the relationship-based strategy supports the development of fixed preferences that lead to a long-term relationship between a customer and his supplier and therefore to less supplier switches. Furthermore, if the customer places more value on the past performance of suppliers, significantly fewer supplier switches and a more stable supply chain structure can be observed, even when suppliers fulfil orders using the FIFO strategy.

These studies show that the main advantage of developing models concerning the supplier selection problem using ABS is mainly because ABS can capture the internal state of mind of an agent to reflect its evaluations of the supplier's performance and adaptions to the choice of suppliers over time.

2.5 Chapter Summary

The purpose of this chapter was to provide a starting point for further research on LHC by reviewing the relevant existing academic literature. The literature review work was carried out in two different research fields.

The review work first investigated the literature related to logistics collaboration in supply chain management. In particular, it thoroughly examined the state of art development in LHC and concluded that the development of literature in this field is still in its infancy, with very few studies and limited focus. By reviewing the literature, the study identified a number of knowledge gaps which require future study. Based on the extant literature and the research gaps identified, three research questions were developed to guide this research towards specific issues in LHC.

To inform the development of a methodology for this study, the literature review also encompassed a review of the ABS literature in SCM. A survey of the relevant ABS works in SCM was carried out, aiming at understanding how ABS was used to model supply chain problems and how the current use can inform the modelling of LHC in this research.

In next chapter, the thesis moves on to explain the research methodologies and designs that will be applied for this study.

CHAPTER 3
RESEARCH METHODOLOGY

3.1 Introduction

The aim of this chapter is to describe and justify the research methodologies adopted in this study. Logistics and SCM is a problem domain that is complex and multi-faceted. If the supply chain research is to keep up with the dynamic business environment, research methods must be applied with the capability to fully explain supply chain phenomena. The application of a single-method research approach is not always adequate for this task as it confines inquiry to only those research questions that can be answered by those methods (Flint et al. 2012). Hence, researchers of SCM are advised to use mixed methods, in which a researcher, or a team of researchers, integrates qualitative and quantitative research approaches within a single study or a set of closely related studies (Creswell and Clark, 2007, Johnson et al. 2007). The diversity in the usage of methods studying the increasingly complex SCM issues will lead to more robust results (Craighead et al. 2007).

The focus of this study is twofold. On one hand, the study aims to explore and classify the different types of LHC in practice. To address such an empirical problem it is often appropriate for researchers to choose the qualitative research methods in order to investigate the particular events and situations in the real world. On the other hand, the study wants to examine the effects of conducting LHC in supply chain. An application of the quantitative methods would allow for the explicit evaluation of the effects. Thereby, in this study it specifically applies two research methodologies in order to adequately address the research questions posed in Chapter two:

(1) Case studies are used to examine the key elements that are useful for developing logistics horizontal collaboration, and to classify models for collaboration in relation to the different characteristics described by these key elements (research questions 1 & 2).

(2) Agent-based simulation is used to work out what benefits would emerge from participating in horizontal collaboration and how such collaboration might have an

effect on supply chain operations for individuals and the system as a whole (research question 3).

The remainder of this chapter explains the methods for conducting the case studies (Section 3.2); it then describes the application of the agent-based simulation approach (Section 3.3). Although these two aspects of the research design are different, they are complementary to each other within the research project as a whole in terms of developing a comprehensive understanding of horizontal collaboration from design to results. For example, the findings from the case studies serve to indicate some key elements that need to be considered when designing the simulation model, and the model both operationalizes these elements in a simulation environment and explores their consequences when operationalized in this way. Section 3.4 summarizes this chapter.

3.2 The Case Studies

A case study approach is employed to address the first two research questions that aim to understand the key elements relevant to the development of LHC and to classify models for collaboration in relation to these key elements. The case study method is useful when the researcher wants to explore a particular situation or phenomenon in depth (Creswell, 2009). This method allows investigators to retain the holistic and meaningful characteristics of real life events and is particularly suitable when we explore "how" and "why" research questions in respect to contemporary events (Yin, 2009).

3.2.1 The Case Study Design of this Research

In this study, multiple case studies are conducted using data collected from both primary and secondary sources. It is claimed that the use of multiple cases allows more robust conclusions to be drawn from the study (Yin, 2009, Robson, 2002) since the conclusions from one case can be compared and contrasted with the results from the other cases, enabling more diversified and convincing evidence to generalize the study outcomes.

More specifically, for this study the primary aim for conducting the case studies is to clarify and generate options, possibilities and configurations which can help to provide a better understanding of the various structures and models so as to develop the typologies of LHC. In this sense, relying on a single case study would be insufficient, and there is a need to deliberately increase the diversity and quantity of case studies. The case study design, therefore, embraces multiple case studies in order to generate as wide a variety of data as possible. The potential diversity of the case settings and descriptions serves to improve the relevance, utility and workability of the resulting typology.

In addition to primary data, secondary data is also used to form the case studies. This is to overcome the limitations inherent in developing complete original case studies, which requires considerable time and financial expense to collect the primary data (Lewis, 1998), which is not abundant for this research project. In addition, conducting original case studies typically values depth over the breadth of a given problem. This inhibits the diversity of case scenarios and phenomena examined, and can often result in idiosyncratic theories (Larsson, 1993). In order to promote diversified case settings for examination, therefore, while also taking into account the resource and time constraints, secondary data is collected to generate more cases which can effectively supplement the in-depth cases based on primary data, and these are expected to provide the extra breadth and variety of settings for analysis.

Another important element of a multiple case studies design is the utilization of multiple data collection methods. This includes verbal data (interview/focus groups), and observational data (on-site visits) which support a small number of original case analysis, and written documents used as the main data for case examinations. Multiple data collection methods are employed because of the inductive nature of the case studies in this research. Inductive use of the data is the principal approach to theory generation, which in this research's focus is to develop the typologies that can classify the key forms and strategies for LHC. As contended by McCutcheon and Meredith (1993), inductive case research typically employs triangulation, using multiple data sources and analytical techniques to improve the representational accuracy of the resulting theory. Moreover, the study of many SCM topics often involves complex human, technical and organizational systems and their dynamic interrelationships, which requires the study to be carried out from different angles, e.g. using verbal data to reflect the personal views/experiences vs visiting on-site to observe the reality of operations in practice. For this reason, using a single data collection method to conduct the case studies can potentially limit the research angles that can be studied and compared during the induction, and hence restrict the resulting theory for wider application.

Furthermore, the output of the multiple case studies (the typologies of LHC) is also an important source of input to derive a better simulation model for later stages of the research, since in its development process the model needs to be clear about how the collaboration could be structured and operated. The various characteristics and forms described by the LHC typologies can provide a strong and practical reference to inform better model development.

3.2.2 Case Definition and Unit of Analysis

One important consideration in conducting case study research is where to draw the line, defining the boundary of a case (Harrison, 2002). Given that horizontal collaboration is an inter-firm matter, it is unlikely that studying a single firm will provide a good case. Instead, the study of several firms working together in a partnership network would be necessary in order to fully reveal the collaboration that is being investigated. Hence, the case defined in this study should be one entailing collaboration in which two or more firms jointly participate.

Since this study collects data from multiple sources, there are various units of observations: individual people, groups, companies, etc. Consequently, the units of analysis are also at different levels. For the analysis of verbal data, the units of analysis can be either the individual people or groups subject to the data generated by a person or reflecting the group input. Similarly, for observational data, the analysis can be based on the company's own operations or coordinated operations between multiple companies. There are hence different units of analysis in the case studies given the different nature of the data. These different units of analysis serve to identify different aspects of the issues under investigation, allowing the development of a fuller understanding of LHC practice.

The following subsection provides more specific illustrations and discussions of the case studies according to whether the data collected for those studies is derived from primary or secondary data.

3.2.3 Case Studies Based on Primary Data

A total of twenty-eight cases are studied (see Appendix I for a fuller description). According to Yin (2003), the multiple case studies should follow the replication logic that is analogous to that used in multiple experiments. Each case must be carefully selected so that it either (a) predicts similar results (a literal replication) or (b) predict different results but for predictable reasons (a theoretical replication). Given that the aim of the study is to explore the different types of LHC in practice, it selects the cases with a theoretical replication principle that they are not the simple replication of the similar practice but they are thought to different from and complement to each other to enable the fuller examination of the dynamic collaboration practice and settings, such as:

- different role players (e.g. suppliers, manufactures, or logistics service providers)
- different sectors (e.g. manufacturing, E-commerce, grocery)
- different logistics functions (e.g. distribution, warehousing, intermodality)
- different collaboration strategies (e.g. capacity sharing joint purchasing)
- different regions (e.g. UK, Belgium, China)

The number of case studies is mainly subject to available data if the main scope of the logistics activities for collaboration is covered, and also takes into account the data availability from the primary or secondary sources and the various other industry and regional characteristics.

Among the total cases, twelve cases are based upon the primary data from expert discussions, on-site observation, and a review of company documents. These twelve cases are in-depth cases because of the presence of detailed documentation of the collaboration cases from the project design phase right through to operations. In addition, seven of them are further investigated by adding input from interview/focus groups and on-site observations. None of these documents are publicly available. Table 3.1 shows the data sources used for generating the cases.

Table 3.1 Data sources used for each primary case

Case No.	Company Name	Interview/ Focus Group	On-site (shipping dock) Observation	Company Document
1	HP & Foxconn & Inventec & Quanta	√	√	√
2	HP & Foxconn & Innolux & Quanta	√	√	√
3	Airbag & Foxconn & Quanta	√	√	√
4	HP & China-based ODMs	√		√
5	HP & China-based ODMs	√		√
6	Everlink & Waimao & DB Schenker	√	√	√
7	HP & Palm	√		√
8	Hammerwerk & JSP			√
9	Coruyt & Baxter & Ontext & Eternit			√
10	Mars & UB & Saupiquet & Wrigley			√
11	PepsiCo & Nestle			√
12	Spar & Inbound Suppliers			√

In the following subsections, the various primary data collection methods are discussed in more detail.

3.2.3.1 Interviews and Focus Groups

Expert discussion is an important part of the original case studies, and this includes both interviews and focus groups. These generate two different outputs: (1) expert opinions about the key elements and issues in LHC; (2) information and discussion connected to specific cases of collaborative practice.

First, an interview is typically a one-to-one interaction between a researcher and a study participant. Interviews are a very effective method to allow researchers to explore individual experiences and perceptions in great detail (DiCicco, Bloom and Crabtree, 2006, Patton, 2002, Britten, 1995).

Semi-structured interviews are conducted with professionals from a number of companies in the IT manufacturing industry in China (Table 3.2 describes the interview arrangements). There are two reasons why this particular industry is chosen for study. First, for the sake of convenience and to be pragmatic, these companies are accessible through my social network which was built when I worked in one of these companies. Interviews with people from these companies can therefore be conducted in a more natural way because of the strong relationships between the researcher and respondents, which have already been built in the past, promoting candour in respect to the interview topics, and facilitating high quality interviews and results. Second, IT manufacturing is an industry where LHC is exercised, or is increasingly being considered to deal with the challenges in its logistics, which are characterized by high volumes and a very speed- and efficiency-driven environment.

Table 3.2 Information regarding the interviewees

Type	Interviewee	Number
Individual interview (remotely conducted in 2013)	OBM[a] logistics manager at ODMs[b] (1) (2) (3)	3
	Logistics manager of ODM (1) (2)	2
	VMI[c] hub manager of OBM/ODM	1
	Supply chain project manager of OBM	2
	Account manager of LSP[d] (1) (2)	2
Workshop (remotely conducted in 2013)	OBM operations manager at ODMs (1) (2)	2
	OBM logistics manager at ODMs (1) (2) (3)	3
	OBM order execution manager	1
Workshop (face-to-face during factory visit in 2014)	Logistics manager of ODMs (1) (2) (3)	3
	OBM logistics & operations manager at ODMs (1) (2) (3)	3
	VMI[c] hub manager of OBM/ODM	1

[a] OBM: original brand manufacturer. This stands for the original manufacturer who owns the brand of the product (e.g. Apple/HP).

[b] ODM: original design manufacturer. This stands for the manufacturer specialized in providing the outsourced designing and manufacturing services. They do not own the brand of the product (e.g. Foxconn/Flextronics)

[c] VMI: vendor managed inventory. VMI hub is a warehouse as well as a distribution centre for all manufacturers (OBM/ODM), run by a third party service provider. The inventory in

a VMI warehouse is initially owned by suppliers until customers release the purchasing orders.

[d] LSP: logistics service provider (e.g. TNT/UPS)

Note ──

An OBM logistics or operations manager "at" ODM means these people are working on-site at an ODM factory to manage and coordinate OBM's outsourced business to ODM.

To some extent, the interviewed companies are all connected to each other through the same supply chain network (i.e. producing and delivering Notebook/ Desktop computers and handheld devices, as shown in Figure 3.1). The nature of these connections really depends on the focused area of business and products, however. These companies are also different from each other when they interact with the different suppliers or customers. For example, when one manufacturer produces PCs he will be the part of the PC manufacturing supply chain; when he produces smart phones, he becomes a member of the mobile phone supply chain. The viewpoints of professionals regarding horizontal collaboration will probably hold true in other supply chain contexts.

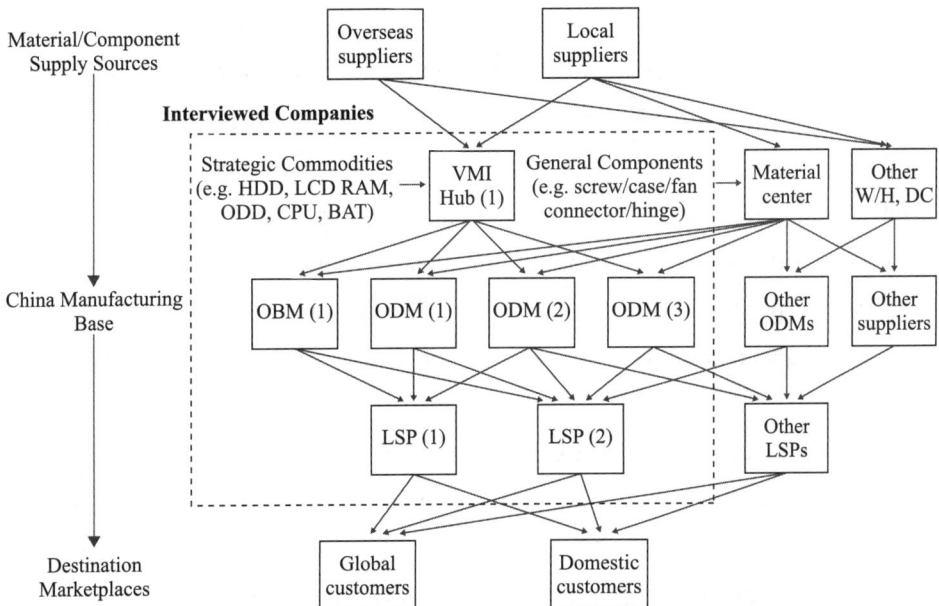

Figure 3.1 Network view of interviewed companies in PC supply chain

The interviewees are selected from a range of positions in these companies having a stake in logistics operations and collaboration. The basic criterion for interviewees is that they should have a good understanding of the subject area (i.e. logistics and supply chain management). The scope includes all main logistics functions: e.g. logistics planning, warehouse management, carrier management, cost management, and information systems. Operations professionals working in other business functions closely related to the logistics are also included for the interview, such as order planning and manufacturing operations. This allows different perspectives to be studied.

In addition to the individual interviews, a focus group meeting was held. Focus groups are guided discussions among a small group of people who share a common characteristic central to the topic of interest (Krueger and Casey, 2000, Mandrik et al. 1998). The key purpose of a focus group meeting is to supplement the individual interviews where the data generation is constrained by individual respondents or the one-to-one discussion context. The focus group is a research technique that takes advantage of group interactions to produce new and additional data on the realities that are defined in a group context, or on interpretations of events that reflect the group input (Frey and Fontana, 1991). Focus groups are appropriate when the goal is to understand differences in perspectives between groups or categories of people or to uncover factors that influence opinions or behaviour (Krueger and Casey, 2000). In addition, focus groups can be a source of validation for events observed and for individual interview data (Frey and Fontana, 1991). Bringing respondents together who have previously been interviewed separately, stimulates the comparison and re-evaluation of a previous position or statement. Focus groups are also less costly than the one-to-one interviews simply because more respondents are interviewed at the same time.

As shown in Table 3.2, the respondents selected for the focus group include the logistics managers who were previously interviewed in order to allow the cross-checking of ideas, while also incorporating experts who are specialized in other supply chain functions to facilitate more system-wide opinions. Another important consideration for selecting the respondents for the focus group is their inter-relationships. These people have strong collaborative connections in their daily work, and some of them are upstream-downstream counterparts/partners who are working at the same/near place. These pre-existing conditions naturally create a participative atmosphere for ideas exchange and discussions. The interviews are implemented prior to the group meeting in this research design because they offer a dedicated opportunity for one single respondent to express his or her own viewpoint without being affected by other people's opinions, while the focus group is useful mainly for the exchange of ideas and the stimulation of new insights in the group context.

Due to the fact that the study is conducted in a UK university, there are constraints in respect to finding a suitable time during university terms for both the interviewer and interviewees to meet face-to-face (e.g. the researcher has teaching duties, and the interviewees are typically busy in the peak season, or involved in business travel/ service support at other company's sites). Initially, therefore (Oct.-Nov. 2013), the interviews and focus groups were conducted remotely using a video conferencing tool with a desk sharing function in order to present the relevant materials during the discussions. The remote interview has been considered as an alternative approach to the conventional face-to-face interview, and has been used, for example, in social scientific research for many years (King and Horrocks, 2010). Table 3.3 shows the typical forms of remote interviews that can be used for data collection.

Table 3.3 Main forms of remote interview (source: King and Horrocks, 2010)

Remote interview form	Time frame	Data type
Telephone	Synchronous	Verbal
Remote video (Video-conferencing and webcams)	Synchronous	Verbal & Visual
E-mail	Asynchronous	Written
Instant messaging	Synchronous	Written

In this study, the remote interview based on video-conferencing is not a major limitation due to the pre-existing mature relationship between the interviewer and the interviewees, allowing effective discussions without being physically face-to-face. There may still be some potential limitations, however (e.g. people might pay less attention during the communication process remotely). To compensate for the pitfalls of such remote work, a face-to-face workshop (see Table 3.2) was held during July

2014 when the researcher was in China, in order to recap the interview questions previously discussed to allow the researcher to verify the understandings gleaned from the remote communication. Furthermore, since the communication is coupled with on-site observation, some new discussions and case information was captured at this stage, which effectively compensates for any shortfalls in the initial remote discussions.

The interview and focus groups are guided by a semi-structured questionnaire and last for about two hours. The questionnaire begins with an introduction to the study topic. Then the professionals are asked to discuss how their roles are linked to logistics, and to explain their opinions in relation to the opportunities for and elements of LHC. Further more detailed discussions are evoked if an actual case of collaboration is identified or there appears to be attractive opportunities for setting up a collaboration project.

The same list of questions is used for the interview and focus groups as they are key to the study of collaboration elements and models. They are developed based on the review of the previous literature and on the secondary case data and advice given by a professional in logistics. The questions covered in the interviews/focus groups are listed below:

(1) What are the logistics characteristics of the company, (e.g. sensitive to cost, time, scale, or frequency), and how is the logistics process conducted?

(2) What are the drivers/issues in a company that would encourage horizontal collaboration? Examples of these may be:

a. Cost reduction

b. Improved service levels

c. Scale/Sustainability

d. Smaller more frequent deliveries, etc.

(3) What are the barriers to collaboration and how might these be overcome? An example of these may be:

a. Difficult to find suitable partners/align objectives

b. Difficult to estimate collaboration gains

c. Technical/operational incompatibility/internal alignment

d. Lack of trust

(4) What type of companies and their supply chain characteristics are suited to horizontal collaboration?

(5) What do you consider to be the most important elements for designing a practical horizontal collaboration?

(6) What are promising areas for horizontal collaboration, with whom and what are the collaboration models for implementation? (If there is a real case, share the case story).

(7) Which types of information are shared in the collaboration? How can the sharing of information assist logistics horizontal collaboration?

(8) How can vertical collaboration be useful for horizontal collaboration?

(9) What is the time horizon suitable for collaboration?

3.2.3.2 On-site Observations

Observational data collection involves the systematic, detailed observation of people and events to learn about behaviours and interactions in natural settings (Curry et al. 2009). There are many reasons to conduct observational data collection in this study. First, this method is very useful to study a case or phenomenon that is hidden from the public, and is appropriate for use when something is not easy to be described orally, especially when involving tacit knowledge. Second, logistics and SCM belong to one problem domain that is complex and multi-faceted, which naturally calls for study from different angles. Interview is one means for such study but constitute only a part of the story. While interviews focus heavily on verbal data generation that is often related to respondents' personal views, efforts are also needed to watch the real practice, in order to facilitate more practical ways of thinking about the issues under study. Third, since the research interests are mostly concerned with "ways of doing thing", active observations are intuitively beneficial. It is also often the case that the conversation with respondents only makes sense if conducted in conjunction with seeing the objects, such as through a plant tour. Performing on-site observation is in addition a way to encourage socialization in order to stimulate more productive discussions and to uncover potentially important phenomena that may otherwise not be accessible to the researcher.

The on-site studies in China, arranged through the researcher's personal connections, include a rail distribution terminal, a VMI hub, factories of three top PC/display ODMs (original design manufacturers), and one factory of a leading American PC/handheld OBM (original brand manufacturer). A visit was also paid in the UK to a distribution centre for a leading British grocery retailer.

Notes were taken during and after the tours in order to capture any useful insights that emerged and useful information related to the research. For example, by observing at the loading docks of ODMs it was found that many trucks were shipped with less-than-truck loads (LTLs). Further communication with the operational staff confirmed the root cause as being a lack of a consistent pace in the receipt of orders from customers (professionally known as "order linearity"), which is a result of applying a BTO (build-to-order) production model wherein factories only produce PCs when customers place the actual orders. Also, individual consumers can place orders directly to factories through an online system without intermediaries to form order batches based on full-truck-load (FTLs) units. These observations show the unpredictability of logistics orders and how this affects the efficiency level. These issues are very difficult to resolve by changing internal rules and behaviours. When different factories sharing the same problem are located near to each other, however, the opportunity for collaboration (e.g. by sharing trucks) is evident and it is then easier to extend the scope of collaboration. Technically, this is not difficult since they all produce similar PCs/displays. With just a minor package alignment the PC pallets from one factory can be easily stacked on the pallets of products (e.g. displays) from another one to increase the truck utilization. A similar situation was also observed in the food distribution centre in the UK. This distribution centre is dedicated to one retailer but a very low utilization level was observed for all kinds of operations. The use of logistics equipment and units of measures that are very standardized and which can be easily shared with another retailer to improve efficiency (e.g. rolling cages are widely adopted, which allows for efficient physical consolidation of cartons with varied sizes and shapes from different suppliers. These can be pre-staged at the loading gate before tuck docking, meaning no tighter planning alignment is needed and collaboration is easy. This is an advantage compared to PC manufacturers' collaborations who adopt pallet-stretch wrapping to build up loads, which requires seamless coordination of the shipping schedule and forklift loading).

Consequently, these visits help a lot to build up understandings of practical issues in logistics and stimulate thinking and discussion of how to practice horizontal collaboration. It also helps to provide additional information for issues discussed in the interview and focus groups (e.g. collaboration objectives). Through the fieldwork it apparently shows that collaboration isn't just for cost reduction. There are many more objectives such as speed/quick turnaround as the other critical concerns for collaboration. Also, the observation at shipping dock gives the chance to look at a fragment of the actual operations for collaboration (e.g. aligned shipment pickup windows with other shippers for rail transport).

3.2.3.3 Documents

Besides the verbal and observational data, written materials are intentionally gathered and serve as a valuable source of data. Written documents often contain richer information to explain situations or configurations of cases. Good documentation can offer comprehensive and structural information to explain certain phenomena. To say the least, studying the various available documents widens the vision of the study. According to Patton (2002), documents include, but are not limited to, institutional documents (clinical, programmatic, or organizational records), personal documents (diaries, letters, artistic expressions), and public historical documents (legislative testimony, legal documents).

It is worth noting that collecting documents during the field work is one type of the primary data collation, because primary data does not necessarily mean people speaking only. Using the connections with interviewees, seven in-depth documents were obtained. These are project documents and SOPs (standard operating procedures), highly relevant to the operational practice of LHC. In addition to the interviewed companies, there are another six in-depth project reports obtained privately through an industry project team who are implementing pilot projects for freight LHC in Europe. All these written documents are about collaboration projects between a number of firms and illustrate the details from design to operations. These project reports might, however, be written to favour the successful elements of horizontal collaboration since none of the reported projects are ultimately failures.

3.2.4 Case Studies Based on Secondary Data

As discussed in the case study design in Section 3.2.1, developing case studies using primary data requires considerable time and resources, which is a key constraint for this research. In addition to the primary data driven cases that generate in-depth insights into the design and operation of collaboration projects, therefore, the development of a comprehensive typology also values broader understandings of the alternative forms and configurations of collaboration. There is therefore a need to increase the diversity and quantity of the collaboration cases for the purposes of classification. Collecting and studying materials from secondary sources appears to be a good strategy that could help to provide the extra breadth and variety of settings for collaborative practice.

The secondary documents collected are related to specific collaboration projects jointly performed between two or more companies and describe more different collaboration practice in the different sectors which complement to the primary cases mainly explored in the manufacturing sector. The documents are gathered from trade journals, company reports, conference reports, and publications from logistics professional organizations such as CILT (Chartered Institute of Logistics and Transport), ECR UK/Europe (Efficient Consumer Response), IGD (Institute of Grocery Distribution). Using this secondary data generates an additional sixteen case studies of horizontal collaboration in logistics and freight transport. The details of the data sources for each case can be referred to Appendix I.

Secondary data has potential limitations in respect to the lack of direct control over the original data generation and analysis. For instance, the secondary case materials might not address fully or precisely the desired issues and aspects that this study wants to explore. Also, the collected documents about a collaboration project might not describe its full picture of configuration and might over emphasise the successful parts of the collaboration while understating the negative outcomes.

Hence, the data quality is less certain in respect to secondary sources. In spite of these limitations, the secondary cases provide additional and valuable insights into the diverse characteristics and forms of LHC in practice.

3.2.5 Data Analysis

Since data is generated from multiple cases as well as multiple data sources, it is important to perform careful data triangulation work in order to link all the data together for more rigorous analysis and interpretations. This study applies the inductive approach informed by the concept of "iterative triangulation" suggested by Lewis (1998). Iterative triangulation employs systematic iterations between data collected from the various sources, comparing and contrasting the emerging constructs, and searching for patterns across diverse case settings. The key purpose of this iterative analysis is to develop a chain of triangulated evidence that may enhance the scientific value of the resulting constructs and theory, and improve their validity, reliability and logical consistency.

The various collected data eventually comprised 12 primary and 16 secondary cases (see Appendix I for the fuller description and the data source) related to the specific collaboration projects implemented. In addition to these specific cases, there are also a number of expert opinions collected concerning the key elements and issues in LHC. The subsequent data analysis employs a five-step procedure (see Table 3.4) following the major guidelines for analysing qualitative data (Bryman, 2012, Gillham, 2000, Charmaz, 2006).

Table 3.4 Steps for data analysis in this study
(adapted from the general guideline in Bryman, 2012, Gillham, 2000, Charmaz, 2006)

Step	Activity
1 Sorting & consolidation	Collate and transform the relevant data obtained from various sources (e.g. interviews, documents) into the standardized transcripts/notes for formal recording, and perform the appropriate sorting and consolidation based on the types and sources of information.

Continued

Step	Activity
2 Reading & labelling	Read through the collected materials several times to become familiarized with the data and story. Then try to make marginal notes such as key words, phrases, or names to serve as a general index to represent certain portions of the data and descriptions, based on which the relevant ideas and issues can be identified and defined.
3 Coding	Cut up the collected data into chunk files based on the different issues and meanings captured in step two and then apply a unique code to each of them. Then reorganize these chunk files through a coding process. During the initial coding sequence the data are broken apart analytically to perceive actions in each segment of the data. The codes are selected when a complete idea or concept is apparent within the data. After the initial coding, a more abstract level of coding is performed to discover the categories and subcategories codes. This is based on comparing and contrasting the initial codes to enable the similarities and differences become apparent, allowing categories to emerge, which can lead to a greater understanding of the cases. Examples of codes can be found in Table 3.5.
4 Iterative comparison & analysis	Iteratively compare and contrast the instances and characteristics between the coded data. Identify the core elements and understand the underlying meaning or patterns found in each element. Figure 3.2 below shows an example of how the data gathered from the different sources and/or cases are iteratively compared and integrated to generate a consolidated view of the benefits of shared warehouses.
5 Develop variance models	Classify the dynamic patterns and constructs in each element to develop variance models. Connect the variance models of different elements to form a structured typology for LHC.

Table 3.5 Examples of code information

Category	Code	Description
Logistics characteristics	DIST VOL PLC VAR CC SQ VS …	**Distance:** the physical distance to deliver goods to customers **Volume:** the scale of the logistics demand **Product life cycle:** the speed of a product devaluation over time **Variation:** the degree to which the logistics demand can be anticipated **Cost control:** the extent to which the logistics cost is concerned **Service quality:** the extent to which the logistics service is concerned **Volume sensitive:** the extent to which the shipping volume is concerned …

Continued

Category	Code	Description
Collaboration KPIs	CR SPD FRQ FLX RELIA ENVO PRE CVG …	**Cost reduction:** a collaboration objective which enables the reduced logistics cost **Speed:** a collaboration objective which enables the faster delivery service **Frequency:** a collaboration objective which enables the higher transportation frequency **Flexibility:** a collaboration objective which increases the flexibility for logistics operations **Reliability:** a collaboration objective which increases the reliability of delivery and operations **Environment:** a collaboration objective which improves the environmental performance as resulted from the collaboration **Predictability:** a collaboration objective which increases the demand predictability **Coverage:** a collaboration objective which increases the geographical and market coverage …
Information sharing	POS OHO OHC OFCST BLOG EST …	**Point-of-sales:** share end-market demand information with partners **On-hand orders:** share current customer orders information with partners **On-hand capacity:** share current capacity information with partners **Order forecast:** share demand forecast or marketing/promotion plans with partners **Backlog:** share back orders information with partners **Estimated shipping time:** share expected delivery time information with partners …
Initiator/Leading actor	GSUPP GSELL CUST LSP	**Goods supplier:** collaboration led by suppliers **Goods seller:** collaboration led by distributors

Continued

Category	Code	Description
Initiator/Leading actor	TCT ...	**Customer:** collaboration led by customers **Logistics service provider:** collaboration led by the 3rd party logistics provider **Third party control tower:** collaboration led by the 3rd party coordinator/trustee ...
...	...	...

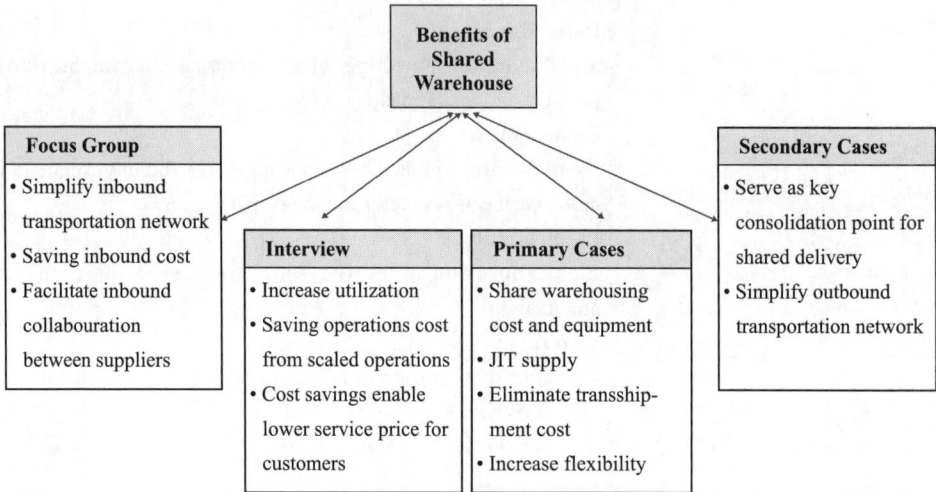

Figure 3.2 Example of comparing and analysing data from different sources

For any empirical social research, it is pertinent to ensure the quality of the research by adopting the four tests as suggested by Yin (2009). These are summarised in Table 3.6.

Table 3.6 Tactics for evaluating the research quality

Test	Tactics applied	Research stage
Construct validity	Use multiple sources of evidence (i.e. verbal, written, and observational data). The data gathered from the various sources was transcribed and transferred into a structured database using the spreadsheet and software. Notes taken during the interview were sent to participants for their confirmation and feedback.	Data collection

Continued

Test	Tactics applied	Research stage
Internal validity	The data gathered were analysed to identify patterns from the various cases. The data gathered were analysed by cross-comparing the patterns identified from the various cases. The group meeting and on-site observation were used to verify the data gathered from remote interviews.	Data analysis
External validity	Four global and major PC manufacturers who participated in the empirical study, representing more than half of the global manufacturing capacity, together with two global leading LSPs and one warehouse/DC operator. In documents research, a total of 28 cases were examined, representing many different sectors (manufacturing, E-commerce, grocery, FMCG), different logistics functions (e.g. distribution, warehousing, inter-modal transport), and different countries (e.g. UK, Belgium, China, Spain, Netherland).	Research design
Reliability	A protocol was developed to conduct the interview. The same data collection procedure (introduction, consistent questions, feedback) was followed in each interview. Develop case study database to store and manage the collected data.	Data collection

Using these analytic procedures, the case study analysis could develop a systematic typological analysis for LHC which takes into account the various elements critical to the collaboration. In addition, the insights generated into key elements such as collaboration strategies, structures and KPIs are useful in informing the next stage of the research, i.e. applying the agent-based simulation, which is described in the following section.

3.3 Agent-based Simulation

The third research question aims to understand the explicit effect of LHC on supply chain performance. To quantify the effects of collaboration, agent-based simulation (ABS) is adopted in order to explicitly model the behaviours and decisions made in the collaboration and to explore their operational consequences.

3.3.1 Why Agent-based Simulation?

ABS undertakes a bottom-up approach to the modelling of individual agents and the way they act and interact. The overall dynamics emerge from the collective interactions between agents. Compared to other types of modelling methods, ABS is recognized as being more suitable for studying complex systems that have a high degree of localization and distribution (Macal and North, 2010, Behdani, 2012). Supply chains fall into this category, since a supply chain system is not centrally controlled and contains many individual organizations who can act and make decisions autonomously. Such characteristics therefore enable the supply chain system to be a good application area of ABS.

From the methodological perspective, ABS is a proven approach which is useful for studying supply chain problems. As indicated in the literature review, ABS has been used to study a wide range of issues in the supply chain management context. Some of these studies investigate the methods for developing the supply chain models which enable more accurate representations of supply chain behaviours (Macal and North, 2006, Behdani, 2012, Arunachalam and Sadeh, 2005, Allwood and Lee, 2005), while others focus on applying ABS to study the specific supply chain problems, such as information sharing and the development of trust between the supply chain partners (Kim, 2009, Chan and Chan, 2005, Lin et al. 2002, Caridi et al. 2005).

Also, the study focuses on the collaboration issues in the supply chain. Collaboration involves a group of independent firms, who while attempting to achieve their self-interested objectives, also decide to collaborate and pursue common goals and interests. Hence they coordinate through different types of collaborative strategies in which they communicate and consult with each other through exchange of information and resources in ways that can promote dynamic interactions. These features fit well with the characteristics of an ABS model.

The most important reason that ABS is selected as the methodology is its capability to explicitly model the collaboration behaviours and decision-making specific to individuals (in this study the individual firms in a supply chain network) and explore how these individuals can collectively affect the collaboration gains and operations in the supply chain system. Without such explicit representation of individuals it would be very difficult to study the effect of horizontal collaboration. There is a major limitation for the empirical survey or interview based studies, in that they concentrate on using statistical correlations or human perceptions to explain the collaboration effects, rather than the mechanisms that actually produce it. The core of any effects and patterns emerging in the course of the collaboration is the mechanism exercised, which is made by the explicit individual decisions, behaviours, and their interactions.

3.3.2 How Do Case Studies Inform Agent-based Simulation?

The development of an ABS model often needs to be guided by and compared to existing systems, which serve to provide indicators to inform the micro-configuration of the model (Grimm et al. 2005). These indicators refer to a set of essential information that needs to be considered, such as agent behaviours, agent attributes and agent relationships, or how the simulation output can be measured. Case study findings from real systems can be helpful to determine the required parameters and to set up the behaviour rules for agents, which will make the developed model more realistic with a basis on practical information. More specifically, there are five different uses as regards to the empirical data collected through case studies as indicated by the various researchers, and of these, three types of empirical data usage are adopted in this study.

(1) Inform the micro process of model configurations (e.g. Berger and Schreinemachers (2006).

In this research, for instance, by undertaking the empirical study the modeller will know much better how the collaboration is set up and performed in the practice. These sorts of useful and practical information will serve as the important guidance for the modeller who will have therefore a clearer idea to configure the collaboration rules and parameters in the process of model development.

(2) Document the macro patterns for model validation, e.g. Evans and Kelley (2004); Giannakis and Louis (2011).

In this research, for instance, the various collaboration benefits and effects identified in the empirical context can be compared to and validated by the simulation, the outcomes of which represent the macro performance patterns arising from the micro behaviours among agents.

(3) Falsify/Test models that have been developed previously by other researchers, e.g. Roorda et al. (2010).

(4) Capture emerging management issues/themes that are of relevance and interest for modelling, e.g. Siebers et al. (2007).

In this research, for instance, the empirical study has indicated the potentiality of combining horizontal collaboration with vertical collaboration. The subsequent model designing, therefore, might take into account this interesting element for modelling and testing.

(5) Replicate real cases and scenarios, e.g. assessing one specific policy in practice under certain scenarios.

3.3.3 Steps in a Simulation Study

This section introduces the typical process for conducting a simulation study, which is followed by this study. For the ABS model applied for this research topic, the detailed illustration of the model design and configurations will be presented in Chapter 5.

A simulation study can be conducted following a step-wise approach, as can be shown in Figure 3.3. At the early stage of the research, both a literature review and empirical case studies are conducted to study LHC in current literature and business practice, based on which the main modelling objectives are established.

After that, a conceptual supply chain model is developed, taking into consideration the findings and implications from the literature and case studies. The conceptual model itself can be represented in a number of ways such as by text, diagrams, or in combination form to indicate the overall workflow of the model.

The next step is to translate the conceptual model into a computer simulation model through programming. Verification and validation of the model were conducted at the end of this step. A debugging process was conducted to ensure that the program works correctly and is error free. This process is split into two parts: a unit test (UT) and an integrative test (IT). In the unit test, all the modules and functions created in the program are verified individually using some specially built testing methods and the resulting data is checked carefully against the design. Then, in an integrated test, the whole simulation program is verified step by step to ensure the correctness of the entire workflow of the model.

After the computer model is programmed, the experimental design is set to alter some alternative configurations and parameters in order to discover their impact on the performance of the supply chain model. In the last step, multiple replication runs of the simulation model are conducted, and the simulation results are analysed and compared with those of other studies. Insights and conclusions are drawn accordingly.

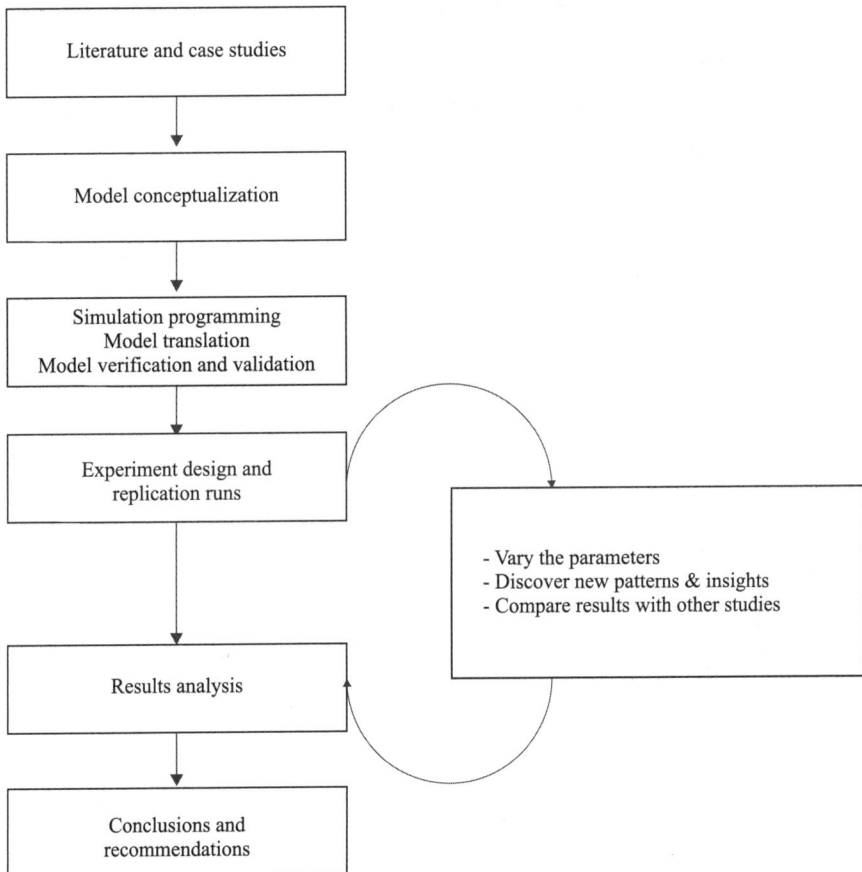

Figure 3.3 Stages in a simulation study — adapted from Robinson et al. (2010)

3.4 Chapter Summary

This chapter explains the two research methodologies adopted for carrying out this research, i.e. case studies and agent-based simulation. In regard to the case studies, the chapter explains why case studies are chosen as the research methodology for this research and sets out the case study design and unit of analysis. The case studies are categorized into primary and secondary cases for analysis, and multiple data collection methods are employed. The data analysis procedures are illustrated in the end. Second, it describes the role of agent-based simulation in this research and justifies why agent-based simulation is appropriate for this research topic. The inter-connections between case studies and agent-based simulation are also clarified. Finally, the main steps for carrying out the simulation study used in this research are demonstrated.

In the next chapter, the thesis moves on to examine the research findings from the empirical case studies.

CHAPTER 4
CASE STUDIES

4.1 Introduction

This chapter presents the findings from case studies. By analysing the collected data it identifies a number of key elements critical to the design of an LHC project. Based on these key elements, a comprehensive typological analysis is conducted to explain the different characteristics and types of collaboration encountered in wider supply chain practice (i.e. not solely concerned with LSPs collaboration which was discussed most in prior studies).

The remainder of this chapter is organized as follows. In section 4.2, a discussion and classification of the key elements for developing effective horizontal collaboration is presented. In section 4.3, a comprehensive typological study is conducted, taking into consideration the varying characteristics of each key element. Section 4.4 concludes the findings, highlighting the main contributions and the elements taken forward into the subsequent simulation study.

4.2 Key Elements for Developing Logistics Horizontal Collaboration

A first step towards the fuller understanding of the different types of LHC is to identify the key elements critical to the LHC development. Through the data collection described in Section 3.2, the study was able to gather many data from the expert discussions and case examinations, which covered various aspects of issues pertaining to designing and operating LHC.

Following the data analysis process described in Section 3.2.5, the interesting and related issues captured from the various expert discussions and case examinations were analysed and categorized. Afterwards, by iteratively comparing and contrasting the different instances and categories of issues, the study identified that "collaboration structures" "collaboration objectives" "collaboration intensity" and "collaboration modes" are the four key elements that are of great importance to characterize the design and implementation of a LHC project in practice. These elements can assist to form a framework for analysing the types of LHC in a more systematic way. As shown in Figure 4.1, each element represents an important aspect of the collaboration development and exhibits many different characteristics and forms.

It is worthwhile to note that the identification of the key elements was mostly based on the empirical data collected. There wasn't a pre-defined list of elements based on the literature as the study desires to explore the relevant elements from the case studies of direct practice in LHC. On the other hand, when analysing the empirical data collected, some of the prior literature had been used to support the analysis of the important elements for LHC development. For instance, the objectives of LHC were widely discussed in the literature, which were also evident in the case studies, suggesting it as an important element for developing LHC. Also, it is difficult to consider all the elements emerging from the case studies. The study concentrated on the key elements relevant to the operational design of LHC which can provide the best opportunities to explore the different kinds of LHC practice (see Figure 4.1)

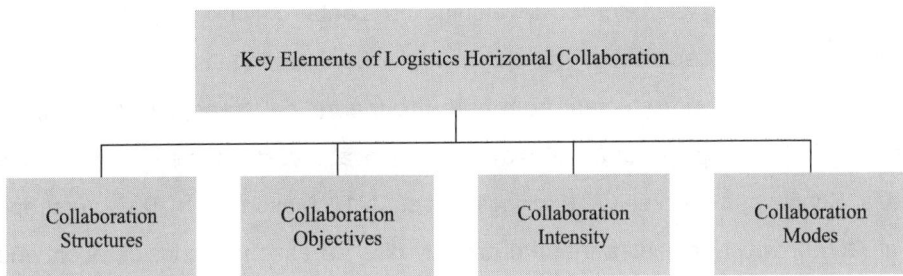

Figure 4.1 Key elements for developing logistics horizontal collaboration

In the remainder of this section, a brief summary of the key elements is given, with a detailed typological analysis of each collaboration element being presented in the following sections.

The first key element describes the structure of the connections and relationships between supply chain players when implementing LHC. It is specifically concerned with whom to collaborate with if there is a need for horizontal collaboration, and the interactions with other supply chain players.

It was found that most prior studies limit the examination of collaboration to the context of the LSPs, such as opportunities and impediments (Cruijssen et al. 2007a), efficiency (Cruijssen et al. 2010), cost distribution (Krajewska et al. 2008), governance (Wallenburg and Raue, 2011). However, the case studies revealed a fact that within a broader supply chain context there are many different stakeholders who can get involved in horizontal collaboration. For instance, not only the LSPs should collaborate. There are cases of upstream players participated in LHC, such two manufacturers (Nestle and United Biscuits) collaborate to explore the backhaul opportunity. Cases also showed that downstream customers can play active roles in LHC. Such as a case of a French retailer (Carrefour) requests their suppliers to collaborate in their goods delivery. Hence it requires a specific consideration of the collaboration setup based on the role players and their relationship structure. Collaboration at the different stages of the supply chain involves different stakeholders and different resources. Therefore, it is quite important to understand the role and characteristics of these stakeholders, and their relationships, as well as the interactions between them.

The second key element for developing horizontal collaboration is centred on the objectives of collaboration. The objectives for participating LHC were extensively addressed by the prior studies, from both the theoretical standpoint (Caputo and Mininno, 1996, Cruijssen et al. 2007b) and empirical investigations (Cruijssen et al. 2007a, Schulz and Blecken, 2010, Hingley et al. 2011, Mason et al. 2007, Verstrepen et al. 2009), which indicates that the objectives is an essential consideration when developing the LHC project. This element was found to be a very important theme among the investigated cases and expert discussions. It was further revealed that companies should consider very carefully why they want to enter into the collaboration. It is important to establish this clarity at the very beginning because it sets the expectations of the benefits the companies would acquire from the collaboration, which will also inform the design of the collaboration strategies and the performance measures used to assess the outcomes of the implementation.

Furthermore, the case studies suggested that the successful horizontal collaboration is very dependent on the symmetry of partners' collaboration objectives.

If partners' objectives are well aligned at some point, they are more likely to trust each other and share the common business objectives, and this will make them a better match for the collaboration, given that they share similar interests in respect to the collaboration. From the expert discussions, it was found that the desire for collaboration is closely related to the current inefficacies in outbound logistics (e.g. ODMs have frequent LTL shipments to airport/rail terminals), meaning that companies with similar issues in their operations are potentially good partners for collaboration. This element was shown to be one of the main business characteristics enabling horizontal collaboration.

The third key element that was evidently found in the case studies is related to the intensity of collaboration.

The case studies revealed that the existing cases of collaboration tend to differ from each other in terms of their input resources. The intensity of the collaboration varies depending on the business environment and the partners' inter-relationships. It is also highlighted that more does not necessarily mean better for some collaboration participants, given the increased cost entailed in invest in collaborative resources (e.g. setting up an inter-organizational ICT system between manufactures in China) and the need to maintain stronger relationships. In some specific cases examined, it would be good enough for some partners to have a "speed dating" kind of collaboration (e.g. offer provisional backhaul loads) or to rely on ad hoc opportunities. On the other hand, higher intensity collaboration can be reserved for more strategically important partners. In this approach there is a wider scope of operational areas included in the collaboration, and higher trust between partners.

It was a fact from case studies that the collaboration practices were implemented at various degrees. However, it's hard to draw the line among the different practices. A set of criteria is needed to support more structural analysis. This is complemented using the existing literature (Lambert et al. 1999, Cruijssen et al. 2007b, Pomponi et al. 2013), which suggested a number of components to analyse the degrees of collaboration among the various cases.

The fourth key element is related to the various implementation forms and strategies of LHC, hereafter referred to as the "collaboration mode". The case studies identified the collaboration mode as a crucial element to characterize the types of LHC and it relates closely to the practicality of the horizontal collaboration. Almost all the interviewees during the discussions were keen to talk about the various designs and the implementation of horizontal collaboration and how that collaboration could be carried out in the different logistics functions and supply chain configurations.

Horizontal collaboration is a recent business practice, and there is therefore limited knowledge about the ways to operationalize this business concept. The existing research on the forms and strategies of LHC are quite limited, as it mainly emphasizes the illustration of potential cost savings through the transport bundling (Cruijssen et al. 2007c, Hingley et al. 2011, Bahrami, 2002b, Hageback et al. 2004). Analysis of further approaches to improve the performance in horizontal collaboration could not be found, however. This reveals the limited understanding pertaining to the operational management of LHC in current contributions.

From the expert discussions it was found that most of them were more familiar with vertical collaboration, while horizontally some of them perceived more chance of competition, particularly between LSP companies and OBM manufactures. When discussing the possible collaboration scenarios based upon their daily experiences, and via examining the case of collaborative practices in a wider industry however, it was found that there are potentially a number of good collaboration modes which can be useful for practitioners seeking to implement horizontal collaboration.

4.3 A Typology of Logistics Horizontal Collaboration

The examination of the key collaboration elements has indicated that the nature and structure of horizontal collaboration networks tends to differ widely. To understand these different structures and characteristics of horizontal collaboration better, this section presents a typological analysis as a means to classify and compare the different types of horizontal collaboration arising from the case studies, thereby supporting the design and positioning of specific collaboration projects and studies. Although there are many elements which can be used as a basis upon which to classify horizontal collaboration, this study does not intend to make the typology exhaustive, developing it instead based on the key elements identified in the last section. These elements represent the key considerations when designing a collaboration, and can collectively determine the key features that a particular type of horizontal collaboration will exhibit in practice. Examples of case studies are illustrated where appropriate, with the case reference number, and all case studies are listed in Appendix I.

In the next four subsections, the typological analysis is illustrated in detail according to each of the key elements.

4.3.1 Collaboration Structure

The first element for the typological analysis concerns the basic structures of LHC. It describes at a high level the types of stakeholders in the supply chain who form horizontal collaborative relationships, and their interactions with other stakeholders outside the horizontal partnership. The case studies show how many different types of business parties engage fully or partially in the collaboration process, ranging from component suppliers and product manufacturers to carriers and retailers. With a perspective of an end-to-end inbound and outbound logistics process in the supply chain, the study developed a generalization of stakeholder types into three distinctive roles as shown in Table 4.1. Then, by analysing the possible collaboration scenarios among these key stakeholders, three generalized collaboration structures were identified, as presented in Figure 4.2, as well as one hybrid LHC, shown in Figure 4.3.

Table 4.1 Key stakeholders in logistics industry

Stakeholder	Explanation	Examples
Shipper	The party who initiates the outbound distribution of goods to various customers at lower levels of the supply chain. Often these are suppliers/ manufacturers, but they can also be distributors/ retailers who do not own the manufacturing but who sell/deliver products to end customers. In some cases where manufacturing/supply is fully/ partially outsourced (e.g. ODM/OEM), shippers can simultaneously be both the outsourcing manufacturer and the brand-owning producer.	HP, Apple, Samsung Foxconn, Quanta, Inventec Nestle, United Biscuits Amazon.com, JD.com

Continued

Stakeholder	Explanation	Examples
Customer	The party who receives inbound products from the upstream shippers. Typically, these are retailers and end-consumers, but they could also be manufacturers or suppliers if they also receive inbound products and materials from further upstream sources. In some cases, where the customer owns the inbound logistics (e.g. Ex-Works), the customer is simultaneously a shipper and a customer if the shipments are inbound to its own facilities. Otherwise it might act as a "co-shipper" if goods are directly outbound to the customer's customer (e.g. Foxconn+HP → Best-Buy shops).	Walmart, Best-Buy Carrefour, Tesco Verizon, AT&T Office Depot, Costco
LSP	The party who offers logistics-related services to the buyers. The buyers could be either the shipper or the customer depending on who performs the logistics in the supply chain. The LSP can be further segmented into several different roles in the marketplace according to its functions, as presented in the examples.	Forwarder (Panalpina, FedEx, UPS, DHL), Carriers (TNT, Maersk, APL, Cosco) Broker (Flextronics), Warehouse & terminal operator (DB Schenker) Logistics equipment & technology provider (CHEP/Cainiao), 4PL (UPS-SCS)

4.3.1.1 Collaboration Structure 1 (shipper-centric collaboration)

There are three variations of this collaboration structure as indicated in Figure 4.2. In the first, shown as a double-headed arrow between shippers, a horizontal collaboration takes place exclusively between shippers with a common goal to improve their outbound logistics performance, such as the transportation cost, the vehicle fill-rate, and the customer service. For example, two shippers from the JSP & Hammerwerk case study actively collaborate to synchronize and bundle their freight flow to improve the vehicle loading utilization (Case 8). The two shippers share information such as production and delivery schedules in order closely to align the operations on both sides, enabling much improved freight consolidation and distribution. A second example is Nestle and United Biscuits, who are direct competitors but who also form a close partnership to improve the utilization of transportation assets and reduce empty miles (Case 13). The two shippers began to regularly share trucks to transport each other's loads when they spot a complementary front and backhaul route, resulting not only in a well-balanced roundtrip, but also significant environmental benefits from CO_2 reduction due to the elimination of empty trucking, leading to a striking example of successful collaboration between competitive shippers.

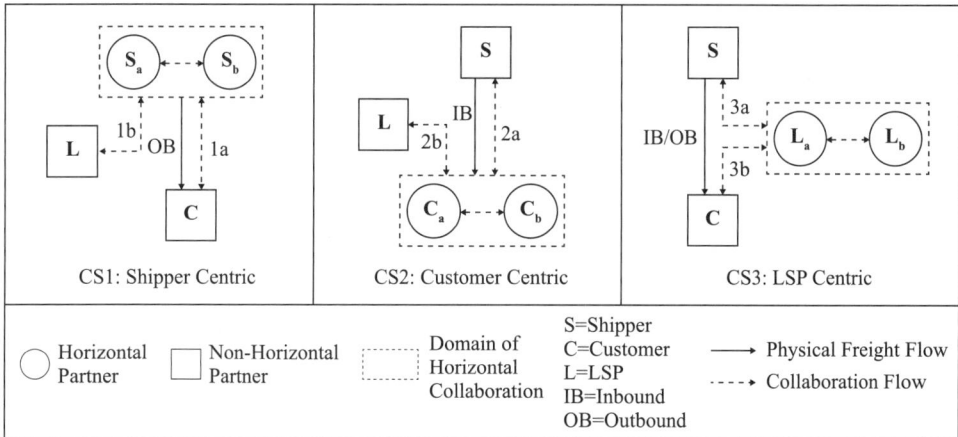

Figure 4.2 Structures of logistics horizontal collaboration

The second variation (highlighted as CS1b in Figure 4.2) happens when an LSP supports collaboration between shippers. As one interviewed LSP suggested, this additional collaborative interaction would happen in a supply chain system where the logistics service in a large part is outsourced to a third party logistics (3PL) provider. The support from the LSP will further ensure a greater visibility for the planning of the capacity and shipping schedule, which guarantees an executable collaboration plan for shipper partners. The third variation (highlighted as CS1a in Figure 4.2) may occur when shippers gain vertical customer support, particularly common customers. Obtaining such collaboration support is quite important from the shipper's perspective as highlighted by two factory operations managers who concern about the delivery performance. Also there was a LHC pilot project in Europe which expressed the desire to obtain customer support for a smarter synchronized delivery (Case 11). The customer in such scenario could offer help by means of order/delivery synchronization to each of the collaborative shippers so that the shippers could align their production and shipping schedule more easily. Another practical example of this can be found in the collaboration between Nestle & Mars with active facilitation by their common customer — Tesco (Case 14).

4.3.1.2 Collaboration Structure 2 (customer-centric collaboration)

In the second collaboration structure, customers collaborate better to control and optimize the inbound logistics from their vendors. According to the interviewed ODM logistics managers, such collaboration is viable in the situation when customers manage goods deliveries from factories (or more generally upstream shippers) and own the associated cost. This approach of customers taking control of the goods transportation has been widely adopted in the supply chain of some industries (e.g. the IT/grocery sector). The Incoterm behind such an approach is often referred to as "FCA shipper's dock" or "Ex-Works". The interviewed OBM often adopted this approach to ship cargos from ODM factories taking the advantage of their robust global logistics network. Potter et al. (2007) found that several leading British retailers, such as Tesco and Sainsbury's, have begun to implement "factory gate pricing" (FGP) similar to "Ex-Works" for a part of their product range, allowing the receiving retailers to take greater control of their primary and secondary inbound distribution, and to make the best use of the available vehicle fleet. Effectively, the experts of interview suggested that this gives potential collaborative opportunities for horizontal customers to integrate their respective inbound logistics network and resources. One case of how Dutch retailers collaborate under FGP to achieve considerable cost savings was studied by Le Blanc et al. (2006). Another British retailer, Marks & Spencer, has also begun trials with other retailers to share the warehouse space in a couple of specific distribution centres (Marle, 2012).

Likewise, effective collaboration between customers also calls for strong vertical support from shippers (see CS2a in Figure 4.2), who would adapt their production and pickup schedule according to the retailers' joint plan for goods collection and consolidation. The LSPs would also be actively involved in the planning and coordination between collaborative retailers for the optimal planning and use of the logistics capacity (see CS2b in Figure 4.2). This can benefit LSPs in terms of their operating efficiency as well as customers who can have lower delivery costs and higher service levels.

4.3.1.3 Collaboration Structure 3 (LSP-centric collaboration)

CS3 is primarily related to collaboration between LSPs. LSPs can join forces to make use of each other's capacity and networks to deliver improved capacity utilization and consequently better performance in cost savings. This is, as has been mentioned, the most studied LHC structure in the literature and is recognized by the interviewed LSPs as a promising approach for increasing the capacity utilization and customer responsiveness.

For instance, there is a collaborative service jointly managed by three LSPs aiming at improving the operational efficiency, connectivity and visibility of the pre-carriage logistics from factories to the railway terminal (Case 6). In this case, two customs brokers who manage the information flow of customs procedures actively coordinate with another freight forwarder who controls the physical flow of trucks and shipments. The seamless integration of information and physical flows between brokers and freight forwarders has succeeded in making the collaborative service cost-efficient for themselves and service-effective for the customers (the factories).

Given the intermediary role of LSPs, the logistics activities managed by them can be either inbound or outbound, depending upon whom they supply services to. The interviewed LSP managers believed that shippers or customers as the service buyers should play an important role in supporting collaboration between LSPs. This is because of the fact that they are the actual parties to initiate the logistics demand to LSPs and are likely to require LSPs to integrate with their operational process. Multiple LSP collaborations would further complicate the network operations and linkages with their customers, therefore shippers and customers have to be actively involved in the collaboration between LSPs to facilitate better flexibility and efficiency in the planning and execution of logistics activities (see CS3a/3b in Figure 4.2).

4.3.1.4 Hybrid Collaboration Structure

A hybrid collaboration structure can be formed by the combination of at least two of CS1-3. In this structure the LHC is not limited to one type of stakeholder but can be organized simultaneously across different parties in a multi-echelon supply chain network. One of the possible hybrid structures is shown in Figure 4.3. In an ideal case, close collaboration links exist between the different LHC communities, allowing members from the different groups to work together to drive excellence in the synchronization of logistics activities (see CS 4a/4b/4c in Figure 4.3). Although, unquestionably, such extended collaborative networks are much more complex and difficult to manage, most interviewees thought that the synergy gains can be significantly higher when all relevant parties' operations in the logistics system are synchronized well enough to eliminate any wasteful activities and sub-optimal decision making. One such collaboration can be specified from a collaboration test case conducted in a horizontal collaboration initiative project in Europe (Case 9), which describes how an orchestrated intermodal transport partnership was created and managed between four shippers, two LSPs and a neutral logistics coordinator. This resulted in several positive outcomes, including reduced transportation costs and CO_2 emissions, and more stable and predictable demands that ultimately benefited all parties.

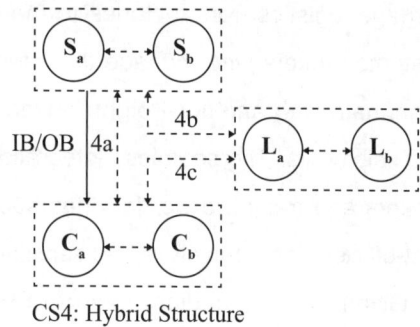

CS4: Hybrid Structure

Figure 4.3 An example of a hybrid horizontal collaboration structure

4.3.2 Collaboration Objectives

The second typological element concerns the different objectives driving the collaboration. LHC in practice is driven by varied business objectives, reflected by the changing and competitive business environment, or environmental/social pressures. A good match for these objectives between companies enables a better setup of the collaborative process and a higher chance of success. Based on case studies, the common types of collaboration objectives that are often considered in LHC practice are classified as follows.

4.3.2.1 Objective 1: Reduce Logistics Operations Cost

Reducing the cost of logistics is in many case studies the primary objective for companies to participate in horizontal collaboration. The top causes of high logistics distribution costs suggested by interviewed practitioners are mainly related to the operations inefficiency (e.g. low asset utilization/low throughput), non-economical modes of transport (e.g. the heavy use of air-freight in IT supply chain), high transportation costs (e.g. Just-in-time delivery requires shippers to deliver the orders with higher frequency but with a smaller load volume), and rising fuel prices.

The expert discussions also indicate that different collaborations might have a different focus to drive down costs. Often, the strategy for shippers and customers to reduce costs is to increase the asset utilization rate, reduce empty running miles and lower the inventory level. The strategy for LSPs will be more concerned with how to improve the transport cost efficiency within their operating network and to minimize asset repositioning costs between services (e.g. pallets/containers after use, filling backhaul loads for trucks), as well as service costs reduction for the customers.

A successful example of cost reduction can be found in a case of retail collaboration in France (Case 10). A group of four grocery shippers led by Mars proactively collaborated to consolidate their goods for full truck loads (FTLs) using a joint warehouse. From this joint warehouse, collaborative deliveries were made to the various retail warehouses in France. This collaboration has on average contributed to more than a 30% cost reduction for the distribution operations for these four shippers (as shown in Figure 4.4), compared to the original cost when the distributions were performed individually.

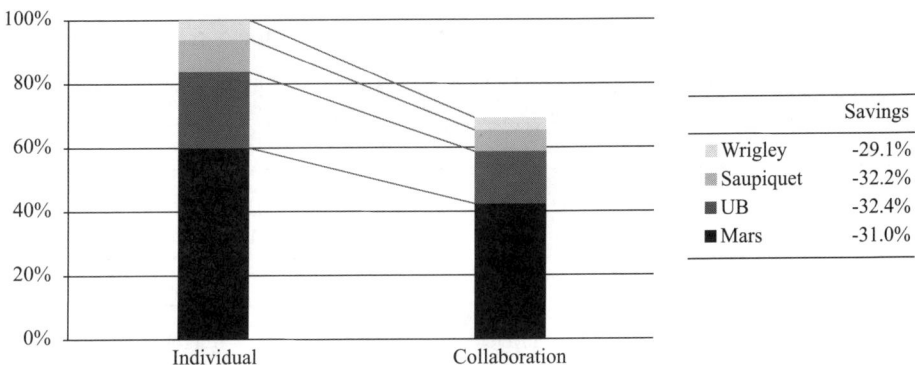

Figure 4.4 Example of cost reduction in a French retail collaboration (source: Case 10)

4.3.2.2 Objective 2: Increase Capacity Utilization

In many cases capacity utilization is the primary performance indicator for evaluating the logistics operation's efficiency level. The capacity utilization is closely tied to the cost performance and possibly can affect the customer service level as often concerned by the interviewed LSP managers. They further explained that the utilization rate could be measured differently depending on the situations, such as the vehicle/container fill rate, empty running miles, the equipment/inventory turnover rate, the percentage of operating time spent idle, warehouse space utilization, and other related labour and equipment usage efficiency issues. Hence, there should be different strategies to improve the utilization of people and resources deployed for logistics operations.

One successful case of capacity utilization improvement is found in the horizontal collaboration between Hammerwerk and JSP for road bundling (Case 8). The two shippers are neighbours in an industrial park in the Czech Republic and they found out that they had an overlapping freight flow to Germany, which created a promising opportunity for collaboration to combine the goods shipment together for more efficient logistics. They subsequently jointly developed a collaboration plan to routinely bundle their shipments for transport. It was found that by just reactively combining the loads of both shippers when they occurred in the same week (so they could be consolidated without active synchronization or service level flexibility) would already contribute to a significant increase in truck capacity utilization. This helped to reduce the number of transports necessary by more than 20%, as shown in Figure 4.5.

Company	#Transports current situation	#Solo transports while bundling	Bundled transports
Hammerwerk	111	79	32
JSP	34	3	32
Total:	145	114	
Difference:		-21.38%	

Figure 4.5 Capacity utilization improvement through collaborative freight bundling between Hammerwerk and JSP (source: Case 8)

The two shippers also realized that this utilization improvement could be higher still if the flexibility in load planning increased and if optimal load combinations were constructed through proactive shipping date synchronization and volume optimization ("smart bundling").

4.3.2.3 Objective 3: Improve Service Level

The expert interviews and industrywide case examinations have revealed an important fact that the customer's requirements for logistics services are very differentiated, largely depending upon the characteristics of their products and orders. In broad terms, there are three categories of logistics orders identified, each of which requires a different focus in designing the logistics service and collaborative operations. These can be characterized as:

1) Speed sensitive

These types of orders often refer to perishable products that spoil with time such as fruits, meats, medical supplies, or products experiencing quick upgrading/ technology advancement causing the current models devaluate fast over time such as consumer electronics. Normally these types of products and orders are speed-driven and require higher priority for shipping and a higher logistics service level (e.g. 90% orders delivered within the targeted lead time). In these cases, the collaboration and capacity sharing must be focused on increasing the shipping speed and the frequency of shipping.

2) Cost sensitive

These shipments are normally associated with non-perishable products such as raw materials, frozen and canned foods, or standard/baseline product models that do not experience a short life cycle and have a slower pace of innovation and upgrading. For these types of products, managing the shipping and delivery at a slower speed is to some extent acceptable. Some of these products, however, are quite sensitive to the cost of logistics as an excess cost might greatly affect their market performance and profitability (e.g. low value products). From the collaboration perspective, therefore, this kind of shipment must be managed to build a higher level of freight aggregation in order to exploit economies of scale in the transport. This might sometimes entail a modal shift to a more economical mode of transport such as rail and ocean, instead of using more expensive air and road transport modes.

3) Required shipping time

These types of orders often require a specific time for the logistics service, in order to fit with the customer's operations planning. This type of logistics service requirements is increasingly in demand in the IT/FMCG industry, where customers require JIT goods delivery at the right time and the right place with the right volume, such as fresh food distribution for hotels and restaurants. When such orders are received early they might not be prioritized until the required shipping time is approaching, at which point their priority for execution and collaboration is escalated.

In today's marketplace, a logistics service that meets the requirement of only one type of demand will not help shippers/LSPs become competitive and sustainable in their business. In order to become the order winner they should develop the integrated capability to cope with all the different types of demand, being simultaneously excellent in cost-efficiency, speed, flexibility and reliability. Achieving these requirements is not an easy task for a single company relying on its own resources but through tight collaboration and integration with external horizontal partners it might become an achievable business proposition.

Since the logistics service targets differ widely, it is crucially important to understand the use of the different performance measures (KPIs) when designing the collaboration project. This ensures close tracking of the performance and evaluates how well the collaborative operations satisfy customers. Drawn from expert opinions and case examinations, Table 4.2 lists the most frequently adopted performance indicators for assessing and improving the logistics service level for customers.

Table 4.2 Performance indicators for measuring service levels

KPIs	Explanation
Delivery reliability	Measures how well the supply of logistics capacity is managed against the customer demand within a specified time window (e.g. 90% of orders shipped on-time).
Lead time	An indicator to assess the speed of a particular end to end the logistics process (e.g. factory cycle time from order receiving to shipping, last mile distribution).

Continued

KPIs	Explanation
Service frequency	Some industries require more frequent logistics services, such as the manufacturing firms adopting JIT operations, or products that are time sensitive (e.g. food, IT).
Stock availability	Examples such as shelf availability at the customer side. Particularly affected by the shipper's replenishment policy and logistics capability.
Lower inventory	To prevent over-stocking at customers, but might conflict with other KPIs (e.g. shelf availability). Often measured as the inventory turnover rate, average on hand and pipeline inventory.
Exception handling	Being able to respond quickly/flexibly to any dynamic and unusual changes from customers (e.g. demand upside/downside, order delivery expedition).
Customization	Capable of meeting varied logistics requirements (e.g. deliver large shipping volumes or FTL to the distribution centre, or the small frequent volume for store level/end customer delivery).
Visibility	Providing customers with better network visibility (e.g. capacity supply of shippers and LSPs, shipment in-transit status).

4.3.2.4 Objective 4: Improve Predictability and Flexibility

Predictability as shown by the case studies is an important indicator for logistics operations, particularly because logistics is at the last stage of the supply chain process where the operation itself is facing a great uncertainty from the upstream operations and is often reactive. As the interviewed LSP and ODM logistics managers emphasized, a key point for the logistics operations is to plan a better demand supply matching between the capacity being first positioned in the market and the actual demand that can be attracted to fill this capacity. Collaboration would benefit logistics execution parties by proactively creating the long term dense, stable and structural freight flows for more accurate planning and efficient use of capacity. It is particularly meaningful to the scale-sensitive modes of transport such as rail and ocean which require a baseline commitment for a sufficiently high and balanced critical mass in order to sustain a commercial level of service, as exemplified by the inter-modal collaboration project described in Case 1, Case 2 and Case 9.

The flexibility to react to the exceptional and last minute changes is often an important capability for the successful logistics operations. This capability is especially highlighted by the ODM/OBM logistics managers who were often troubled by the delayed shipment due to the issue of quality hold or production late output. By collaborating, more resources, information and skills can be deployed and shared at the network level enabling greater flexibility to respond to predictable/unpredictable events (e.g. swap quality hold shipment to avoid dead freight costs). A unique case study can be found from an exception management collaboration process in which multiple shippers/LSPs closely coordinate to ensure the on time delivery of railway shipments (Case 2).

4.3.2.5 Objective 5: Reduce CO_2 Emissions

The environment and global pollution are increasingly gaining attention. Logistics is one of the sectors that emits most greenhouse gases (EC, 2001). Whilst the focus on improving the logistics service and minimizing the cost of day-to-day operations activities is an on-going challenge, being able to understand the carbon footprint in advance and to integrate this into the strategic decision-making has clear advantages. Considering the carbon footprint of transport modes allows the efficiency of the logistics operations and networks to be evaluated in terms of their environmental performance, and ensures the design of the logistics process and infrastructure are efficient as well as sustainable and mutually compatible.

The case studies have shown that in the freight transport sector road transport is by far the most widely adopted mode of transport due to the high availability of service and the flexibility for companies to plan their logistics to connect better with their business plan. It is also surprisingly found that there is heavy reliance on air freight in some industries. For example, the interviewed notebook PC manufacturers ship 70%—90% of their products through air freight, which is not only costly but also harmful for the environment. In general, when evaluating the carbon emission performance in terms of per tonnage km (see Figure 4.6), air and road transport produces far greater carbon emissions compared to other means of transport. Decreasing the amount of air and road transport and substituting it with some other more environmentally friendly transport modes, like rail and waterborne, could be one way to reduce the negative environmental effects. These eco-transport modes in many circumstances are also more cost-efficient if the commercial level of operations can be established and maintained.

Emissions factors by transport modes
(per tonne km compared to sea freight)

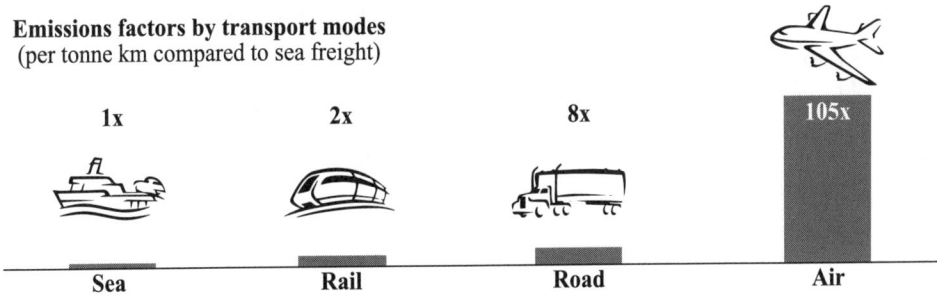

1x	2x	8x	105x
Sea	Rail	Road	Air

Figure 4.6 CO_2 emissions comparison between the modes of transport (source: Hindley, 2013)

As the awareness of eco-logistics is growing, many companies are putting increasing efforts, including collaboration, into reducing their carbon footprint as part of their sustainable environment policy. This is nowadays a very important practice that directly affects their brand image and customer recognition. An even greater determinant could be the introduction of taxation and subsidy policies for CO_2 emissions in many countries. A typical example is the tax legislation for CO_2 emissions (Ecotaxe Poids Lourds') in France. This means that in the near future CO_2 emission savings are highly likely to be monetized in the wider industrial practice and companies that can effectively save on CO_2 emissions through collaboration will have an advantage over their competitors and be able to significantly drive up their profits.

Industry examples of horizontal collaboration successfully reducing CO_2 emissions are growing in recent practice. For instance, the collaboration between Nestle and United Biscuits for sharing the use of empty trucks has saved an annual 250 tonnes of CO_2 emissions (Case 13). In another case, shown in Figure 4.7, JSP through active freight consolidation with its partner HWK has realized more than a 30% CO_2 reduction in distribution operations (Case 8).

Truck	JSP Bags	HWK boxes	JSP Calc CO_2(g)	HWK Calc CO_2	Total CO_2 separate (g)	Total CO_2 bundled (g)	CO_2 savings in (g)	% CO_2 savings
Pliot1	16	8	312.250	477.485	789.735	546.243	-243.492	-31%
Pliot2	18	12	320.091	507.072	827.164	542.486	-284.678	-34%

Figure 4.7 Example of CO_2 emissions through collaborative transport (source: Case 8)

4.3.2.6 Objective 6: Increase Market Coverage

Horizontal collaboration in a fragmented marketplace would be particularly valuable (Cruijssen et al. 2010). Partners seeking for collaboration can share and leverage their respective strengths and resources so as to improve their overall capabilities and negotiation power to serve a wider range of more demanding customers.

A case study can be found from the Chinese E-commerce industry where Cainiao Network forms an intensive collaboration with China's top five logistics companies to increase delivery service coverage and speed in China, with the aim of delivering online shopping orders to any places in China within 24 hours (Case 21). Relying on this magnificent collaborative logistics system, China's E-commerce giant (Alibaba) was able to attract massive shopping orders during China's "Double Eleven" shopping day, even greater than the total orders delivered for "Thanksgiving" "Black Friday" and "Cyber Monday" in the USA (fortune.com).

4.3.2.7 Objective 7: Reduce Logistics Procurement Cost

Coalitions of shippers or customers offer the opportunity to generate large and structural freight flows rather than spot flows to LSPs, thereby putting the collaboration community in a stronger position to negotiate with LSPs for lower service procurement prices.

Multi-shipper/customer partnerships also help to rationalize the selection of LSPs, by potential switching to one common, or a smaller number of LSPs, to perform the consolidated logistics services for the whole community and reduce the cost through sharing capacity. One case of a shared user fleet is found in the collaboration between Wincanton, Sainsbury's and Panasonic (Case 17).

4.3.3 Collaboration Intensity

Another important typological element in LHC is related to the intensity of collaboration. This varies depending on the business environment and partners' inter-relationships. In the literature, Lambert et al. (1999) defined three levels of logistics partnerships, while Cruijssen (2006) translated this into the LHC context. By integrating their frameworks with the empirical findings drawn from case studies, a more enhanced typology is developed based on three dimensions: the collaboration relationship for decision making and coordination, the scope of collaborative activities, and the time horizon against which the collaborative activities are planned, as shown in Figure 4.8.

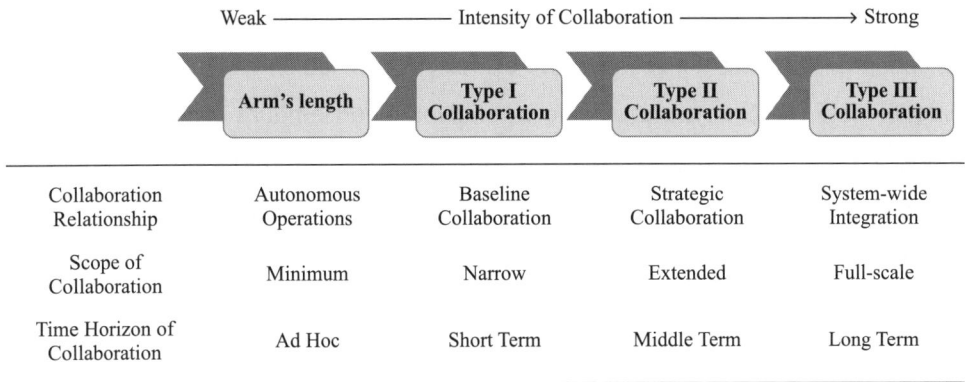

Weak ———————— Intensity of Collaboration ————————→ Strong

	Arm's length	Type I Collaboration	Type II Collaboration	Type III Collaboration
Collaboration Relationship	Autonomous Operations	Baseline Collaboration	Strategic Collaboration	System-wide Integration
Scope of Collaboration	Minimum	Narrow	Extended	Full-scale
Time Horizon of Collaboration	Ad Hoc	Short Term	Middle Term	Long Term

Figure 4.8 Intensity of Collaboration: adapted from Lambert et al. (1999); Cruijssen (2006)

4.3.3.1 Autonomy

Autonomy represents the minimum level of collaboration. Each stakeholder's operation is in a large part self-organized, and is reliant on local objectives, information and rules of action in their decision making process, rather than seeking the optimal solutions for the entire supply chain network. The number of activities and stakeholders to be coordinated is very limited. There is no strong sense of information exchange and joint operations, and no standard rules to drive the coordination. The shared information is limited and low value to generate appealing synergies. A typical collaboration case in logistics operations would be a freight forwarder who sub-contracts the trucking service to a road haulage company, involving only basic transactions such as transport orders following the standard service offerings.

4.3.3.2 Baseline Collaboration

Baseline collaboration comprises more collaborative elements in comparison to autonomy. Stakeholders will regard each other as more important partners and begin to coordinate their planning and activities. A certain level of trust facilitates the sharing of more useful information in order to improve partners' operational performance, both within individuals and across partners, as a result of more proactive communication.

In terms of collaboration scope, the baseline level of collaboration might target a greater number of coordinated activities and stakeholder participation but they usually focus on limited functional areas such as shipping/transportation planning.

In terms of the time horizon of the collaboration, this would be largely short term focused, which means the collaborative exercise is planned only within the operational time window (1—5 days), providing a relatively short amount of time in which to react to issues and plans for solutions. A typical example in logistics collaboration would be the case of dealing with sudden pull-in orders for expedited shipping due to unexpected surges in demand, which is often encountered by the studied OBM/ODM factories.

4.3.3.3 Strategic Collaboration

Participants in strategic collaboration not only facilitate a better quality of communication and coordination, but also integrate part of their business processes to a higher orchestration level. The significantly increased level of trust and commitment among partners allows more extensive collaboration in decision making and process alignment.

The scope of strategic collaboration would extend to multi-functional activities, supported by a higher quality of information sharing. This enhanced information sharing means that partners do not merely focus their collaboration on the direct interfacing activities, but also on other indirect or upstream activities that might have a close connection to the collaborated activities in logistics functions. This, in practical logistics operations as suggested by the experts in logistics/order planning, could often involve sharing information such as demand forecast data for future logistics capacity projections and production/order planning for logistics scheduling.

In terms of the time horizon of the collaboration, strategic collaboration might target both the short-term operational time window (1—5 days) and the middle-term tactical time window (1—3 weeks) in order to retain sufficient time and flexibility for more proactive planning and execution. The expert discussions suggested that the extended time window can be very useful for collaborative operations such as joint distribution. In addition to the traditional method of consolidation, where goods are reactively consolidated based on short-term opportunities, collaboration over the longer planning horizon enables more active and smart consolidation by properly shifting orders and delivery schedules between partners to reach better freight flow synchronization, as also indicated by Case 8 and Case 11.

4.3.3.4 System-wide Integration

System-wide integration represents the highest level of collaboration. Partners are supposed to have a significant level of integration over their business processes and treat each other as natural extension of their own operations.

Almost all relevant stakeholders and activities are involved at this level of collaboration, coupled with the highest proactivity to drive full-scale information transparency and joint decision-making in order to streamline all their planning and operational strategies. Such a collaborative network aims to pursue optimal solutions for the entire end-to-end supply chain network by taking into proper consideration all of the constraints and issues within individual participants.

In terms of the time horizon of this collaboration, system-wide integration aims to target all levels, ranging from the short-term operational (1—5 days), to the middle-term tactical (1—3 weeks), and ultimately to the long-term strategic window (above 6 weeks). An example of such full-scale collaboration can be found in Case 3. In this case, horizontal collaboration was established between two types of shippers (several PC manufacturing suppliers and a PC package supplier). The collaboration concerned information sharing and coordination for the package materials supply and integration with the manufacturing. A simplified workflow of the collaboration is shown in Table 4.3.

Table 4.3 Example of full-scale information sharing in PC manufacturing collaboration
(source: Case 3)

Long-term forecast	• Manufacturing suppliers share a monthly rolling forecast for the next 8 weeks of trains. • The forecast focuses on predicting the number of trains and the expected containers. • The package supplier uses this forecast to plan the materials supply and buffer by each specific train.
Mid-term forecast	• Manufacturing suppliers share the weekly volume forecast for one specific train. • A forecast is published 9 working days before the shipment pickup day, and focuses on the explicit order quantity received for one specific train. • The package supplier uses this forecast to estimate the number of pallets required and ships the package materials to each factory prior to the pickup day.
Short-term forecast	• Manufacturing suppliers share the daily advanced shipping notice (ASN) for one specific train. • A forecast is published every day before 12a.m. and lasts until the pickup day, focusing on the actual consolidated shipment (pallet count) for each container. • The package supplier uses this forecast to schedule the work orders for packaging at each manufacturing supplier's factory.

4.3.4 Collaboration Modes

How to implement horizontal collaboration? This is a truly important and pragmatic question. But, this "how" question is difficult to address when interviewing practitioners. Some interviewees tend to be very vague when discussing the implementation modes and know-how. This is perhaps because they are not familiar with this new way of collaboration, since in most cases their collaboration experiences and knowledge are limited to vertical collaboration. Horizontally, the companies more often treat each other as competitors rather than collaborators, especially between LSP companies and OBM manufactures who compete directly in the final marketplace based on brand image.

Nevertheless, the study identified a number of successful cases from the interviewed companies and gathered many good points from practitioners based on their daily experiences and issues encountered. Several successful and ongoing collaboration cases (although not termed as "LHC") were also specified from reviewing the documents that were collected from the various sources. It turns out that there are many different ways to implement horizontal collaboration in practice. This section, therefore, develops a typology which generalizes these manifestations into five key modes for horizontal collaboration in freight logistics which have a wide application base.

4.3.4.1 Collaborative Distribution

The case studies identify that collaborative distribution is the most common and applicable collaboration modes. Many alternative terms are used in practice, such as "transport consolidation" "freight flow bundling" "joint/shared distribution" or "common delivery". The advantages of shared distribution are: relatively higher service fill-rate and/or frequencies, higher loading levels and/or greater economies of scale, less transportation trips and lower CO_2 emissions, and possibly also the smoothing of handling peaks and troughs in the demand. Freight load consolidation is not new and is common practice in the logistics industry. However, past practice has mainly focused on such consolidation within a company's own facilities and networks. Collaborative load consolidation and distribution by partnering with external companies is rare due to the issues of mistrust, competition and the increased complexity of coordination.

High costs and low logistics efficiency are worldwide problems. Recently, a call for consolidation among shippers has been advocated by the European Union (Commission, 2011) which aims to help the European logistics sectors become more efficient and sustainable. In China, collaborative distribution is increasingly promoted by the government in order to cut down the cost of logistics in proportion to GDP and to reduce the serious traffic congestion in many big cities.

The interviewed experts suggest that collaborative distribution is best applicable in the case of regional and urban logistics, where the demand is from many customers scattered at different locations, making the individual delivery for this last 1—10 miles very costly. Since many shippers and LSPs serving the same region/city tend to overlap with each other in terms of their distribution networks, there is a good chance to implement collaborative distribution. From a high level, this is possible by employing one of the following three collaboration modes.

Mode 1: The shipper mode

Mode 1 (Figure 4.9) is described as a collaboration mode where proactive shippers collaborate directly using the milk-run strategy for goods consolidation and distribution. In the traditional mode (as depicted to the left in Figure 4.9), shippers usually adopt a point-to-point distribution strategy for their customers at various locations. This method requires large and stable volumes from a single customer to guarantee an efficient and daily service. Most often, however, customers will not be able to satisfy this requirement (for example retailers who have tight inventory control and space limitations). Consequently, a large number of distribution trips are required, many of which are less efficient. This is the key industry pain point, especially for the case of relatively short distance deliveries such as the urban and last mile distribution where it is impossible to build intermediate stations for consolidation.

The solution for this problem can come from collaboration (as depicted to the right in Figure 4.9). Instead of shipping the loads separately at the different time and with low efficiency, a better strategy would be to consolidate the separate loads into better utilized collaborative distribution. Loads from the compatible shippers can be collected and merged through the milk-run and delivery time synchronization, and a consolidated distribution trip is created and shared for the common parts of the transportation. Finally, the milk-run delivery is conducted to ensure customers can receive their goods

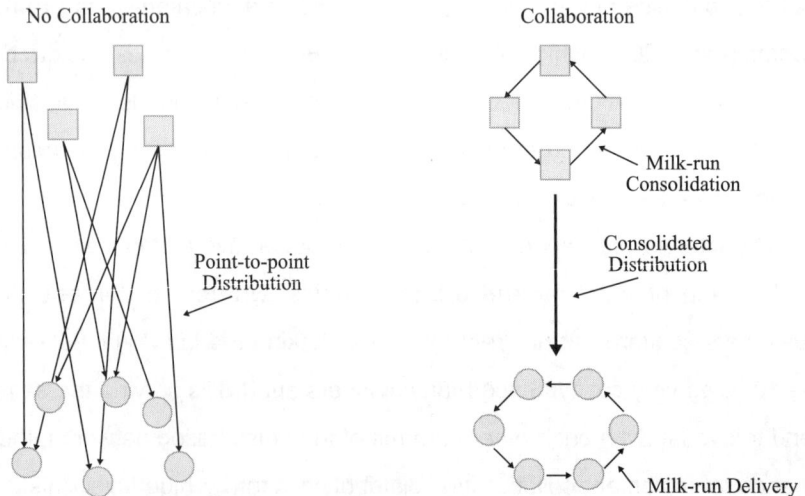

Figure 4.9 The shipper mode

more quickly than usual and with higher frequency but smaller orders.

One case which well demonstrates "the shipper mode" is found in the collaborative distribution between grocery shippers in Belgium (Case 11). The shippers initially organized their distributions separately for their customers (as shown in the "No Collaboration" scenario in Figure 4.10—on the bottom right are the shippers' location, and on the upper left are the customer addresses). They often faced the problem of frequent LTL deliveries to customers due to the specific needs of customers and the limited amount of possible combinations within one company's own portfolio. This resulted in the logistics costs of fresh and chilled products to be highly variable, making these flows a big source of uncertainty in cost calculations. The five potential shipper partners therefore began to evaluate the potential for collaboration.

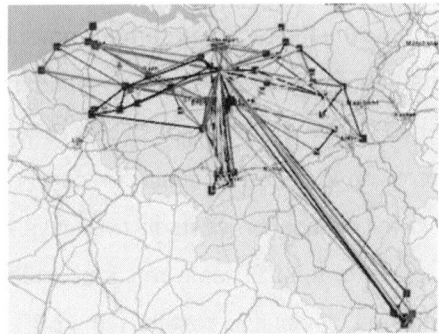

An analysis of the logistics data showed that the shippers' distribution networks were highly overlapped, and that their retail customers had similar requirements in terms of the product delivery service level. These features created good conditions to consolidate the distribution operations. Through active collaboration in distributions, where the shippers act as a unified community and efforts are made to achieve the maximum synchronization for goods pickup and delivery, the required number of transportation journeys can be greatly reduced and the vehicle fill-rate can be maximized (as shown in the "Collaboration" scenario in Figure 4.10). This simplified distribution network led to more stable and lower costs for distribution.

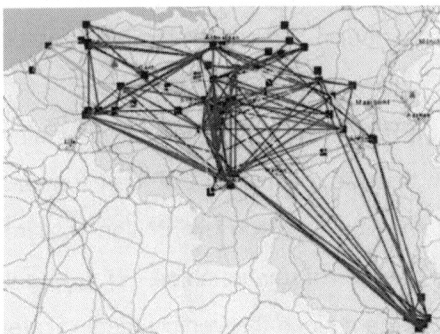

No Collaboration   Collaborative Distribution

Figure 4.10 Example of food distribution collaboration (source: Case 11)

Mode 2: The common LSP mode

Mode 2 (Figure 4.11) is described as a collaboration mode where the collaboration is operationalized through the use of a common LSP. This mode corresponds to a scenario where the logistics are outsourced and managed by the LSPs. In the traditional mode of third party logistics (as depicted to the left in Figure 4.11), a logistics service provider signs a one-to-one contract with each shipper and therefore one single shipper's shipments are not allowed to be mixed with others in the delivery. For this reason LSPs have to increase spend to deploy more logistics assets (e.g. trucks/people) in order to serve more customers. These one-to-one contractual relationships also lead to a large number of less efficient delivery trips that serve to increase the operational costs of LSP and therefore the service cost for shippers. In a usual logistics marketplace, shippers' contracted LSPs often differ from each other due to competition on price, strength of relationship and other factors. This creates fragmentation which leads to many parallel distributions organized at the same time, increasing the inefficiency. In addition, many shippers, especially large shippers, often prefer to contract more than one LSP to serve their shipping needs, in order to split the risk between the alternatives. This also creates more distribution journeys from the origin to destinations, which also increases the total cost and traffic congestion.

To counter these inefficiencies, adopting collaborative distribution through a common LSP (as depicted to the right in Figure 4.11) is a solution. In the common LSP mode, shippers collaboratively appoint one common service provider to manage all their distribution needs. The service contract would be changed from a one-to-one to a multilateral agreement among the partners. Based on this collaboration agreement, LSPs could actively bundle the freight flows of each shipper and enable FTL journeys as far as possible, reducing the total distribution journeys required. According to expert discussions, collaboration through a common LSP can contribute to lower distribution costs in two ways: (1) saving the inbound distribution cost from shippers to the LSP as a result of a reduced number of relationships; (2) saving the outbound distribution cost from the LSP to customers since the vehicle loading rate is increased by consolidation and delivery trips are reduced due to the centralization of the LSP service.

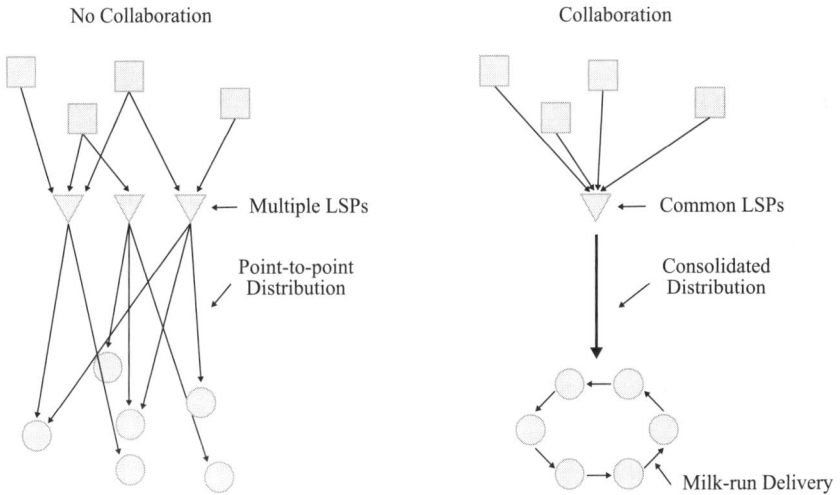

No Collaboration   Collaboration

← Multiple LSPs   ← Common LSPs

Point-to-point Distribution   Consolidated Distribution

Milk-run Delivery

Figure 4.11 The common LSP mode

Mode 3: The LSP mode

Mode 3 (Figure 4.12) is described as a collaboration mode where LSPs proactively work together to build the milk-run consolidations for their distribution trips. In traditional LSP operations (as depicted to the left in Figure 4.12), LSPs often have to be reactive in their distribution operations due to the fact that they are not the ones who initiate the demand for transportation but the shippers. Such an operational structure will always create a mismatch between the actual demand and the planned logistics supply that inevitably leads to additional costs to the LSP operations. Inefficiency is even increased if a single LSP is facing multiple shippers and their demand profile is unpredictable. Also, LSPs competing in the same region/ marketplace might have a high percentage of overlap in their distribution routes: this can produce a lot of parallel distributions towards the same/similar destinations which leads to low efficiency across the whole distribution network. Traffic congestion and CO_2 emissions are also increased for this reason.

The experts have mentioned a recent trend that that more and more small to medium LSPs have begun to collaborate as a means to increase slim profit margins and their level of competitiveness. The ability of an LSP, especially a small- to medium-sized one, to make a profit in a highly volatile yet competitive market hinges, therefore, on its ability to minimize its costs through a collaborative network. The specific way for collaboration could consider the milk-run consolidations across LSPs to enable FTL journeys as far as possible (as depicted to the right in Figure 4.12). It is worth noting that one important pre-condition for The LSP Mode is the management of the LSP's relationships with shippers (i.e. that shippers would not mind having their goods consolidated with others by the LSP and/or having a LSP different from their usual contracted one shipping their goods). This will help LSPs seek proactive collaboration to minimize their operational costs.

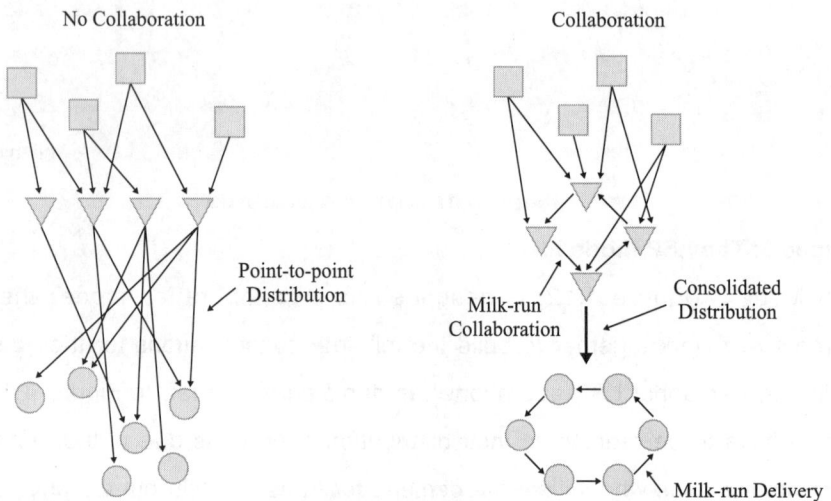

Figure 4.12 The LSP mode

4.3.4.2 Sharing Logistics Assets and Facilities

An alternative mode for horizontal collaboration is the sharing of logistics assets and facilities. This is quite a simple and straightforward approach that the majority companies can implement in order to improve their efficiency level. Two specific collaboration modes were most often identified from the case documents examinations as well as the expert discussions: (1) sharing empty trucks for fronthaul/ backhaul opportunities; (2) shared warehouse either between shippers or customers.

1) Collaboration on empty front/backhauls

This collaboration mode (Figure 4.13) is used to solve the empty running problem in either the front- or backhaul transportation. The former corresponds to the journey for goods collection with empty trucks, the cost of which can be substantial if the transportation distance is long. For instance, many inland factories in China order empty containers from the ocean ports to collect their shipments due to an imbalanced flow of container supply between the regions. This means hundreds of miles of empty running costs are incurred before the loaded backhauls. The empty backhaul, on the other hand, is seen everywhere in the industry for shippers and LSPs. This is also called the asset repositioning cost, and is traditionally treated as an inevitable expense added to the standard logistics costs.

Collaboration through a truck sharing approach encourages shippers or LSPs to consider working proactively to spot opportunities for sharing empty trucks during front- or backhauls. Freight routes travelling in opposite directions can be glued together to create a balanced closed loop shipping corridor containing complementary loads from shippers or LSP partners. In such cases, partners will make full use of the trucks during the movement, reducing the overall number of trucks in use and the number of transportation trips. An important condition for making this collaboration mode effective is that partners must align their planning of transportation as much as possible in order to create seamless connections between the journeys and to minimize costs and waiting times, as particularly highlighted by the LSP managers.

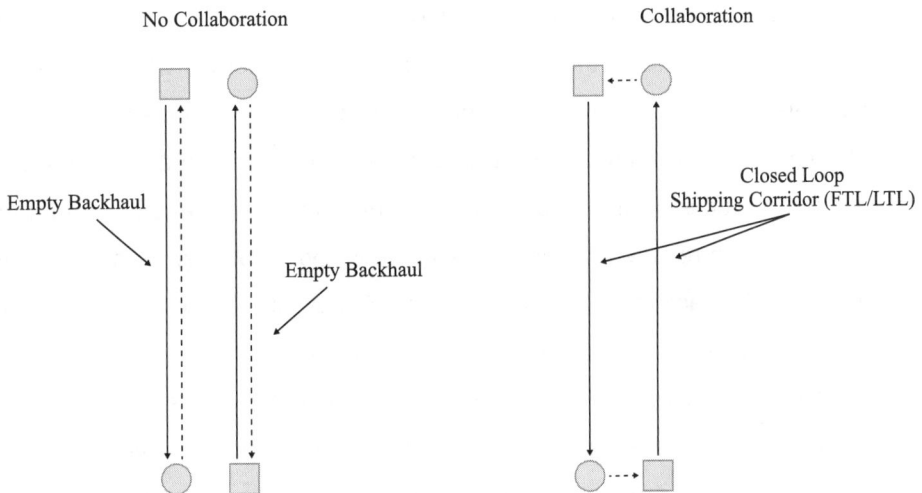

Figure 4.13 Collaboration on front/back empty hauls

2) Collaboration on a shared warehouse

Collaboration on a shared warehouse (Figure 4.14) is quite a common approach adopted by industrial companies, particularly small- and medium-sized companies, with the primary aim to drive down the warehousing cost and/or increase the warehouse utilization efficiency. In the traditional mode (as depicted to the left in Figure 4.14), due to the competition and the lack of business connections between shippers, the use of a warehouse is often dedicated for one single shipper. Individually speaking either to self-own a warehouse or lease it from an LSP can be a substantial cost. From the overall network perspective, the dispersion of warehouses further complicates the inbound and outbound transportation networks, which increases the total system cost and inefficiencies.

The major reason for shippers to consider shifting to a shared warehouse is highlighted by the issues of low volumes, uncertain demands or seasonal operational fluctuations. Collaboration on shared warehousing allows the shipper partners to enjoy the benefits of a larger operation at significantly less costs. Especially, many small- and medium-sized shippers lack a sufficient scale to deploy and run a warehouse, and thus they usually have to apply the cost for direct shipment for the customers.

Collaboration on a shared warehouse (as depicted to the right in Figure 4.14) provides shipper partners with the opportunity to pay only for the space they need, with more flexible access to the additional space and resources when and if their business requirements change. In a multi-user shared warehouse, capacity is carefully planned and optimized so that the cost can be minimized and shared between the multiple partners to maximize operational efficiencies. Additional benefits include the readily available infrastructure and resources for sharing such as equipment, IT infrastructure, management staff and skilled warehouse personnel, and also the access to the storage facilities which need specialized requirements such as temperature controlled storage, which is costly to build for small businesses. Potentially, collaborative warehousing can also be helpful to simplify the inbound and outbound transportation network, especially when shippers have common customers. Instead of shipping the goods separately from the respective warehouses, collaborative warehouses drive the possibility to build consolidated distribution originating from a single point for common and nearby customers, which also saves significantly on cost.

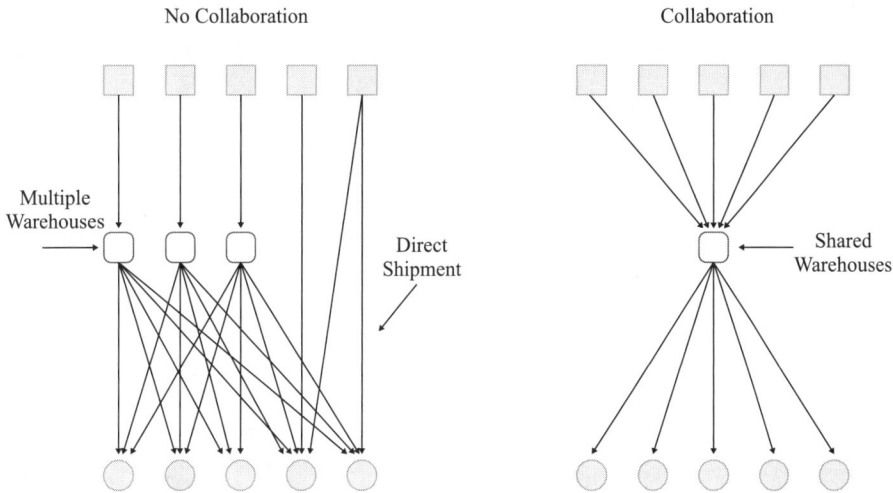

Figure 4.14 Collaboration on shared warehouse

One such collaborative warehousing was identified from an interview with an operations manager who manages a VMI hub for multiple suppliers and manufacturers in China (Case 5). The collaboration to use one single inventory location was primarily driven by the customer who aimed to simplify the upstream logistics network and reduce the warehousing and transportation costs, which were not optimal due to fragmentation. Hence, manufacturing suppliers were brought together to share the use of the same warehouse to store their raw materials (see Figure 4.15). Since this warehouse is geographically near to every manufacturer, the component supply for production can be pulled on a JIT basis, which is a benefit in addition to the cost savings from inventory pooling. Another major benefit comes from the top quality of the warehousing facilities and services operated by a world leading warehouse providers. Negotiating a favourable contract with such a top level LSP is never an easy business if the volume and operational scale does not meet their threshold. This is not something the individual companies can commit to.

Since the manufacturers for some of their inventory also implement the VMI (vendor managed inventory), in which their suppliers take the responsibility for inbound logistics, suppliers are also brought together to ship the goods to the shared warehouse. From the network perspective, this simplifies the inbound networks to manufacturers and saves the warehousing/transportation cost. A further advantage is that inventory ownership can be instantly transferred between suppliers and manufactures or between manufacturers (when they collaborate to share component supply) without the need to move the inventory from one warehouse to another. No trans-shipment costs are occurred, which are often high when the warehouses are widely spread and the cross-balancing/re-balancing for inventory locations is frequently planned.

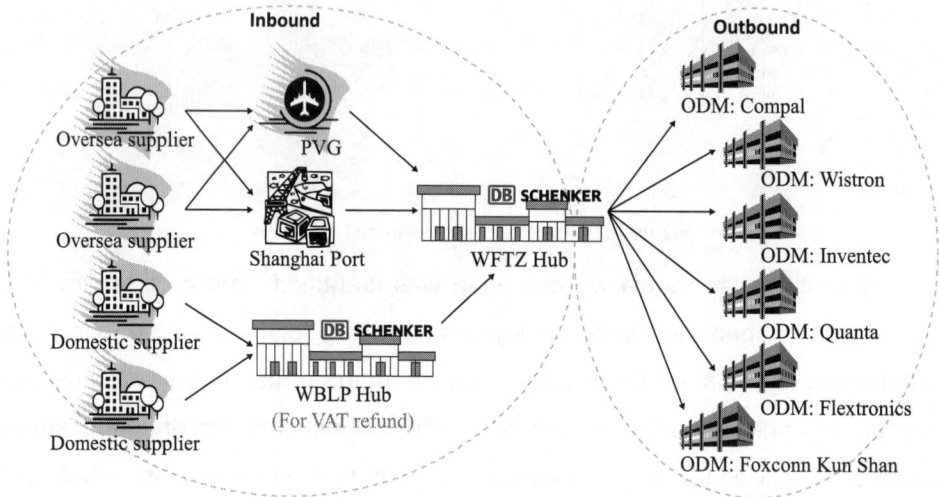

Figure 4.15 Example of collaboration through a shared warehouse (source: Case 5)

4.3.4.3 Freight Modal Shift

Freight modal shift is another form of horizontal collaboration for which there is a growing awareness and need among shippers shown in case studies. This collaboration mode corresponds to the context of long distance and/or trunk hauls where shippers collaborate to enable the switch to more cost-efficient modes of transport such as rail and waterways.

For freight logistics, road transport is nowadays the predominant mode of transport on a global scale. In Europe, about 76% of all tonnes/kilometre movements are made by road with the remainder sent by rail and water (see Figure 4.16).

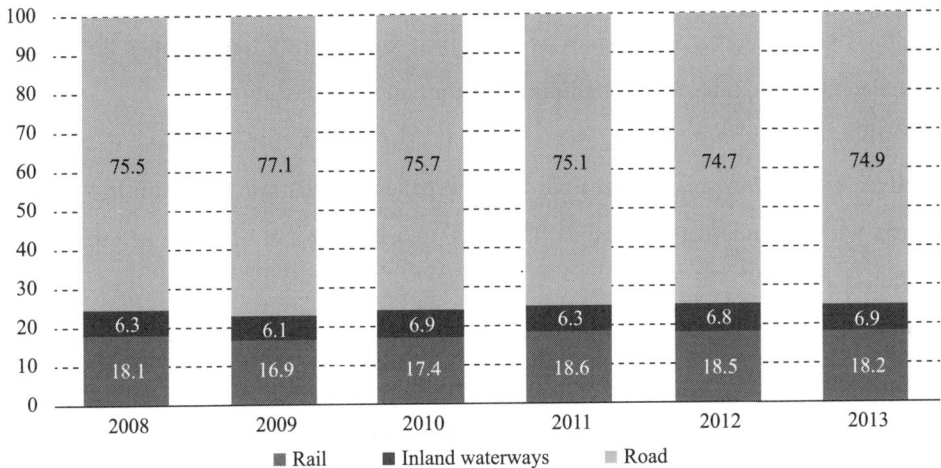

EU aggregates contain estimated data for rail for 2012—2013(BE, LU), inland waterways for 2008 (BG,RO) and exclude road freight transport for MT(negligible).

Figure 4.16 Modal split in EU 28 (source: Eurostat)

From a cost perspective, for the same volume travelling the same distance, road transport generally incurs much higher costs compared to rail and waterway. Environmentally speaking, transportation is one of the sectors that emits most greenhouse gases (EC, 2001) and road transportation accounts for the dominant part and is increasing year by year (EC, 2009). The increased traffic jams and congestions also add to the cost of transporting cargos by road. Consequently, the EU is encouraging a move away from road to other means of transport that are more environmentally friendly and cost-efficient, but the percentage of road use has only reduced slightly over many years, as shown in Figure 4.16.

The examination of case documents and expert discussions has revealed a number of key reasons why shippers and LSPs are resistant to using rail or waterway transport but stick to road transport, even at the price of a complicated and inefficient road transport network (as depicted to the left in Figure 4.17).

• First, the inability to build sufficient scale is the top reason preventing the use of rail or waterway transport solutions, which have a significantly higher volume threshold for service. Large and structural freight loads, however, are not easy to generate within a short time window, especially for small- and medium-sized shippers. Shippers usually face the tight shipping lead-times required by customers and they are not likely to sacrifice the service level for cheaper modes of transport as it requires significantly longer times for volume accumulation and possibly longer transportation times (e.g. waterway).

- There is also an increasing demand for JIT logistics services that require shippers to deliver orders with smaller sizes but higher frequency. This movement further restricts shippers when considering a modal shift to stick to relatively more flexible and responsive road transportation.

- In addition, shippers often experience low frequency and unreliable service when using the rail/waterway transport. For instance, one shipper in China used to use the rail service to ship goods from their inland factory to the ocean port. But they experienced delays in the train departure on a number of occasions, which caused them to miss catching up with the vessels. Also, the frequency of service is not stabilized and the service running time is often changed, forcing some shippers to quickly hire in road based vehicles as a backup.

- For rail /waterway service providers, a classic challenge is to attract sufficient and stable volumes in order to achieve profitable operations. The high fixed costs of rail and waterway capacity in comparison with road transport makes it difficult and risky to commit a regular service and/or with higher service frequency. As a result, rail/waterway carriers seldom have direct commercial connections with shippers but rely on the freight forwarders who are better able to attract volume. This pattern of business, however, limits the possibility to bundle freight loads proactively at the source of origin to create dense, balanced and synchronized transport volumes with long-term stability.

The solution for these problems can come from horizontal collaboration (as depicted to the right in Figure 4.17) where shippers can proactively collaborate to consolidate their freight flows at the source of origin so that the modal shift becomes an economically viable measure. LTL or FTL shipments from different shippers but travelling in the same direction can be routinely combined into one trunk haul on a vehicle (i.e. train or vessel) with a greater capacity. Usually the consolidation for the rail and waterway shipments is much simpler as the shipments are usually consolidated at the container level and that is often sufficient to meet the volume requirements by the carrier. This feature also allows shipper's shipments to be quickly consolidated/de-consolidated at the terminal, enabling, if required, a quicker connection with a feeder service.

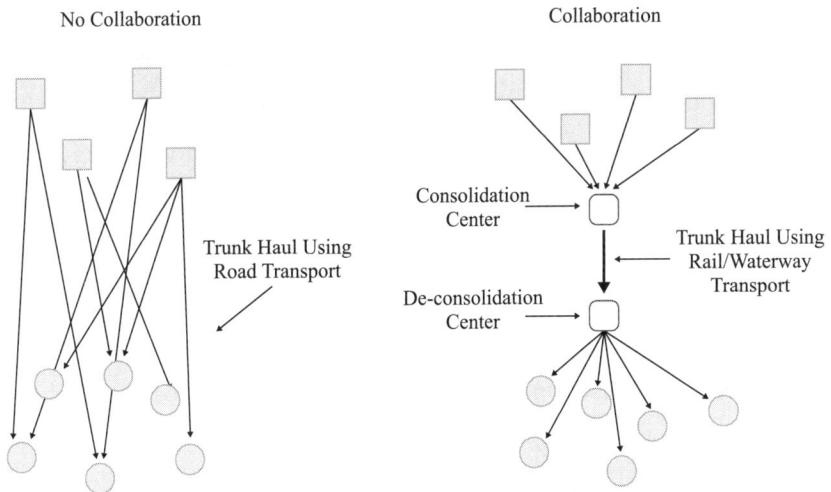

No Collaboration

Collaboration

Consolidation Center

Trunk Haul Using Road Transport

Trunk Haul Using Rail/Waterway Transport

De-consolidation Center

Figure 4.17 Collaboration on freight modal shift

An amazingly successful example of horizontal collaboration in terms of freight modal shift was found in one of the interviewed companies (Case 2). Hewlett-Packard (HP), and its outsourced manufacturers (ODMs), initiated a novel logistics project in 2011 called "Trans-Eurasian-Rail (TER)" aiming at developing a rail transport solution for the Notebook PCs (NBs) produced in China and shipped to the European marketplace. This project was set with an ambition to transfer a great portion of its NB shipments to the rail freight that had previously usually been transported by air or ocean. An important driver behind this modal shift effort lies in the fact that using air freight transport is very expensive, costing about six or seven times higher in comparison with rail, while using ocean freight is too slow to transport the NB products that are characterized by a short life cycle and therefore devalue over time (ocean freight normally takes 39—45 days to move products from China to Europe). Therefore, HP decided to shift to rail transport as it was comparable in terms of cost to ocean transport but takes significantly less time (only 15 days from China to Europe).

The pilot runs of the rail project were organized in 2011 with dozens of trains chartered by HP and ODMs. The initial running test pointed out some serious operational issues which could be a show stopper for such a modal shift. As shown in Figure 4.18, the biggest problem was lack of a sufficient and stabilized demand volume to support the weekly running of the train. The train required a certain volume threshold otherwise the cost target could not be met and the train would have to be cancelled and the shipments transported by other means. It was very difficult for NB manufactures to commit to a rail carrier with such a high volume every week. The orders manufacturers received from customers were highly uncertain due to the severe market competition and seasonal influences. Supply chain issues occurring upstream, such as material shortages and quality holds might also delay the shipments, thereby leading to insufficient volume to allow the train to run. Reduced service levels were also reported for some shipments. This occurred when the freight demand was strong enough to exceed the capacity of the train. The volume in excess had to be kept in a warehouse until another train became available. Thus, at least one extra week was added to the original lead time committed to customers.

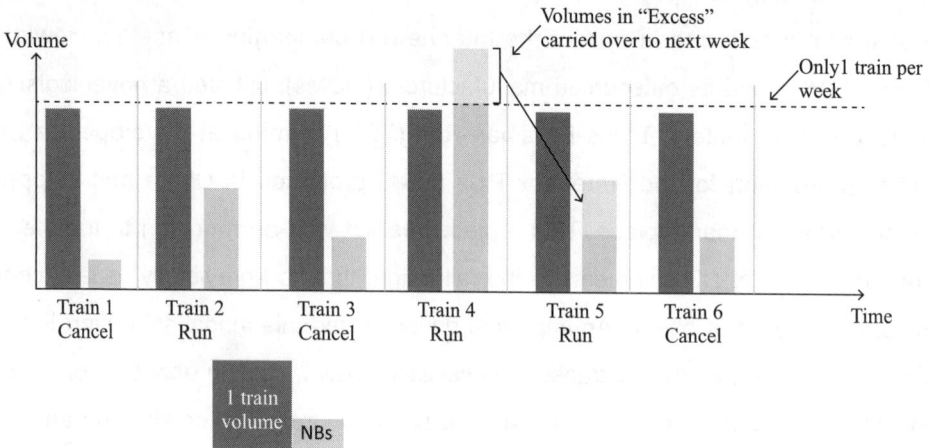

Figure 4.18 Collaboration on freight modal shift

The lessons learnt in the 2011 pilot runs forced NB manufacturers to think about countermeasures. In 2012, they decided to collaborate with a nearby shipper (Innolux) who was producing displays and had weekly volume shipped to Europe. After setting up the collaboration, the shippers' shipments were closely coordinated and combined for the train service (see Figure 4.19).

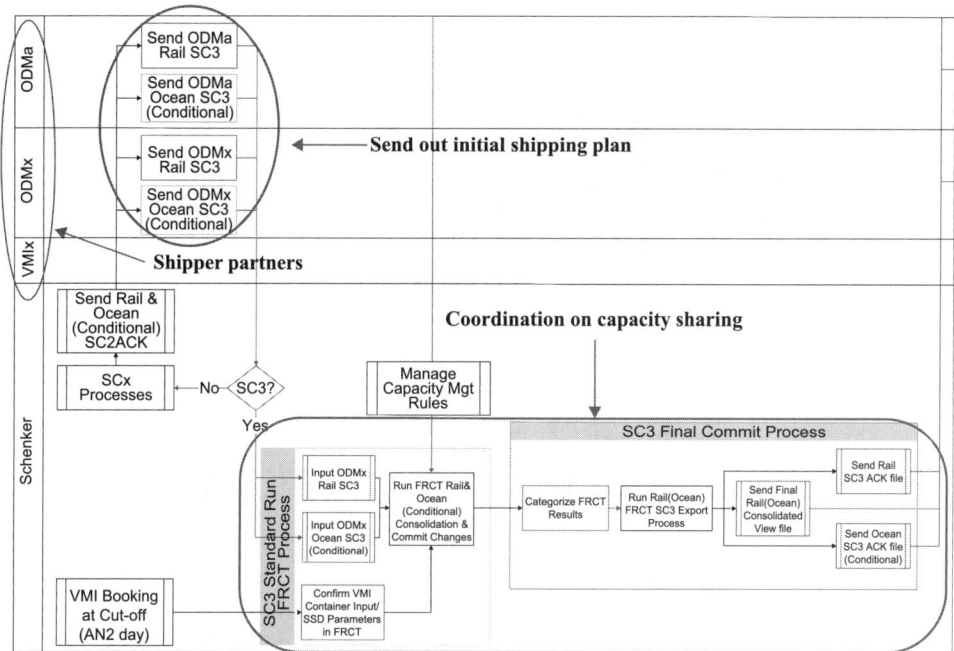

Figure 4.19 A screenshot of the coordinated capacity allocation process
in rail transport collaboration (source: Case 2)

From then on these shippers were backing up each other in respect to the train volume. This resulted in an exceptionally good performance (see Figure 4.20). The turbulence in the shipping demand was greatly reduced because the collaboration extended the source of demand which helped to increase the volume in each demand cycle and reduced the chance of train cancellation/dead freight costs. Hence, a more stabilized train service was able to establish, which in turn attracted many more shippers to join in the collaboration (e.g. shippers with accessories shipments also considered participation, and shippers at the destination side were evaluating the collaboration opportunity for backhaul). As scale increased, the train service frequency was able to be increased. This brought some additional benefits such as shortened lead time, flexibility to ship smaller orders quicker, and less working capital tied to the on-hand and pipeline inventory, less chance of delayed shipments piled into the warehouse and hence blocking the production output. More importantly, the shipper partners shared the cost of running the train which made the rail freight more cost competitive and sustainable.

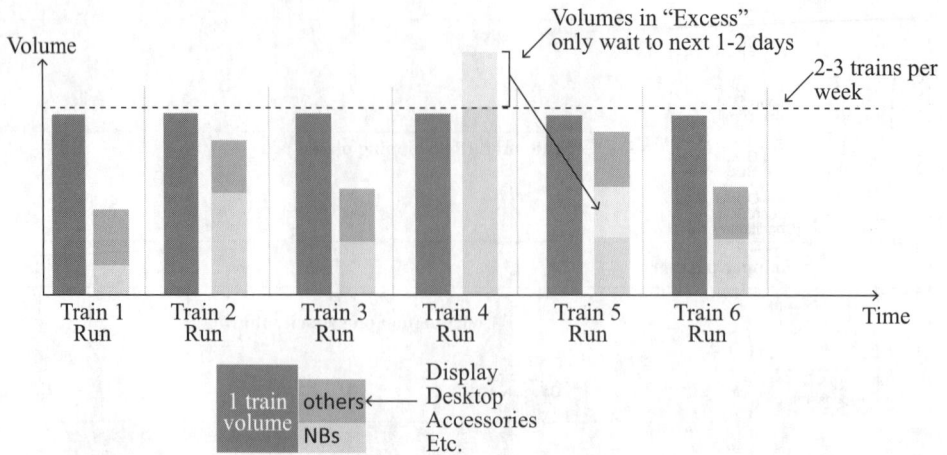

Figure 4.20 Collaboration on freight modal shift

4.3.4.4 Collaborative Purchasing

As opposed to collaboration in the downstream distribution operations, this mode concerns purchasing collaboration that is a more upstream activity performed in the logistics process. Collaboration in logistics purchasing is very similar to the concept of group purchasing, where a group of shippers collaborate horizontally to form a bigger buyer entity in order to purchase a specific logistics service. The typical advantages of horizontal collaborative purchasing are, among other things, lower purchase prices for the required logistics services, due to economies of scale, and lower transaction costs, due to reduced duplication of efforts and activities. Thus, in an appropriate context, horizontal collaborative purchasing can be quite a beneficial concept for acquiring logistics services with a lower cost and higher quality.

1) The strategic level of purchasing collaboration

Purchasing collaboration at the strategic level focuses on the sourcing of the service supplier. Small individual partners' buying power is consolidated together to make the purchasing group a very attractive business customer for service providers. This allows small shippers to access the quality LSPs or LSPs with the desired service at an affordable price, which they could not achieve individually. From the perspective of LSPs, a collaborative purchasing group can also help reduce their cost for operations, thus indirectly bringing cost savings for their customers. As one of the interviewed LSP managers said, "the reason why we could reduce our cost is because our labour, equipment and facilities cost is spread among many sharing customers. The business volume aggregated by these small sharing customers is just as big as the ones brought by the large customers, so that we can fully leverage the advantage of scaled economy in the operations and save costs. These cost savings, in turn, allows our company to implement more favourable low-price policies."

2) Operational level of purchasing collaboration

Purchasing collaboration at the operational level concerns sharing the freight demand data for joint purchasing of transport capacity. This is a demand orchestration strategy driven by the collaborative approach, and generates benefits for both the shippers and LSPs. First, during the off-peak season, multiple shippers can consolidate their small and fragmented demand to form aggregated demands that can help to purchase transport capacity more cost efficiently. Second, multi-shippers demand orchestration and purchasing help to reduce the number of demand streams that LSPs have to manage. Traditionally (as depicted to the left in Figure 4.21), LSPs sign one-to-one contracts with each of the shippers and perform the forecasting and capacity planning based on separate and individual transactions. Such fragmentation in the planning process creates significant distortions in forecasting the total required capacity because forecasting errors are inevitable and the multiple forecasts involved here therefore compound errors. The buffer strategy specific to each individual customer collectively might also increase such distortions in the capacity planning.

With collaborative group purchasing (as depicted to the right in Figure 4.21), multiple shippers consolidate all the demand into one integrated body facing the LSP. This significantly simplifies the demand network and helps LSPs to improve their ability to predict demand, reduce the demand amplification effect, and make it easier to plan capacity utilization with greater accuracy.

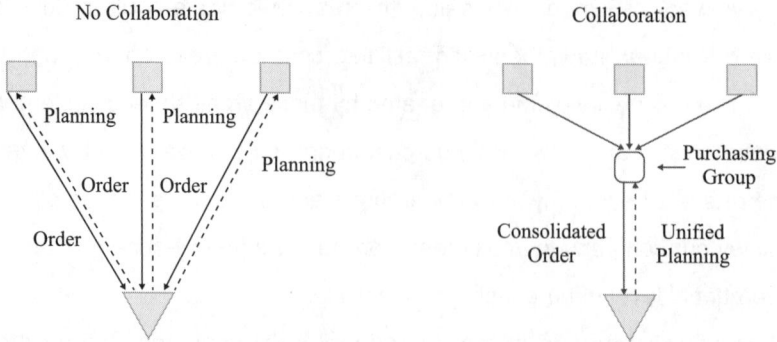

No Collaboration   Collaboration

Figure 4.21 Collaborative group purchasing

4.3.4.5 Collaborative Service

Collaborative service is another powerful business mode for horizontal collaboration. From the supply perspective, this mode encourages shippers or LSPs to collaborate by pooling their individual logistics assets to form a larger and unified service body that can offer services to customers that would be too large or complex for any individual company to undertake.

Collaborative service at the strategic level targets the tendering of the customer service contract. If the customer's contract is large in terms of the demand volume, then a collaborative tender-group can be a strong candidate for winning this contract. Within a collaborative tender-group, the transport equipment and/or the warehousing facilities can be highly integrated to form a bigger unified servicing body that contains the aggregated capacity and is able to reach the required level of scale. If the customer requires complex and diversified services, these are unlikely to be satisfied by any individual service providers, but through collaborative tendering, participants of a collaborative tender-group can share their unique network resources and expertise to provide customers with a one-stop shopping solution. A typical example could be the case when a road haulier collaborates with a rail or waterway carrier to set up an intermodal transport solution for the customer. Another case could be found from the interviewed companies where two customer brokers closely collaborate with a freight forwarder to build an efficient goods exporting solution for factories (Case 6). In short, collaborative tendering and service enable small- and medium-sized companies to jointly compete against large and powerful companies, and facilitates individual companies to jointly perform mega and complex contracts.

Collaborative service from the operational perspective mainly concerns setting up a capacity or service pool that aims to improve the efficiency and flexibility of the daily service operations. In many circumstances, demand for logistics is unstable and subject to seasonal influence. On the other hand, the operation of logistics is very reactive due to the fact that it is a derived demand and it is at the final stage of the supply chain process, hence facing the greater uncertainty cumulatively contributed by the upstream supply chain operations. This makes it difficult for companies to utilize their assets and capacity fully: the individual companies always have their own pool of trucks and containers, which are separately managed and operated. If companies start to think about connecting their assets and capacity to form a bigger integrated pool, this pool could certainly be utilized much more efficiently. Also, the total pool can be downsized to better align with customer demand and reduce the working capital. From the customer's perspective, a collaborative service pool offers them more flexibility without adding to the cost. Instead of being tied to only the incumbent supplier, they could enjoy more differentiated service offerings provided by a group of suppliers in the collaboration network, and could also flexibly switch among the different suppliers subject to their status of operations or performance (see Figure 4.22).

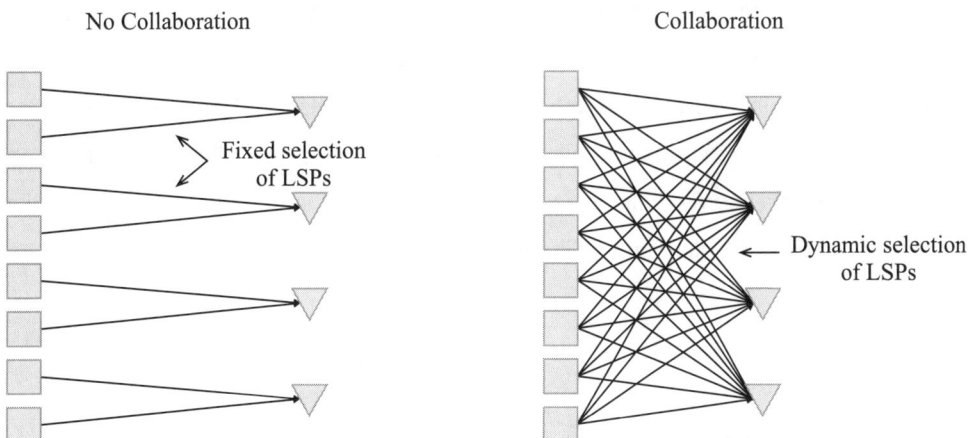

Figure 4.22 Collaborative service network

Note ──

Customers can also select shippers if shippers are service suppliers.

Some innovative practices in terms of collaborative service in operations are happening in China. The internet/e-commerce industry in China is developing very fast and goes hand-in-hand with a strong trend for integrating the online and offline (O2O) retailing business, often based on horizontal collaboration between online and offline retailers. Because of the need for a better customer response and better shopping experiences such as home delivery, online retailers are thinking about putting the inventory of goods nearer to the customers. Instead of using the traditional B2C E-commerce strategy like Amazon/Ocado, whereby central and regional warehouses are set up for order fulfilment, now many online retailers (e.g. JD.com) are directly collaborating with offline shops/supermarkets (e.g. Walmart/Yonghui) and use their space to store goods and/or to share inventory. This collaborative business helps online retailers save the huge costs inherent in setting up and running warehouses. Just as importantly, it significantly reduces the time in which customers can receive their orders, which helps to retain customers and encourages them to order more frequently because of the reduced home delivery time, better convenience, and guaranteed high quality products managed by the offline stores (e.g. fresh products). Offline retailers can also benefit a lot from such collaborative service and integration. Through collaboration with online retailers, they are able to connect their business to the online marketplace, to perform online marketing and order receiving, which in turn extends their sales channels, visiting traffic and customer reach, and ultimately increases their sales revenue. Horizontal collaboration in terms of O2O integration seems to be a win-win business that changes the traditional hostile relationship between online and offline retailers.

4.4 Conclusion

Based on empirical evidence, this chapter provides a typological analysis aimed at understanding the various forms and characteristics of LHC between companies.

It represents a step forward in respect to both knowledge and theory development in the issues regarding the development and operations of different types of horizontal collaboration in practice.

The typological analysis began by exploring the four key elements for developing horizontal collaboration, identified based on the instances that emerged in both the interview discussions and the analysis of the similarities and differences between the many horizontal collaboration cases encountered in practice. Each element represents an important aspect of the collaboration and contains dynamic characteristics and variation forms. The variations forms and characteristics within each element were then defined and classified so that they might, together, explain the different types of horizontal collaboration in practice.

This chapter has added to the existing literature by providing a comprehensive typological analysis for LHC that takes into account the key collaboration elements and their various forms, recognizing that this is crucial to a better understanding of why different types of collaboration fit different situations. The contribution is particularly evident since most prior works have been concerned with only one form, or one fragment, of LHC (e.g. LSP-centric), whereas this work systematically identifies several alternative forms of LHC, which paves the way to a fuller understanding of the structure and dynamics of such collaborative practice. According to the typologies arrived at in this study, most collaboration projects can be properly positioned and their relevant attributes described. This can help practitioners to obtain a more systematic understanding of how to plan and operate different types of LHC in real world business settings. There is strong practical value for the typologies since they are entirely based on the empirical evidence. For researchers, this chapter assists in determining a particular scope for studying LHC, allowing the clearer positioning of different collaboration studies and easier comparison of results.

At this point, the study has investigated the various forms, issues and characteristics in LHC from an empirical and qualitative perspective. To gain a further understanding of LHC in action, the next chapter will aim to quantify the benefits that can be attained through horizontal collaboration, and how its implementation can affect the behaviour of the supply chain system. This will be done by developing an agent-based simulation model.

The key collaboration elements discussed in this chapter will help to inform the development of the model. More specifically, the typology of collaboration structures provides options for configuring the structure of the connections and relationships between supply chain agents. The typology of collaboration objectives informs the typical performance measures (KPIs) that can be set as the simulation output to analyse the collaboration performance and impact. The typology of collaboration intensity informs the configuration of the strength of the relationship and the extent of information sharing between agents. The typology of collaboration modes allows the selection of a particular type of collaboration activity to model (e.g. sharing transport capacity, collaborative intermodal transport). These configurations are key to developing an agent-based model. The next chapter will describe the operationalization of the related empirical elements into the simulation model.

CHAPTER 5
SIMULATION MODELLING

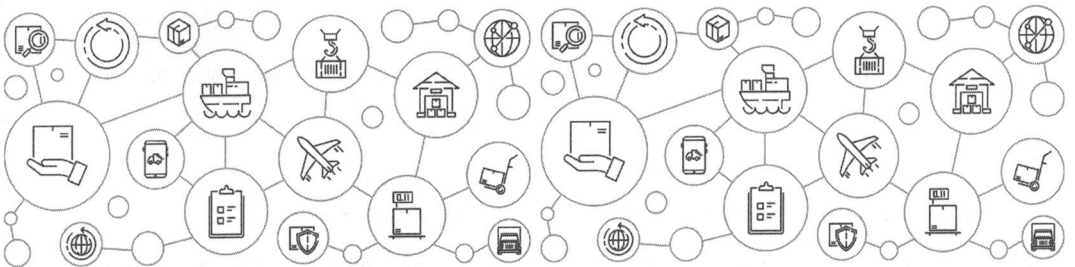

5.1 The Agent-based Supply Chain Model

The literature review in chapter two has indicated the limitations in the existing literature on LHC. Earlier research in this field has generally adopted empirical methods and tends to analyse horizontal collaboration mainly from the qualitative aspects, such as culture, opportunities and impediments. Research that systematically and rigorously examines the effect of participating in horizontal collaboration on participants' supply chain operations, such as capacity utilization and order fulfilment, is scarce, however. Many questions remain to be answered. For example, will companies fulfil customer orders better if they join a LHC network? Will participating in horizontal collaboration have a positive or negative effect on the participants' logistics cost and service level? Will the benefits of joining horizontal collaboration be different for different participants?

Hence, there are problems in quantifying the actual effects of horizontal collaboration in the logistics supply system and these constitute a major barrier for the further development of this body of knowledge. The aim of this chapter is to build the explicit intuition on, and to actually model, the impact of horizontal collaboration in supply chain. As explained earlier, the specific modelling tool is agent-based simulation. Informed by the prior literature review and empirical study, a simulation model is developed aiming at studying the various strategies for collaboration and how the relevant strategies and behaviours might affect the collaboration gains, as well as the operations in the supply chain system as a whole. The specific connections between the simulation model configurations and the elements taken from the literature and case studies will also be illustrated in the following subsections.

5.1.1 Basic Model Structure and Configurations

The agent-based supply chain model is constructed on the basis of a general-purpose supply chain framework. Figure 5.1 shows a class diagram of the implemented supply chain framework. Class names are given in the boxes. The Network Observer class controls the running of the model and provides various visual analyses and data collection tools. The Supply Chain Network class defines the structure of the supply chain, the role of the agents and the relationships between the different agents. The customer agent is an agent class at the downstream supply chain who is responsible for generating and allocating the demand for upstream suppliers. The shipper agent is another agent class who serves as the supplier of customers and provides the logistics supply to fulfil the demand from customers. These two agents interact with each other through orders. The coordinator agent represents a fictitious agent who implements the collaboration mechanisms between shippers.

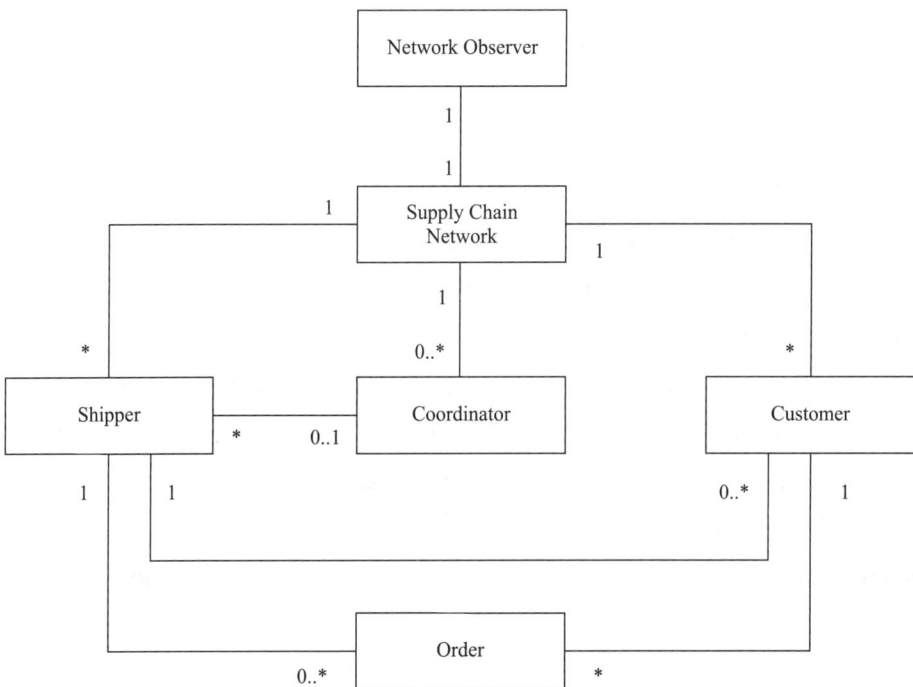

Figure 5.1 Class diagram of the supply chain framework

As can be seen from the class diagram in Figure 5.1, the model sets the rule that one supply chain network can contain multiple shipper agents, multiple customer agents, and zero or more coordinator agents depending on the collaboration arrangements between shippers. At any one time one customer can generate more than one demand order but all orders have to be placed to one of the shippers only. One shipper at a time can receive and fulfil orders from zero or more customers. It is evident that the model structure described in Figure 5.1 represents a classic two-tier supply chain system involving shippers as the upstream agents and customers as the downstream agents. Since the focus of this study is horizontal collaboration rather than vertical collaboration, it is not necessary to construct a multiple-tier supply chain system.

Concerning the collaboration settings, the model first considers the LHC at the shipper's stage. This design corresponds to the case studies of Collaboration Structure in LHC (i.e. the first variation form of CS1—shipper-centric collaboration), discussed in Section 4.3.1.1. The study chooses to model the collaboration between shippers since they are acknowledged as the active role to initiate and practice horizontal collaboration. This was found to be the most common type of collaborative relationship in the case studies of this research in comparison to the LSP-centric collaboration that most prior studies focus on. Second, horizontal collaboration is modelled in the form of capacity sharing between shippers. The study chooses to model this specific form of collaboration because it represents the most common and applicable collaboration in practice, as exemplified by the many empirical examples listed in Appendix I. The goal of such collaboration is to attain larger economies of scale that would help to cut down the distribution cost and increase the flexibility and availability of supply so as to serve customers better.

Agents in this model operate in discrete time steps, with the following sequence of actions being performed during each time step. Figure 5.2 visualizes such workflow.

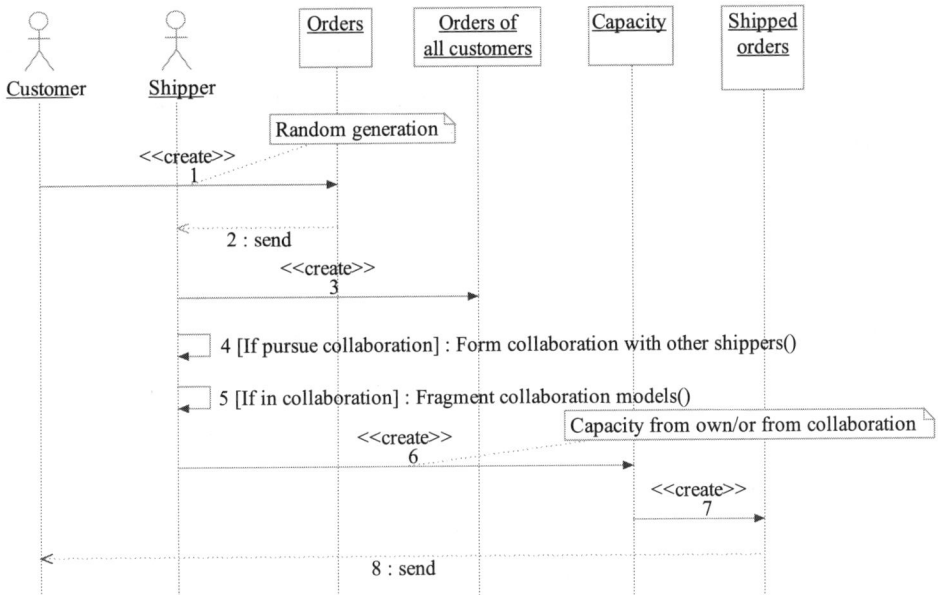

Figure 5.2 Sequence diagram of agent actions in the supply chain process

(Human icon = agent, rectangle box = a class of object (or entity) that contains certain information such as a document about customer orders. An arrow line will cause an operation to be invoked, raise a signal, or cause an object to be created or transmitted.)

Note ———

Ignore all brackets such as (),<<>>, which do not indicate any specific meanings in the diagrams in this chapter.

(1) At the beginning of each time step, the customer agent generates a random demand and passes the demand to the shipper agent in the form of orders. The stochastic demand mechanism is designed to model the demand variability often seen in logistics operations, which can affect the efficiency of the logistics and service (e.g. in Case 2 due to the highly uncertain demand the logistics operations are frequently troubled by excess capacity or shortages). At any one time one customer can only select one shipper for order fulfilment and partially splitting orders to different shippers is not allowed. Multiple shipper selection rules are applied, which will be explained in Section 5.1.3.

(2) The shipper agent receives orders from different customers and adds up all

orders that need to be fulfilled. The shipper agent also generates a random logistics capacity to be used in delivering the customer orders. This stochastic configuration represents a finding from empirical study that the availability of capacity supply is dynamic and subject to a particular time window in the operations (e.g. in Case 3, the packaging supplier calculates and adjusts the capacity plan specifically for every future delivery). For the sake of simplicity, the model considers a volume-based capacity which does not associate with the number of individual power units (e.g. trucks/trailers), but rather the total volume available through these power units. It also assumes that the shipper has no production process (e.g. a circulation industry like E-commerce) or the production is not a constraint and can be instantly completed.

(3) Next, shippers fulfil the delivery of customer's orders using the logistics capacity. Non-collaborative shippers fulfil the customer's orders straightaway using their own capacity. Collaborative shippers fulfil the orders using a collaborative approach. Multiple collaboration strategies are applied, which will be explained in Section 5.1.2. In this model, collaborative shippers can dynamically form collaborations with each other and there can be more than one collaboration network (represented by the coordinator agents) at every time step. This configuration is to take account of the empirical findings that the compatibility for shippers to collaborate is not always constant. In the real practice, the feasibility of collaboration depends on a lot of conditions, such as the overlap of distribution routes and customers, pickup and delivery time windows, and logistics conditions for products (e.g. whether they are temperature-controlled). These conditions are not always constant thereby affecting the operational compatibility between shippers.

(4) In the end, customers receive the orders delivered by shippers in the form of shipments. Any unsatisfied orders will be lost and no backlog is considered in the model. A new cycle back to step one begins.

5.1.2 Horizontal Collaboration Strategies

The effect of joining horizontal collaboration is measured by the difference in a shipper's performances in the collaborative scenario and the traditional self-operating scenario.

In the self-operating scenario, shippers solely rely on their own logistics capacity to fulfil customer orders, while in the collaborative scenario logistics capacity is shared among all shipper partners. Since shippers in the collaborative scenario can share their logistics capacity, they need a strategy for doing that. On the basis of the prior literature/empirical studies, the simulation model considers three distinctive capacity sharing strategies that have the wide application base. These are the: (1) Equal capacity sharing strategy; (2) Proportional capacity sharing strategy; (3) Excess capacity sharing strategy.

1) Equal capacity sharing strategy

In the equal strategy, it is assumed that partners do not share any information due to the fear of leaking sensitive data and opportunism in the course of collaboration (Hingley et al, 2011, Verstrepen and Bossche, 2015). With low information transparency, the only way for a sensible collaboration to occur is to share the capacity equally between partners so that no one could complain about unfairness or misjudgement. The high-level collaboration process is visualized in Figure 5.3. At every time step the following sequential steps will take place.

Step 1 Shipper partners generate their capacity and put them into the collaboration community to form the community's total capacity. As described earlier, on each occasion there can be more than one collaboration community formed depending on the operations symmetry between shippers. In order to collaborate, a shipper can join an existing community or form a new community with other shippers. This micro interaction process is governed by a matchmaking mechanism between two or more shipper agents. This mechanism also enables the collaboration to be extended beyond just two partners to represent more realistic collaboration scenarios (most empirical case examples in Appendix I showed more than two shippers participated in a collaboration network).

Step 2 The collaboration community (the coordinator agent) divides the community total capacity equally for every collaboration partner (as "allocated capacity" in Figure 5.3), regardless of whether that partner has the demand and/or how big the demand is.

Step 3 Each partner uses the allocated capacity to fulfil his customer orders.

Unused capacity will be returned back to the community again.

Step 4 The collaboration community performs the equal allocation process again for the shippers who have outstanding orders. This will be an iterative process until all partners' orders are fulfilled/or all the community capacity is used.

Step 5 The collaboration community divides the total unused capacity equally for every partner, if any, after the order fulfilment.

Step 6 Partners calculate and report the performance metrics.

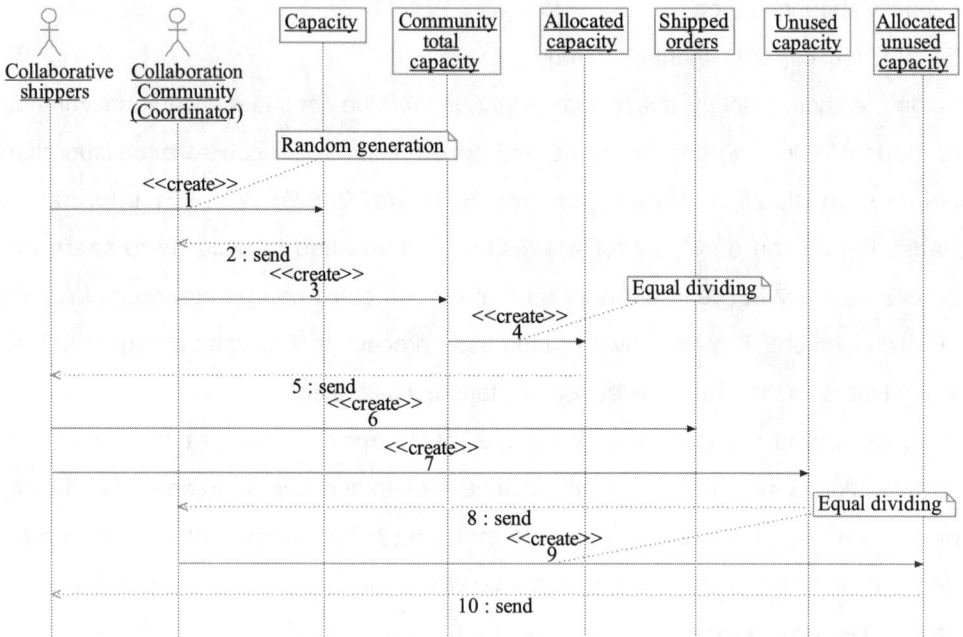

Figure 5.3 Sequence diagram for the equal capacity sharing model

As can be seen, the basic rule for the equal strategy indicates that partners will not only equally enjoy the benefits of capacity sharing in the community, and do so on a fair give- and -take basis, but they also equally share the unused capacity in the community, which becomes the cost of collaboration from time to time, the amount of which depends on the demand and supply dynamics in the supply chain network. Also, service level issues can arise when adopting the equal sharing of capacity (e.g. who gets priority in the case of capacity bottlenecks).

2) Proportional capacity sharing strategy

In the proportional strategy, it is assumed that the collaborating shippers are willing to share their demand data, indicating a higher level of trust between partners. Hence, the collaboration involves more proactive information sharing for planning the capacity sharing. Because of this increased information transparency, the community total capacity can be distributed proportionally according to each partner's demand volume. Only a one-off distribution is conducted. Once the community capacity is distributed, the distributed capacity for each partner is the final capacity given to that partner who will then use it to fulfil his own customer orders. This collaboration strategy is similar to the case study examples such as the train collaboration between PC and display manufacturers in China (Case 2) and the road bundling collaboration between two Czech manufacturers (Case 8), in which the active demand information is exchanged in order to plan the logistics capacity sharing. The high level workflow of this collaboration strategy is shown in Figure 5.4 with the following steps:

Step 1 Shipper partners generate their capacity and put them in the collaboration community to form the community total capacity. In addition, shippers report their demand volume (orders received from customers).

Step 2 The collaboration community (the coordinator agent) divides the community total capacity proportionally for every collaborating partner according to his reported demand (as "allocated capacity" in Figure 5.4). If there is no demand for the whole community, then there is no need for partners to share the capacity.

Step 3 Each partner uses the allocated capacity to fulfil his customer orders. Any unused capacity or unmet orders will be counted into his own account.

Step 4 Partners calculate and report the performance metrics.

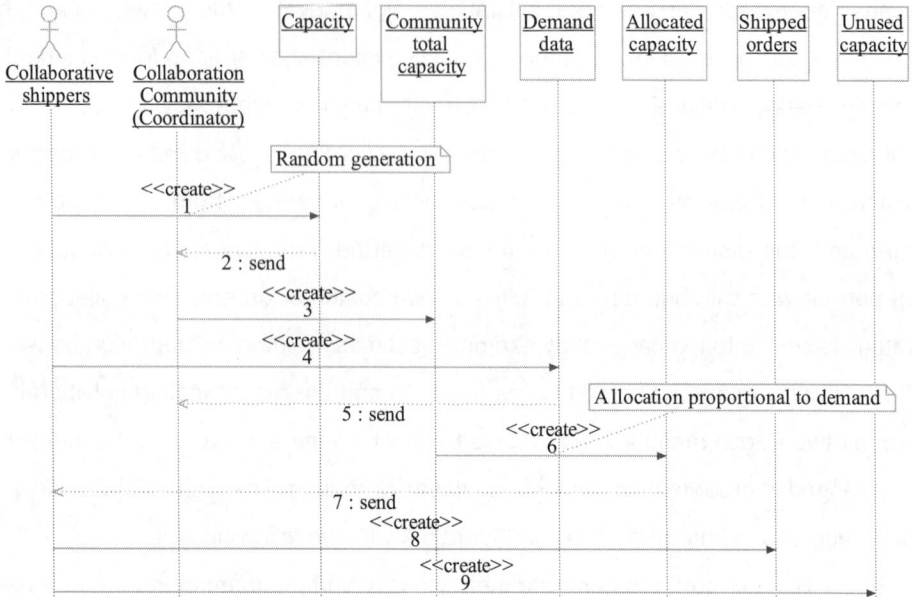

Figure 5.4 Sequence diagram for the proportional capacity sharing strategy

As can be seen for the proportional strategy, the additional information sharing regarding demand enables the distribution of the capacity in such a way as to more closely match each partner's demand profile. The evident benefit is that if one shipper has more orders, he will basically receive more shared capacity hence he can satisfy more customer orders than by using his own capacity. Similar to the equal strategy, however, the collaboration also entails a risk of committing to significantly higher unused capacity, particularly in a situation when other partners' demand orders are smaller in size but the total capacity supply of the community is very high.

3) Excess capacity sharing strategy

For the excess sharing strategy, the biggest difference compared to the initial two strategies lies in the fact that the collaborative shippers will only collaborate to share excess capacity. In other words, collaborative shippers will fulfil the customer orders using their own on-hand capacity in the first place, and pursue the collaboration if they have excess capacity/or unmet orders. This kind of setting corresponds to the LTL (less-than-truck-load) logistics marketplace in which only the LTL shipments are collaborated. This collaboration strategy design is informed by the case study of Asia carrier hub (Case 4) and the LTL carrier collaboration model described by Peeta and Hernandez (2011).

Similar to the proportional strategy, information sharing is the core of the excess strategy. Sharing demand information such as POS data or demand forecasts is by far the most common type of information shared in the supply chain collaboration (Sawaya, 2006). The extent of the overall information exchange in collaboration is much more than just the shared demand information, however. In this collaboration strategy, supply information in terms of the spare capacity is shared in the community. The high level workflow is shown in Figure 5.5 with the following steps:

Step 1 Collaborative shippers generate their own capacity and use this to fulfil customer orders.

Step 2 After the initial order fulfilment, collaborative shippers might decide to collaborate if they have spare capacity/or excess orders. If there are no excess orders or spare capacity in the community, then there is no chance for shippers to collaborate.

Step 3 Collaborative shippers who have spare capacity share the most up to date availability of their spare capacity to the partners.

Step 4 Collaborative shippers who have excess orders will select a partner who has the largest uncommitted spare capacity at the time of pursuing shared capacity (Note that shippers with spare capacity do not have full visibility of the excess orders of all shippers. Only the excess orders of the shipper who is involved in the negotiation can share such information. Hence shippers with extra capacity cannot compare and choose the "best" partners).

Step 5 Spare capacity is used by the partner to fulfil his excess orders. His counterpart then updates the status of on-hand spare capacity to the community, and waits for collaboration with the next possible partner.

Step 6 Partners calculate and report the performance metrics.

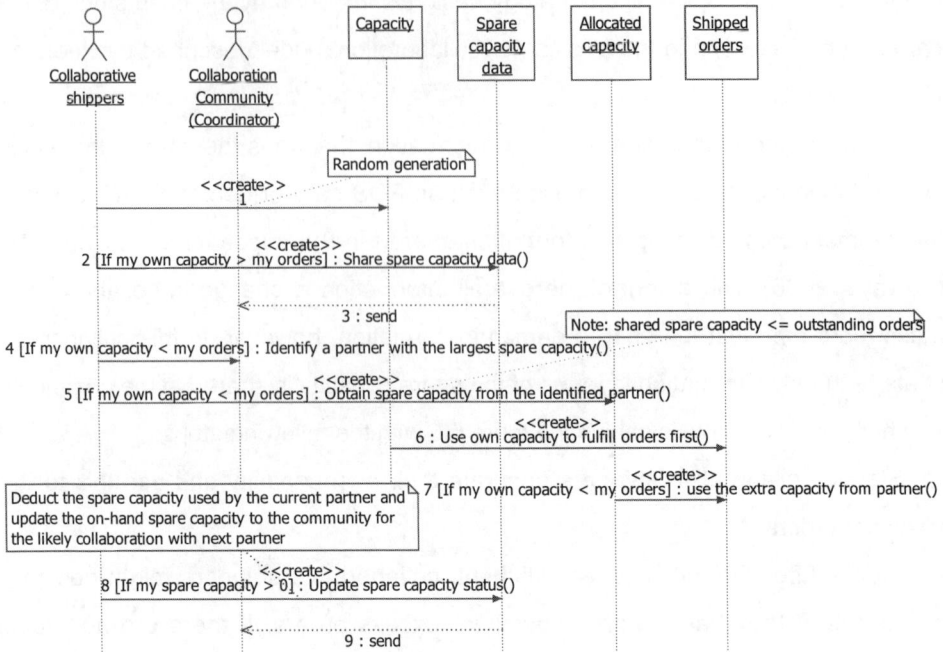

Figure 5.5 Sequence diagram for the excess capacity sharing strategy

As can be seen, there is no capacity sharing and redistribution work made to the partners prior to their initial order fulfilment in the excess strategy. This means that shippers under this collaboration strategy could act more independently in that they can determine in the first place how to use their own capacity to fulfil orders from their customers. Partners do not need to undertake the extra unused capacity from the community since only the spare capacity is shared for excess orders. In this case, the collaboration can only help to increase the number of satisfied orders and capacity utilization, but will not affect the individual planning for the customer order fulfilment. On the other hand, since the opportunities for collaboration are assessed by individual shippers locally, collaboration is not initiated between every partner and/or at every time step.

As can be seen, the key distinction between the horizontal collaboration strategies is whether partners share the information or not, and what kinds of information are shared for collaborative decision-making. This setup reflects the prior literature/ empirical findings, indicating that information sharing is a critical factor for the success of horizontal collaboration. On the positive side, the sharing of information between the collaborating companies is an enabler for collaboration, which allows partners to have greater visibility to coordinate the planning and execution. Zhu et al. (2014) has identified four types of horizontal partnership involving different levels of information sharing and suggest that full-scale information transparency can better support the aim to pursue optimal collaboration results for the entire end-to-end supply chain network, by taking into proper consideration all the constraints and issues from the individual collaborating companies.

The downside of sharing information is also worth careful consideration. This is mainly related to security and legal issues. A survey by Eye for transport (2011) has noticed that the most important impediment for logistics horizontal collaboration is the fear of sharing information with competitors. Hingley et al. (2011) further identify that UK retailers tend to have a strong emphasis on protecting sensitive sales information and therefore find it difficult to envisage any situation where they would collaborate so much that they shared the distribution management. A similar issue is also encountered in a recent industry case where Spar led an inbound horizontal collaboration (Verstrepen and Bossche, 2015). The operation of the collaboration requires the collection and sharing of large amounts of data and information between the inbound suppliers, some of which will be competition sensitive such as demand volumes, transport prices, commercial terms, etc. For competition and anti-trust reasons, the players in the coalition are discouraged from exchanging competitively sensitive information directly with each other. Palmer et al. (2012) revealed that the majority of those interviewed in a horizontal collaborative partnership were based on a limited exchange of information because of the fear that their knowledge can be used by competitors.

Since there is much concern regarding the issue of sharing information between partners, it is of great importance to use this simulation model to evaluate the extent to which information sharing is necessary and beneficial for the horizontal collaboration.

5.1.3 Supply Chain Configurations

To improve the generality of the results, the study also considers the different supply chain configurations given that supply chain networks in the real world take a wide variety of forms (Chopra and Meindl, 2007).

Built on the basic structure described in Section 5.1.1, three variations of the supply chain configurations are created as the experimental environment for studying the effect of horizontal collaboration. The first one considers a simple random marketplace supply chain (referred to as the random SC hereafter). The second considers a supply chain configuration that is characterized by a focus on short-term performance (referred to as the performance-based SC hereafter), while the third considers a configuration that focuses on long-term relationship development (referred to as the relation-based SC hereafter).

The three configurations represent three classic supply chain systems that are often observed in the manufacturing industry. Taking the interviewed PC supply chain as an example, manufacturers always buy critical components (e.g. LCD/CPU) from strategic partners (i.e. an approved vendor list or AVL). For the less critical materials like screws, connectors and hinge parts, manufacturers choose the suppliers based on their short-term delivery performance. For commodities such as the accessories and packaging, manufacturers choose suppliers freely in the open market with no specific preference due to the low specification requirements and the wide array of suppliers. In this simulation model, the key characteristics that make the supply chain configurations distinctive lie in the customer's ordering strategy and the shipper's order fulfilment strategy, which will be elaborated in detail as follows.

1) Random SC

The first supply chain configuration represents a simplistic scenario. Agents of this supply chain adopt simple rules for the order/or supply allocations. For shippers, they adopt an equal order fulfilment strategy so that when there is more than one customer order from the same shipper, and the shipper will utilize his capacity supply to equally fulfil every customer's order. This is an iterative process until every customer order has been shipped/or the capacity is used up. For customers, agents adopt a simple random strategy for ordering. This means that shippers will be selected at random and customers do not hold a specific preference for ordering from a particular shipper. A random shipper selection strategy represents a situation in which the purchasing customers have little information about the shippers (e.g. capacity availability, service performance), and therefore do not know whom the best is for order placement, simply ordering randomly. This setup typically corresponds to an open market supply chain system under which the transactions are made in an on-demand/ad hoc nature, and the trading agents are typically at an arm's length relationship (Lambert et al. 1999). This supply chain configuration is used as the first experimental environment for studying the effect of horizontal collaboration between shippers, and serves as a benchmark for comparing with the other supply chain configurations.

2) Performance-based SC

The second supply chain configuration is defined as a performance-based supply chain system, under which the customers become sensitive to the short-term performance of shippers. Initially, customers place orders randomly among the available shippers similar to the random SC. Customers can evaluate the shipper's order delivery performance, however, and alter their ordering strategy accordingly. The basic rule is that shippers who fail to deliver an order would be blacklisted by the customer of that order following the negative experience. The customer will then temporarily block this shipper for order placement among the available shippers. The blacklist length is tied to the total number of shipper agents (TotalNr). This means that, at least for the subsequent (TotalNr-1) time steps, the customer will choose other shippers.

Note ——

The TotalNr - 1 logic ensures that customers can always have at least one available shipper to order from.

This cognitive ability is simple but corresponds to a rational decision feedback commonly seen among customers who are disappointed by the performance of shippers. It is assumed, however, that customers do not know the performance of all other shippers due to a lack of information transparency in the supply chain network.

They can therefore only rely on their own experiences and local information (i.e. the blacklist) to support the selection of shippers: a typical bounded rationality (Hindess, 1988, Gigerenzer and Selten, 2002). Shippers, meanwhile, continue to apply the same equal order fulfilment strategy as in the random SC.

If customers are changing their ordering behaviour based on the blacklist, there could potentially be a big impact on the upstream logistics supply systems that are characterized by collaborative/or non-collaborative relationships. The overall effect is not easy to predict, however, because there of the complex interactions in the entire supply chain network. Customers, in this case, can act differently for their order allocations, which is more complicated than the scenario where they universally adopt the simple random rule. Their collective effect on the demand dynamics generated for the upstream shippers is therefore unknown. Further, when customers start to value shipper's short-term performance, increasing interactions can occur between collaborative and non-collaborative shippers for their order fulfilment. This poses the questions, for instance, of how, when non-collaborative shippers are blacklisted more often than collaborative shippers, the consequent changing flow of customers affects the order fulfilment of collaborative shippers? This supply chain system, therefore, contains a more complex demand stream, with increasing interactions between players, both vertically and horizontally. Particularly, the setup of the blacklist ordering policy corresponds to one common type of real world supply chain that is driven by short-term performance. This will be the second supply chain configuration to be used as an experimental environment for studying the effect of horizontal collaboration.

3) Relation-based SC

The third supply chain configuration for experimentation is characterized as a relationship-based supply chain. Under this supply chain system, both the shippers and customers have a learning capability, and they become adaptive over time in their learning process. The term "adaptive" here means that agents can accumulate the past experiences of dealing with one specific shipper or customer, based on which they can adapt decisions on the order/supply allocations.

There are several ways to evaluate the past supply chain performance. The criteria includes factors such as the volume exchanged, the frequency of exchanges and the strength of the relationship that has been built upon, and those associated with the current status of the interacting agents, such as the number of unmet orders/ backlog and the ability to fulfil future orders (Akkermans, 2001, Schieritz and Grobler, 2003, MACAL, 2004). The simulation model here considers the strength of the relationship as the criterion for adjusting the supply and order allocation decisions. The strength of the relationship is built upon one agent's history of doing the business with the other agents, i.e. based on the actual cumulative orders placed or orders successfully delivered. The more a customer orders with a shipper, the more the shipper's trust for this customer will develop over time, and hence the higher the priority his allocation of capacity supply will be to this customer. Conversely, the more successful shipments a customer receives, the more he will start to appreciate this shipper and prioritize his orders for this shipper. This mutual evaluation design would therefore facilitate the development of mutual trust between the supply chain trading agents, and this represents a typical relationship-driven approach to managing the orders and supply in the supply chain network.

The presence of stronger vertical relationships might have a great impact on the collaborative/non-collaborative shippers in their supply system. Many vertical collaboration studies have indicated that supply chain networks based on high trust and long-term relationships can result in better performance. For instance, Kim (2009) used an agent-based model to explain how the variability of inventory levels can be reduced as supply chain players perform transactions based on trust relationships. The value of relationship-driven supply chains remain unclear for the supply chain players engaging in partnerships that are horizontal in nature, however. The question is whether the stronger vertical relationship can facilitate the horizontal collaboration. Or would the benefits of horizontal collaboration become less evident due to the domination of the benefits brought by the vertical collaboration?

This configuration is also informed by the case studies of LHC Collaboration Structure discussed in Section 4.3.1.1 (i.e. the third variation form of CS1 where shippers in horizontal collaboration can obtain vertical support from downstream customers). In fact, to model the horizontal collaboration in a context of a supply chain with stronger vertical relations is also justified by recent empirical studies that have indicated the need to include stronger vertical collaboration in order to facilitate horizontal collaboration. For instance, Zhu et al. (2014), Jacobs et al. (2014) and Verstrepen and Bossche (2015) have pointed out that incorporating vertical collaboration with strong supplier-customer relations could facilitate better planning and execution performance in horizontal collaboration, such as volume projection and scheduling shipment. Jacobs et al. (2013) have revealed a key point, that for horizontal collaboration it is important to select the structural flows rather than spot flows, because their high volume and/or frequency will give partners a certain degree of predictability that will contribute to the stability of the collaborative community. One means to achieve this requirement is that shippers establish a stronger collaborative relationship with customers so as to optimize their demand stream, and the same is true for customers in the case of supply planning. Hence in this model, the vertical collaboration is realized by a collaborative shipper's long-term customers who are committed to provide him with more stable and predictable demand in order to enable the collaboration between shippers.

In summary, the relation-based supply chain contains further complexity in both the demand and supply streams. It represents a typical relation-based supply chain network with an emphasis on long-term collaborative relationship and trust accumulation between the vertical players. This will be the third supply chain configuration for exploring the dynamic effect of horizontal collaboration.

5.1.4 Experiment Design

As can be seen from the simulation model description in the previous sections, in terms of the internal structure for agent behaviours, the simulation model contains two key modules as depicted in Figure 5.6. The first module defines the collaboration rules to be followed by shippers when they collaborate. It contains three scenarios, as explained in Section 5.1.2. The second module determines the shipper-customer trading rules in a supply chain system that contains the customer ordering and shipper fulfilment strategies. Within this module there are three supply chain scenarios designed, which are explained in Section 5.1.3.

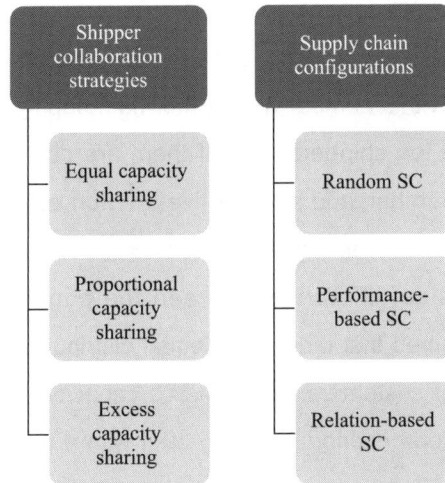

Figure 5.6 The key agent action rules in the simulation model

Once the baseline simulation model is tested, it is used to design a simulation plan with three experiments that are based on the three supply chain configurations. They are different in terms of the customer's ordering rules and the shipper's order fulfilment rules. Since three different collaboration strategies are considered, the comparison is done under each supply chain configuration. In all, a total of nine configurations are considered. Figure 5.7 shows the alteration of configurations characterizing each experimental setting. The collaborative shipper's performances, as measured in each setting, are compared with those measured in the absence of collaboration to evaluate the benefits and patterns arising from the horizontal collaboration dynamics, as well as the effect on the customer's performance.

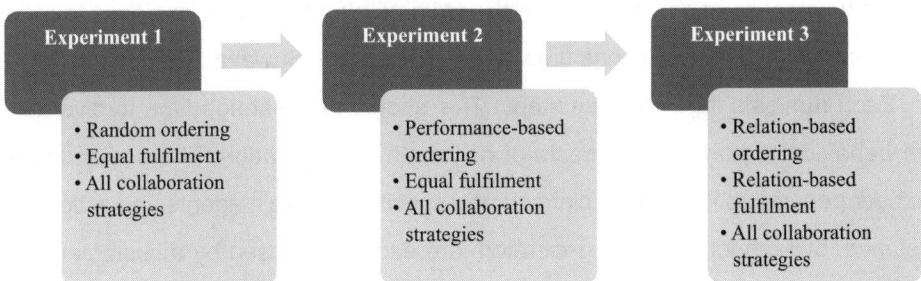

Figure 5.7 Experimental settings across models

This model considers ten shipper agents, ten customer agents, and a variable number of coordinator agents depending on the collaboration arrangements between shippers. The number of agents does not correspond to the population of a real world supply chain network, but this number allows the main supply chain dynamics to be represented. Among the ten shippers, five of them are collaborative shippers who can collaborate with each other, and another five are non-collaborative shippers who maintain the independence in their logistics operations.

In this model, the size difference between the supply chain agents is not considered and it is assumed that there is an equal distribution of capacity supply for shippers, and demand for customers. The logistics capacity of each shipper agent is modelled by using a uniform distribution [200, 300] with a mean equal to 250 and a standard deviation of 28.87. A uniform distribution is used because, in the real world, the logistics capacity is tied to a number of fixed assets such as trucks, the number of which cannot be greatly varied compared to the inventory planning. Each customer's demand is modelled by adopting the same uniform distribution [200, 300] with a mean equal to 250 and standard deviation of 28.87 (This indicates a mature and balanced marketplace which ensures that the total demand in the system is not too high or too low compared to the capacity supply of shippers).

Each model configuration is simulated for 50 replication runs. The same set of random seeds (i.e. common random numbers or CRN) is used to ensure the results are comparable across models, and to alleviate effects of randomness. The method of CRN essentially means putting exactly the same inputs into different model configurations. Therefore, if the stream of random numbers has peculiarities, then both of the configurations must deal with the same elements of randomness to reduce the chance of misinterpretations (Law and Kelton, 2000, Sawaya, 2007).

Each run lasts for 2000 time steps. This should give enough time to give rise to the behaviour patterns and effects of horizontal collaboration. The use of random number generators is carefully planned and specific to certain agents and actions. For instance, two random number generators are exclusively used by a customer agent, one for demand generation and the other for shipper selection.

The model is coded in Netlogo (http://ccl.northwestern.edu/netlogo), which is one of the commonly used agent-based simulation platforms for modelling and studying complex systems in natural and social science. Figure 5.8 shows a screenshot of the user interface of this model. On the left in Figure 5.8 the simulation parameters can be controlled from the sliders and combo boxes. On the right in Figure 5.8 there is a panel to visualize all agents and their interactions in supply chain. Interactions are modelled as the "links" in-between the agents to represent certain activities. For example, the grey directed links shown in the panel are the demand links which can help a customer to place an order to one of the shippers. For the purpose of better display, not all types of links (interactions) are made visible in this panel.

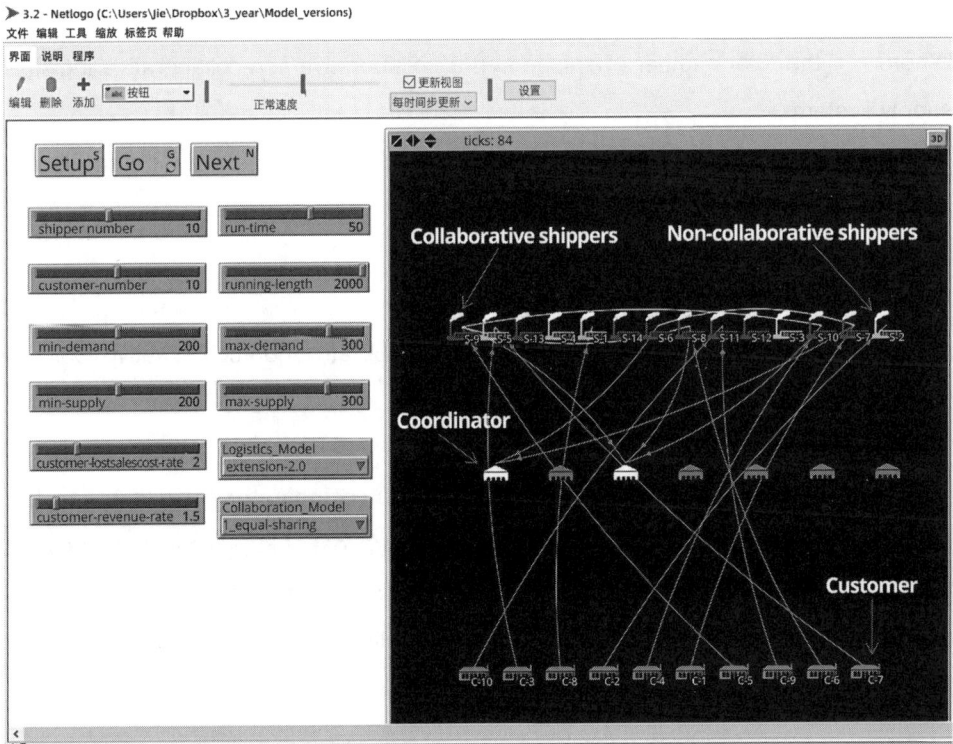

Figure 5.8 Screenshot of the model implemented in Netlogo

To evaluate the effect of horizontal collaboration, the following performance measures (KPIs) are considered. The selection of KPIs is based on case studies of collaboration objectives (Section 4.3.2) and the literature (Section 2.4.2) that indicate the key performance dimensions of interest for horizontal collaboration.

1) Fill-rate of shippers

Fill-rate is commonly used to evaluate the shipper's logistics service level to customers and is also a key driver for collaboration. The fill-rate of a single shipper agent (S_i, where i = 1, 2, 3, ...) at time tv (where v = 1, 2, 3, ...) is calculated as:

$$Fillrate_{S_i, t_v} = \frac{ShippedOrders_{S_i, t_v}}{ReceivedOrders_{S_i, t_v}} \times 100\%$$

The shippers' fill-rate are measured at individual and system level. The individual level of fill-rate at time t_v is measured as the average fill-rate of all individual agents, calculated as:

$$Fillrate_{at\ individual\ level} = \frac{\sum_{i=1}^{i=n} Fillrate_{S_i, t_v}}{n}$$

Where n = the total number of shippers in a collaborative/non-collaborative logistics supply system.

The system level of fill-rate at time t_v is measured as the aggregated fill-rate achieved by the whole system, calculated as:

$$Fillrate_{at\ system\ level} = \frac{\sum_{i=1}^{i=n} ShippedOrders_{S_i, t_v}}{\sum_{i=1}^{i=n} ReceivedOrders_{S_i, t_v}} \times 100\%$$

Where n = the total number of shippers in a collaborative/non-collaborative logistics supply system.

2) Capacity utilization of shippers

Capacity utilization is the primary performance indicator for evaluating the efficiency level of logistics operations. The operating cost of logistics is largely tied to the capacity utilization since logistics is basically an asset driven business. Capacity utilization is measured similar to the fill-rate, as explained above:

$$Utilization_{S_i, t_v} = \frac{ShippedOrders_{S_i, t_v}}{ReceivedCapacity_{S_i, t_v}} \times 100\%$$

Note

Received capacity could be either self-generated or obtained through collaboration.

$$Utilization_{at\ individual\ level} = \frac{\sum_{i=1}^{i=n} Utilization_{S_i, t_v}}{n}$$

$$Utilizaiton_{at\ system\ level} = \frac{\sum_{i=1}^{i=n} ShippedOrders_{S_i, t_v}}{\sum_{i=1}^{i=n} ReceivedCapacity_{S_i, t_v}} \times 100\%$$

3) Total orders satisfied by shippers

This measures the total throughput of customer orders in a given period of time, which can indicate the efficiency of the logistics system in fulfilling customer orders. Shippers' total satisfied orders are calculated as:

$$TotalSatisfiedOrders = \sum_{v=1}^{v=m} \sum_{i=1}^{i=n} ShippedOrders_{S_i,t_v}$$

Where:

n = the total number of shippers in a collaborative/non-collaborative logistics supply system

v = the time step

m = the maximum time step

4) Total order frequency of shippers

This measures the total number of times a shipper is selected by customers, as an indication of a shipper's attractiveness to customers and his likely market share. The calculation is similar to that above:

$$TotalOrderFrequency = \sum_{v=1}^{v=m} \sum_{i=1}^{i=n} OrderReceivingTimes_{S_i,t_v}$$

Note

OrderReceivingTimes = the number of customers who place orders to this shipper at time tv.

5) Total unused capacity of shippers

This measures the exact total amount of capacity wasted in a given period of time. The calculation of shippers' total unused capacity is as below:

$$UnusedCapacity_{S_i,t_v} = ReceivedCapacity_{S_i,t_v} - ShippedOrders_{S_i,t_v}$$

Note

Received capacity could be either self-generated or allocated through collaboration.

$$TotalUnusedCapacity = \sum_{v=1}^{v=m} \sum_{i=1}^{i=n} UnusedCapacity_{S_i,\,t_v}$$

6) Total profits of customers

Customers' profit is used as a means to assess the impact of shipper horizontal collaboration on downstream agents, and is calculated as:

$$Profits_{C_i, t_v} = Revenue_{C_i, t_v} - LostSalesCost_{C_i, t_v}$$

Where:

C_i = Customer i (i = 1, 2, 3,...)

Revenue = total orders of Customer i fulfilled by his selected shipper * rate (1.5)

LostSalesCost = total orders of Customer i unfulfilled by his selected shipper * rate (2)

$$TotalProfits = \sum_{v=1}^{v=m} \sum_{i=1}^{i=n} Profits_{C_i, t_v}$$

Where:

n = the total number of customers

v = the maximum time step

7) Imbalance index

The issue of the unfair distribution of cost and gains is a major impediment for companies considering participating in horizontal collaboration (Cruijssen et al. 2007a, Hingley et al. 2011). In respect to this issue, the imbalance index is used in this model to measure the balance of performance between individual agents. The imbalance index of agents' performance is computed by averaging the difference in absolute values between the agent's performances, as calculated below:

$$ImbalanceIndex = \frac{\sum \begin{array}{c} |Performance_{s_1} - Performance_{s_2}| \cdots + |Performance_{s_1} - Performance_{s_n}| \\ |+Performance_{s_2} - Performance_{s_3} \cdots + |Performance_{s_2} - Performance_{s_n}| \\ +\cdots + |Performance_{s_{n-1}} - Performance_{s_n}| \end{array}}{k}$$

Where:

n = the total number of shippers in a collaborative/non-collaborative logistics supply system

k = the number of absolute values of difference between the agent's performances

The results reported on the performance metrics, i.e. fill-rate and capacity utilization, are averages over the 50 independent runs and across the 2,000 time steps of each run. For those of the KPIs that are cumulative in nature, i.e. the total order frequency/satisfied order/unused capacity/customer profits, the reported results are averages of the final accumulative figures at the last time step over the 50 independent runs.

5.2 Results and Analysis

This section presents the simulation results along with the analysis. Agent performance in the different collaboration strategies is compared with those in the absence of collaboration to examine the effects of participating in horizontal collaboration. Since three supply chain configurations are considered, the effect of horizontal collaboration is evaluated and compared under the different supply chain systems. Detailed results for the random SC, which is used as the baseline supply chain configuration, are presented first in Section 5.2.1. The key results for performance-based SC and the relation-based SC are then given and compared in Section 5.2.2 and Section 5.2.3, respectively.

5.2.1 Random Market Supply Chain

This section studies the simulation results for random SC, under which the supply chain is characterized by customers who adopt a random strategy for order placement in the supply chain. The value and effect of shipper horizontal collaboration is interpreted by investigating five types of performance measures: (1) Fill-rate; (2) Capacity utilization; (3) Cumulative KPIs; (4) Customer profits; (5) Imbalanced Index. To quantify the relative difference in performance between the collaborative and non-collaborative shippers, a "Synergy" variable is calculated, as shown below.

$$Synergy = \frac{CollaborationPerformance - NoCollaborationPerformance}{NoCollaborationPerformance} \times 100\%$$

Such a synergy value in performance can represent the collaboration gains/ performance improvement (if the value is positive, otherwise it represents the loss due to collaboration), which is often measured using the above formula to indicate the (per cent) difference between the performance in the original situation where shippers fulfil their logistics orders individually, and the performance in a system where logistics orders are fulfilled in collaborative ways (Cruijssen et al. 2007c). According to the interviews with logistics experts and the collaboration case studies of various industries, a synergy value that is more than 10% is considered to represent effective and attractive collaboration gains, and a value above 20% would be considered as a very significant performance improvement resulting from the collaboration.

All the performance results under this supply chain configuration are used as the base case results to be further compared with the other two supply chain configurations presented in the later sections, using a similar comparative approach but with the term "Change Percentage" instead of "Synergy", as shown below.

$$ChangePercentag = \frac{PerformanceBasedSCPerformance - RandomSCPerformance}{RandomSCPerformance} \times 100\%$$

$$ChangePercentag = \frac{RelationBasedSCPerformance - RandomSCPerformance}{RandomSCPerformance} \times 100\%$$

5.2.1.1 Fill-rate

The first part of the results analysis looks at the effect of horizontal collaboration on the shipper's order fill-rate; a major indication of the logistics service performance, since a general consensus is identified in the empirical literature that horizontal collaboration can facilitate considerable improvements in the logistics service level for customers. Table 5.1 summarizes the detailed results of fill-rate performance in the baseline supply chain configuration.

Table 5.1 Fill-rate in baseline configuration (random SC)

CS[a]	Equal	Proportional	Excess
System			
Collaborative	0.85[b]	0.85	0.84
Non-collaborative	0.65	0.65	0.65
Synergy	0.30	0.30	0.28
p (C vs NC)[c]	<0.0001	<0.0001	<0.0001
p (IS vs No-IS)[d]		0.6712	<0.0001
Individual			
Collaborative	0.89	0.86	0.88
Non-collaborative	0.73	0.73	0.73
Synergy	0.22	0.18	0.21
p (C vs NC)	<0.0001	<0.0001	<0.0001
p (IS vs No-IS)		<0.0001	<0.0001

[a] CS = Collaboration Strategy

[b] Sample mean

^c P value in paired t-test (C = Collaborative, NC = Non-collaborative)

^d P value in paired t-test (IS = Proportional or Excess, No-IS = Equal)

The first and general outcome in Table 5.1 shows that shippers participating in the collaboration achieve a better fill-rate than their counterparts who maintain the operations independently. The collaboration synergy is significant both at the system and individual levels. In particular, collaborative shippers, as an aggregated supply system, demonstrate a higher synergy value (see synergy value under the title "system"). Further, the synergy is consistently achieved in every collaboration strategy implemented. Such results conform to the theoretical assumption in horizontal collaboration that coordination of capacity sharing would help to reduce the non-fulfilment of orders, due to the extra buffer of capacity supplied by the partners against the demand uncertainty. Under the random supply chain structure, therefore, when shippers are facing completely random customers with a highly dynamic demand stream, the impact of demand dynamics on order fulfilment is filtered more effectively for collaborative shippers than non-collaborative shippers. The collaboration on capacity sharing across the supply chain horizontal partners is therefore proven to be beneficial.

Secondly, the results analysis compares the performance results across the three collaboration strategies implemented. More specifically, the investigation aims to find out if the collaboration strategies supporting active information sharing will produce higher fill-rates. The results from the simulation show that collaboration, whether by sharing demand information (i.e. the proportional strategy) or supply information (i.e. the excess strategy) do not produce higher fill-rates than collaboration with no information sharing (i.e. the equal strategy). In contrast, the equal strategy actually generates the highest fill-rate from either a system/or individual perspective. Thus, under the random SC, it can be concluded that sharing either demand or supply information in the collaboration under this configured supply chain system does not facilitate a better matching of supply to demand when allocating the shared capacity.

The last pattern to be investigated is the measure of imbalance for the fill-rate achieved by individual shippers. The imbalance index is presented in Table 5.2.

Table 5.2 Imbalance index for fill-rate under the random SC

CS	Equal	Proportional	Excess
Collaborative	1.2%	0.9%	1.4%
Non-collaborative	1.6%	1.7%	1.7%
Synergy	−28.2%	−46.2%	−19.5%
p (C vs NC)	<0.0001	<0.0001	<0.0001
p (IS vs No-IS)		<0.0001	<0.0001

Note

For imbalance synergy, the bigger the negative value, the better the synergy perceived in imbalance reduction.

The simulation results show that horizontal collaboration can balance the fill-rate performance better than the absence of collaboration. This ensures that shippers participating in the collaborative logistics network can perform equally well in terms of serving their customers and maintaining long-term sustainable collaboration. In particular, the proportional strategy generates the least imbalance. The rationale behind this lies in the fact that sharing demand information helps to distribute the network capacity in a more proportionally correct way, hence alleviating the discrepancies in the non-fulfilment of orders among partners. From this perspective, therefore, sharing demand information is valuable since a reduction in the imbalances in fill-rate could contribute to a fairer and more sustainable partnership community.

5.2.1.2 Capacity Utilization

This section contains results for capacity utilization, which is a key indicator to determine the efficiency of the logistics. The analysis compares the efficiency level between collaboration and no collaboration, and examines the changes to the efficiency level when different collaboration strategies are implemented. Table 5.3 presents the detailed results.

Table 5.3 Capacity utilization under the random SC

CS	Equal	Proportional	Excess
System			
Collaborative	0.81	0.81	0.80
Non-collaborative	0.63	0.63	0.63
Synergy	0.30	0.30	0.28
p (C vs NC)	<0.0001	<0.0001	<0.0001
p (IS vs No-IS)		0.9036	<0.0001
Individual			
Collaborative	0.70	0.93	0.80
Non-collaborative	0.63	0.63	0.63
Synergy	0.12	0.48	0.27
p (C vs NC)	<0.0001	<0.0001	<0.0001
p (IS vs No-IS)	<0.0001	<0.0001	<0.0001

From Table 5.3, it can be observed that, similar to the fill-rate performance, collaboration helps to drive better capacity utilization both for the system and individuals. This pattern is consistent across the three collaboration strategies. From a shipper's perspective, this means participating in horizontal collaboration is a considerable value-adding activity for increasing the efficiency of the logistics, which can help to reduce the operating cost.

A number of patterns need to be explained in more detail. First, there is no apparent difference between the system and individual utilization for non-collaborative shippers. This is true because, for non-collaborative shippers, there are no capacity sharing and redistribution activities. There is, therefore, always a similar proportion between shipped orders and on-hand capacity, regardless of the totals in the system, or the average across individuals. This utilization pattern of non-collaborative shippers is consistent across the collaboration strategies because the same rule (no collaboration) is adopted.

Second, for the collaborative shippers, there some differences are evident between the system and individual utilization. This is due to the implementation of the specific capacity sharing and re-allocation mechanisms which drive the utilization to be more dynamically different between individuals as opposed to the utilization measured at the aggregated level for the system.

Next, the results analysis compares the utilization performance between the three distinctive collaboration strategies in order to evaluate the effect of information sharing on collaboration synergy.

The results demonstrate two distinct patterns. From the system efficiency perspective, there appears no significant utilization difference between the collaboration strategies. Thus information sharing is not valuable in terms of increasing the system's efficiency level.

With regards to the utilization at an individual level, measured in terms of mean utilization of all partners, a big difference is identified between the collaboration strategies. The equal sharing strategy results in the lowest individual mean utilization. The synergy gain is found to be much smaller than the other two collaboration modes. The cause of this lower individual utilization can be traced back to the capacity sharing and allocation mechanism in this model. As in the equal strategy, partners do not share any information. With low information transparency, the only sensible approach to collaboration is to share the capacity equally so that no one can complain about unfairness and misjudgement. This basic rule indicates that partners will not only equally enjoy the benefits of shared capacity, doing so on a fair give- and -take basis, but they also have to share the unused capacity of the community equally, which becomes the cost of collaboration. Under this collaboration rule, occasionally partners can face the risk of having even lower utilization rates than the original demand capacity ratio due to the responsibility of undertaking the additional unused capacity generated by the collaboration network (hence the additional cost to bear individually). On this occasion, the cost of the collaboration will exceed the benefits and could result in even lower utilization than in the case of no collaboration.

The proportional sharing strategy results in an exceptionally good individual mean utilization, with an average of more than 90%. This is much higher than in the absence of collaboration. Furthermore, the individual mean utilization achieved is significantly higher than the system utilization; revealing the superior value of this particular collaboration strategy for individual efficiency improvement. This is perhaps due to the sharing of demand information between collaborators which allows the capacity supply to be allocated more accurately for individuals, matching closely with their demand. For instance, in a particular period, if one partner has a capacity supply of 200 but only receives 50 orders, while another partner has a capacity of 100 but with 300 orders received, in the event of no collaboration, they will have a utilization of 25% and 100%, respectively. In the event of collaboration, however, the total supply will be divided proportionally according to the demand received by each partner. Hence the two will have a redistributed supply of 43 and 257, respectively, which matches more closely to their demand profile. Hence, in this case, both will have a utilization of 100%, and all capacity will be effectively utilized. This indicates that demand information sharing is very important and has strong value for improving the partner's own efficiency (e.g. a decrease in empty hauling, better usage of fleet/ storage facilities).

The excess sharing strategy results in a very similar individual mean utilization to the system utilization. Both achieve about 27% utilization improvement over the non-collaboration case. The reason why the utilization results are similar between the system and individual measurement should be attributed to the rule of capacity sharing and the allocation mechanism under this collaboration strategy. In the excess strategy, partners are supposed to utilize their own capacity to fulfil the orders first, and only the excess capacity is shared through a bilateral coordination between two partners. This means that there is no responsibility for partners to undertake the additional unused capacity from the collaboration network. As a result of this collaboration rule, there is no capacity sharing and any redistribution of work is undertaken prior to the partner's initial order fulfilment. This means that the amount of the satisfied orders is directly tied to each shipper's available capacity (i.e. when the capacity is already fully loaded, the satisfied orders can only be increased by one unit if one additional unit of supply is obtained from other partners). This means that the measured ratio of the satisfied orders over the capacity supply at the individual level is always similar to the measured utilization ratio at the system level.

The simulation results prove that the excess strategy, although it acts very differently, can also produce considerable value in terms of improvements in capacity utilization. At the system level, its performance is not much lower than either of the other two collaboration modes. At the individual level, it does not work as efficiently as the proportional strategy but significantly outperforms the equal strategy. This suggests that by sharing the supply information, collaborative shippers can attain better synergy than in the case of no information sharing. On the other hand, from a short-term perspective, this collaboration strategy is probably more welcomed by the shippers in the early stage of the collaboration, because each partner under this collaboration method can act more independently; in that they can determine how to use their own capacity to fulfil orders from their own customers. Partners do not need to undertake the extra unused capacity beyond their own order volume since only the excess capacity is shared within the network. In this case, the collaboration synergy serves more like a dessert after the main course, which can help to further increase the utilization, but will not affect the individual planning for the customer order fulfilment. This arrangement is particularly meaningful when some customers are more important than others such that the service level they enjoy should not be affected by the shipper's collaboration. This is why the excess strategy has the highest fill-rate among the Relations-Based Models, under which capacity usage needs to be prioritized for the important customers rather than for the collaboration.

Now, after investigating the main patterns in capacity utilization, the study looks at the issue of imbalance in capacity utilization. The simulation results are produced in Table 5.4.

Table 5.4 Imbalance index for capacity utilization under scenario-R

CS	Equal	Proportional	Excess
Collaborative	1.9%	0.8%	1.8%
Non-collaborative	2.4%	2.4%	2.4%
Synergy	−21.8%	−67.9%	−22.8%
p (C vs NC)	<0.0001	<0.0001	<0.0001
p (IS vs No-IS)		<0.0001	0.5906

It can be seen from the results that the logistics supply system with the presence of horizontal collaboration has contributed to a lower imbalance index value compared to the non-collaborative system. From the customer's perspective, this highlights the greater flexibility of the collaborative logistics system since the low imbalance index value indicates that most of the collaborative shippers are involved in the logistics production process and that therefore their long-term survival and prosperity is guaranteed. Consequently, customers can benefit by having more flexible options when selecting shippers.

Further, it is found that the proportional strategy generates a much lower imbalance index. Recall that this is the same model that achieves the highest mean utilization, and is also the same model that produces the lowest imbalance in fill-rate. The same explanation holds for this pattern, therefore: sharing demand information seems to be particularly beneficial for the collaboration network to reduce imbalances in fill-rate and capacity utilization.

5.2.1.3 Cumulative KPIs

In this section, the analysis compares the total gains or loss between the collaborative and non-collaborative shippers. Table 5.5 presents the simulation results under the random SC.

Table 5.5 Cumulative KPIs under the random SC

CS	Equal	Proportional	Excess
Total order frequency			
Collaborative	10003.62	9992.08	9986.9
Non-collaborative	9996.38	10007.92	10013.1
Synergy	0.1%	−0.2%	−0.3%
p (C vs NC)	0.7070	0.4404	0.1973
p (IS vs No-IS)		0.4079	0.2628
Total satisfied orders[a]			
Collaborative	2,035	2,034	2,005
Non-collaborative	1,563	1,564	1,565
Synergy	30.2%	30.1%	28.1%
p (C vs NC)	<0.0001	<0.0001	<0.0001
p (IS vs No-IS)		0.8057	<0.0001
Total unused capacity[b]			
Collaborative	468	466	495
Non-collaborative	938	937	934

Continued

CS		Equal	Proportional	Excess
	Synergy	−50.1%	−50.3%	−47.0%
	p (C vs NC)	<0.0001	<0.0001	<0.0001
	p (IS vs No-IS)		0.4798	<0.0001

[a] Total satisfied orders: numbers in thousands

[b] Total unused capacity: numbers in thousands. Higher negative figure, higher synergy

Note

Numbers in the table are the totals of all individual agents.

As can been seen from Table 5.5, under the random SC, the total frequency for order placement is the same between the collaborative and non-collaborative shippers. This phenomenon correctly corresponds to the model configurations. Under this model, customers have an equal preference for each shipper and, therefore, in the longer term, the total order frequency of each shipper is going to be very close regardless of whether that shipper is collaborating or not collaborating.

More customer orders are satisfied by the collaborative shippers than the non-collaborative ones. This directly corresponds to the improvement in fill-rate performance. In addition, the magnitude of synergy is found to be similar between the fill-rate and total satisfied orders: both are found to be improved by around 30%. This means that the two KPIs are highly positively correlated under this supply chain network. The increased average daily service fill-rate has been directly transformed into the same level of volume increase for the total satisfied orders in the end; a key indicator for generating the business revenue. On the other hand, collaboration based on the additional sharing of demand or supply information does not make any apparent difference compared to when there is no information sharing in the collaboration. Although more proactive information sharing between partners is found to be helpful for partners to improve their individual capacity utilization, it is not beneficial for achieving higher total throughput of customer orders for the entire collaboration system.

When customer demand is highly random, a significant reduction of underutilized capacity can be achieved by shippers if they are participating in the horizontal collaboration: they could save up to 50% of the operational cost tied to the excess capacity which can frequently be incurred in a highly volatile (random) marketplace. Similarly, sharing information does not help the system to reduce the unused capacity further. Moreover, the excess strategy with sharing of supply data even results in more unused capacity, indicating that sharing supply data has a negative effect when there is long-term collaboration.

Again, the imbalance index is measured for cumulative KPIs. Table 5.6 illustrates the results.

Table 5.6 Imbalance index for cumulative KPIs under the random SC

CS	Equal	Proportional	Excess
Total order frequency			
Collaborative	2.4%	2.7%	2.6%
Non-collaborative	2.5%	2.7%	2.4%
Synergy	−4.3%	1.5%	7.4%
p (C vs NC)	0.5701	0.7801	0.3493
p (IS vs No-IS)		0.1261	0.2335
Total satisfied orders			
Collaborative	2.4%	2.6%	2.4%
Non-collaborative	1.9%	2.1%	2.0%
Synergy	24.0%	24.8%	21.2%
p (C vs NC)	0.0083	0.0004	0.0201
p (IS vs No-IS)		0.1532	0.8903
Total unused capacity			
Collaborative	3.1%	5.4%	4.7%
Non-collaborative	3.3%	3.6%	3.3%
Synergy	−4.4%	50.6%	40.2%
p (C vs NC)	0.5055	<0.0001	0.0002
p (IS vs No-IS)		<0.0001	<0.0001

The imbalance index of the total order frequency is quite similar between the collaborative and non-collaborative shippers. This pattern is valid since customers in this context do not hold a specific preference for the shippers and therefore there is an equal opportunity for customers to select any shipper, meaning that the flow of customers/orders is not able to be concentrated in the hands of just a few shippers, which would cause a big discrepancy.

For the imbalance in total satisfied orders, collaborative shippers are found to have a higher imbalance index than non-collaborative shippers. This should be due to the capacity sharing and re-allocation process among partners, which creates bigger discrepancies than non-collaborative shippers who fulfil their orders independently.

In terms of imbalance in total unused capacity, non-collaborative shippers exhibit consistent imbalance performance of around 3.4%, while the imbalance index for collaborative shippers varies across the collaboration strategies. The proportional and excess strategies report much higher imbalances, while the smallest imbalance is identified for the equal strategy. The equal strategy seems to be particularly useful for preventing the amplification of imbalances between shippers. This is due to the fact that shippers adopting this model are prevented from sharing demand/supply data so they have to undertake the unused capacity equally on a daily basis, which in turn effectively prevents the unused capacity being overloaded onto any individual partners in the network.

Overall, when comparing the imbalance performance between the three collaboration strategies, it can be concluded that sharing information does not facilitate the collaboration to produce a better balance in partners' long-term cumulative performance.

5.2.1.4 Customer Profits

This section presents and discusses customers' profit performance, the amount of which is collectively determined by shippers' order fulfilment. Customer's profit in this model is a means to assess the effect of shipper horizontal collaboration on downstream agents, as well as the effect of customers' own behaviours.

The results of customers' profits and profit imbalance are presented in Table 5.7.

Table 5.7 Customer total profits and imbalance under the random SC

CS	Equal	Proportional	Excess
Total Profits	2,594.0	2,594.2	2,405.2

Continued

CS	Equal	Proportional	Excess
p (IS vs No-IS)		0.9814	<0.0001
Imbalance Index	4.6%	4.2%	4.9%
p (IS vs No-IS)		0.0352	0.2575

Note

customer profits in thousands

Customers' profits are subject to two critical elements: the placed orders that are satisfied and the orders unfulfilled, which can be transformed into the lost sale cost. From the results shown in Table 5.7, it can be seen that customers' profits are very similar when collaborative shippers adopt the equal and proportional strategies, but lower profits are found in the case of the excess strategy. This is mainly due to the lower fill-rate of this model, meaning more lost sale costs are incurred.

There is an imbalance level of around 4.6% for customer profits. This is, in general, higher than most of the shippers' metrics, mainly due to the fact that customers are interacting with shippers of both collaborative and non-collaborative supply systems, which inevitably increases cases of variations in performance. The imbalance level is not greatly different when the various collaboration strategies are implemented, however.

5.2.2 Performance-based Supply Chain

This section contains the results for the performance-based SC, under which the supply chain is characterized by the downstream customers adopting a blacklist policy for order placement based on shipper performance. The performance of shippers who pursue the collaboration is compared to those in the absence of collaboration to determine the value and impact of horizontal collaboration. Further, the results under this supply chain configuration are also compared to the baseline supply chain configuration (the random SC) in order to examine the potential influence of the changing customer behaviours on the upstream logistics supply systems characterized by the presence of collaboration, or no collaboration.

5.2.2.1 Fill-rate

Table 5.8 contains the simulation results for fill-rate. To quantify the relative difference in performance between the random SC and performance-based SC, an additional calculation of the change percentages is presented in Table 5.9.

Table 5.8 Fill-rate under the performance-based SC

CS	Equal	Proportional	Excess
System			
Collaborative	0.81	0.82	0.80
Non-collaborative	0.67	0.66	0.67
Synergy	0.20	0.25	0.20
p (C vs NC)	<0.0001	<0.0001	<0.0001
p (IS vs No-IS)		<0.0001	<0.0001
Individual			
Collaborative	0.86	0.84	0.85
Non-collaborative	0.74	0.73	0.74
Synergy	0.16	0.15	0.16
p (C vs NC)	<0.0001	<0.0001	<0.0001
p (IS vs No-IS)		<0.0001	<0.0001

Table 5.9 Change percentages for fill-rate under the performance-based SC

CS	Equal	Proportional	Excess
System			
Collaborative	−4.8% (<0.0001)[a]	−3.1% (<0.0001)	−4.9% (<0.0001)
Non-collaborative	2.6% (<0.0001)	0.3% (0.0007)	1.7% (<0.0001)
Synergy	−31.5%	−14.8%	−29.5%
Individual			
Collaborative	−3.2% (<0.0001)	−2.9% (<0.0001)	−3.3% (<0.0001)
Non-collaborative	1.4% (<0.0001)	−0.1% (0.04)	0.8% (<0.0001)
Synergy	−25.5%	−18.0%	−23.6%

[a] Change percentage of mean (P value in paired t-test)

Note

Change percentages represent the relative degree of change in agent performance between the supply chain configurations, with the random SC being the comparison basis.

A general pattern that can be concluded from Table 5.8 is that horizontal collaboration enables shippers to achieve higher fill-rate than their counterparts who do not collaborate. The positive value of horizontal collaboration is consistent with that for the random SC. The collaboration synergy is considerably decreased, however, which can be explained by the decrease in change percentages shown in Table 5.9. This reduction in synergy is due to the decrease in the fill-rate performance of collaborative shippers, and the increase for non-collaborative shippers. Such increase/decrease changes are more profound at the system level.

The outcome of the decreasing fill-rate for collaborative shippers suggests that collaborative shippers under this supply chain configuration are more likely to experience bigger orders and higher volatility in the total volume of orders. This can be partly attributed to the lack of fulfilment of orders by non-collaborative shippers, since customers can punish them by putting them into the blacklist. It is sensible to conclude that, at the initial simulation periods, non-collaborative shippers will experience a higher chance of being blacklisted because they do not have access to the external capacity to buffer their supply shortages. This increased blacklisting of non-collaborative shippers will drive customers to switch more frequently to the collaborative shippers. This increasing number of customers for collaborative shippers, however, can significantly enhance the pressure on them to manage the capacity supply when the demand has greatly increased. As the number of non-collaborative shippers in the blacklist increases, many of the customers would start to order solely from collaborative shippers. The coincidence of multiple customers engaging with the same shipper increases leading to a sharp spike in demand, which in turn could result in more frequent cases of shipper's supply becoming over-committed.

The fill-rate change pattern for non-collaborative shippers works in an opposite way. The result shows a slight increase in the fill-rate, but the magnitude of this increase does not correspond with the decrease in the fill-rate of collaborative shippers.

This result can be attributed to the increasing interactions between collaborative and non-collaborative shippers for their order fulfilment under performance-based SC: when non-collaborative shippers serve fewer customers (due to being blacklisted), they have the chance to improve their fill-rate performance considerably. This improvement opportunity, however, interacts with what is happening with the collaborative shippers: as more customers begin to order from collaborative shippers, shortage in capacity is more likely to occur and the blacklist behaviour will drive customers to switch back to non-collaborative shippers, largely offsetting the positive improvement in fill-rate for non-collaborative shippers.

To some extent, there tends to be a pendulum effect in this model. Initially, perhaps more non-collaborative shippers are blacklisted because of their poor ability to fulfil big orders, but as the preference of customers for collaborative shippers increases, high pressure from demand surges with consequent reduced fill-rate, which motivates customers to return to the non-collaborative shippers who have been released from the blacklist. This thereafter can become a cycle that will be iterated due to the customer's blacklist policy. There are also more complex interactions as time progresses: after the initial periods, the individual customer's learning of the order fulfilment performance of each shipper can vary greatly at a specific time, due to the dynamics existing in every shipper-customer couple. From an overall perspective, however, the customer's blacklist policy in the long run actually makes the total demand in the supply chain system more volatile than in the random SC. The negative impact on the collaborative shippers' fill-rates is particularly profound.

On the other hand, a more reduced fill-rate can indirectly reveal the fact that more customers select collaborative shippers. This can lead to the conclusion that in a supply chain system where customers can evaluate the shipper's order delivery performance, horizontal collaboration can help shippers to retain more customers than their counterparts, but at the cost of lower fill-rates. This result is in line with the empirical findings by Cruijssen et al. (2007a) that horizontal collaboration helps to protect the company's market share.

In terms of the fill-rate difference between the collaboration strategies, the pattern is found to be consistent with that in the random SC. Collaboration strategies supported by additional information sharing do not, apparently, outperform collaboration with no information sharing.

Table 5.10 sets out the results for fill-rate imbalance, while Table 5.11 highlights the relative degree of change compared to the random SC.

Table 5.10 Imbalance index for fill-rate under the performance-based SC

CS	Equal	Proportional	Excess
Collaborative	1.0%	1.0%	1.2%
Non-collaborative	1.2%	1.2%	1.2%
Synergy	−18.5%	−20.1%	0.0%
p (C vs NC)	<0.0001	<0.0001	0.9905
p (IS vs No-IS)		0.2232	0.0003

Table 5.11 Change percentages for fill-rate imbalance under the performance-based SC

CS	Equal	Proportional	Excess
Collaborative	−13.3% (0.0007)	4.1% (0.3996)	−11.6% (0.0012)
Non-collaborative	−23.6% (<0.0001)	−30.0% (<0.0001)	−28.8% (<0.0001)
Synergy	−34.4%	−56.6%	−99.8%

Under the performance-based SC, it is found that the imbalance gap becomes very small between the collaboration and non-collaboration case for shippers, although collaboration still slightly outperforms non-collaboration, with the exception of the excess strategy where the two are almost the same. This indicates that the customer's learning and blacklist behaviours have an alleviating effect on the fill-rate imbalance for both collaborative and non-collaborative shippers, since, generally, in both cases the imbalance index is reduced. In particular, non-collaborative shippers experience a greater reduction in imbalance and the blacklist behaviours collectively seem to facilitate a better demand mechanism for balancing shippers' fill-rate performance.

5.2.2.2 Capacity Utilization

This section contains the results for capacity utilization under the performance-based SC. Details for utilization are presented in Table 5.12, while Table 5.13 shows the change percentages compared to the random SC.

Table 5.12 Capacity utilization under the performance-based SC

CS	Equal	Proportional	Excess
System			
Collaborative	0.84	0.82	0.82
Non-collaborative	0.57	0.58	0.58
Synergy	0.47	0.41	0.42
p (C vs NC)	<0.0001	<0.0001	<0.0001
p (IS vs No-IS)		<0.0001	<0.0001
Individual			
Collaborative	0.75	0.94	0.82
Non-collaborative	0.58	0.59	0.58
Synergy	0.30	0.60	0.41
p (C vs NC)	<0.0001	<0.0001	<0.0001
p (IS vs No-IS)		<0.0001	<0.0001

Table 5.13 Change percentages for utilization under the performance-based SC

CS	Equal	Proportional	Excess
System			
Collaborative	3.3% (<0.0001)	0.8% (<0.0001)	2.2% (<0.0001)
Non-collaborative	−8.3% (<0.0001)	−6.8% (<0.0001)	−7.9% (<0.0001)
Synergy	54.3%	35.2%	50.0%
Individual			
Collaborative	5.8% (<0.0001)	0.7% (<0.0001)	2.2% (<0.0001)
Non-collaborative	−8.2% (<0.0001)	−6.7% (<0.0001)	−7.9% (<0.0001)
Synergy	139.1%	24.5%	50.7%

First, the simulation results show that horizontal collaboration under this supply chain configuration produces a higher synergy in capacity utilization compared to the baseline supply chain. This pattern is consistent at both the system and individual levels across the three collaboration strategies implemented, although the level of the synergy increase is different.

The increased capacity utilization is due to the customer blacklist policy. Customers in this case order more frequently from collaborative shippers because they have more robust capacity supply through sharing and thus less chance of being blacklisted. In the longer term, this can lead to more orders being concentrated in the hands of collaborative shippers than when customers select shippers in a completely random way. Consequently, the capacity utilization will be increased for collaborative shippers, but decreased for shippers absent from collaboration.

Although the general pattern is easy to understand, further analysis reveals that the magnitude of the increased utilization of collaborative shippers does not correspond with the reduced utilization of non-collaborative shippers. Non-collaborative shippers are found to experience greater changes (a reduction) in the utilization rate. This is for sure caused by losing customers due to being blacklisted, but this proportion of lost customers are not fully captured by collaborative shippers since they do not experience the same level of utilization increase. This result implies that customers adopting the blacklist policy would come across more failures to get their orders delivered by shippers compared to when they randomly select shippers in the random SC. The cause of this phenomenon will be linked back to the earlier discussion regarding the fill-rate reduction for collaborative shippers under this model. As more non-collaborative shippers are put into the blacklist, customers tend to have a higher preference for collaborative shippers. At some point the demand from all customers can be so strong as to make it unlikely that it can be completely fulfilled by collaborative shippers. In this eventuality, dissatisfied customers will act by turning back to non-collaborative shippers. As a result of such iteration, the overall demand variability is amplified. From a long-term perspective, collaborative shippers will not benefit too much from the increase/decrease in demand, therefore, and their utilization improvement is not strong.

On the other hand, customers will be punished by their blacklist learning behaviours. Although this behaviour is sensible when acting individually, when they act collectively, a negative result (a higher frequency of unmet orders) can be created. Also, the subsequent effect on shippers is different: the blacklist policy can have a larger negative impact on non-collaborative shippers but a smaller positive impact on collaborative shippers in terms of their utilization performance. This suggests that horizontal collaboration is attractive as a means for shippers to increase their efficiency when customers act more realistically and when higher demand variability is exhibited.

In terms of the utilization performance between the three distinctive collaboration strategies, the pattern is similar to that identified in the random SC. There does not appear to be a big difference for system utilization. For mean utilization of individuals, the proportional strategy achieves the highest utilization and the highest synergy. The superior value of sharing demand information for increasing individual utilization also holds under this supply chain system.

Another noticeable change is evident in the equal sharing strategy: this exhibits a stronger increase in the utilization. For system performance, it generates the highest utilization and also the highest synergy. For individual performance, it produces a considerably greater improvement in utilisation. This reflects the fundamental nature of the equal sharing strategy: since in this model there is equal sharing of networked capacity, when the demand is generally increasing for all collaborative shippers, it is easier and more straightforward for the individual partners to improve the utilization. This pattern might also indicate that if the demand is stable and high enough, the equal sharing strategy without information sharing could perform equivalently well in terms of utilization compared to the information driven collaboration.

Lastly, the measure of imbalance in utilization is shown in Table 5.14, and change percentages in Table 5.15.

Table 5.14 Imbalance index for capacity utilization under the performance-based SC

CS	Equal	Proportional	Excess
Collaborative	1.7%	0.8%	1.8%
Non-collaborative	1.9%	1.9%	1.8%
Synergy	−8.4%	−59.0%	1.0%
p (C vs NC)	0.0348	<0.0001	0.8129
p (IS vs No-IS)		<0.0001	0.3625

Table 5.15 Change percentages for utilization imbalance under the performance-based SC

CS	Equal	Proportional	Excess
Collaborative	−8.4% (0.0457)	−0.5% (0.9)	−2.4% (0.5975)
Non-collaborative	−21.8% (<0.0001)	−22.0% (<0.0001)	−25.4% (<0.0001)
Synergy	−61.4%	−13.1%	−104.2%

Under the performance-based SC, although a tiny decrease in imbalance can be noticed for the collaborative shippers, the overall imbalance pattern is very similar to that of the random SC. On the other hand, the customer blacklist ordering policy collectively has a greater effect in terms of reducing the utilization imbalance between non-collaborative shippers.

5.2.2.3 Cumulative KPIs

This section analyses and compares the cumulative KPIs under the Performance-Based SC. Table 5.16 and Table 5.17 present the results and change percentages, respectively.

Table 5.16 Cumulative KPIs under the performance-based SC

CS	Equal	Proportional	Excess
Total order frequency			
Collaborative	10939.66	10525.66	10810.82
Non-collaborative	9060.34	9474.34	9189.18
Synergy	20.7%	11.1%	17.6%
p (C vs NC)	<0.0001	<0.0001	<0.0001
p (IS vs No-IS)		<0.0001	<0.0001
Total satisfied orders			
Collaborative	2,102	2,052	2,050
Non-collaborative	1,433	1,458	1,442
Synergy	46.7%	40.7%	42.2%
p (C vs NC)	<0.0001	<0.0001	<0.0001
p (IS vs No-IS)		<0.0001	<0.0001
Total unused capacity			
Collaborative	400	448	450
Non-collaborative	1,067	1,042	1,058
Synergy	−62.5%	−57.0%	−57.5%
p (C vs NC)	<0.0001	<0.0001	<0.0001
p (IS vs No-IS)		<0.0001	<0.0001

Table 5.17 Change percentages for cumulative KPIs under the performance-based SC

CS	Equal	Proportional	Excess
Total order frequency			
Collaborative	9.4% (<0.0001)	5.3% (<0.0001)	8.3% (<0.0001)
Non-collaborative	−9.4% (<0.0001)	−5.3% (<0.0001)	−8.2% (<0.0001)
Synergy	28539.2%	7110.9%	6844.4%
Total satisfied orders			
Collaborative	3.3% (<0.0001)	0.9% (<0.0001)	2.2% (<0.0001)
Non-collaborative	−8.3% (<0.0001)	−6.8% (<0.0001)	−7.9% (<0.0001)
Synergy	54.5%	35.5%	50.1%
Total unused capacity			
Collaborative	−14.4% (<0.0001)	−3.8% (<0.0001)	−9.0% (<0.0001)
Non-collaborative	13.8% (<0.0001)	11.2% (<0.0001)	13.2% (<0.0001)
Synergy	24.7%	13.3%	22.1%

As can be seen from Table 5.16, collaborative shippers under the performance-based SC tend to have a higher frequency of customer ordering than non-collaborative shippers. This pattern justifies the configuration of the blacklist policy, and therefore validates the previous conclusions made in respect to the fill-rate and capacity utilization under this supply chain. In fact, from a long-term perspective, sharing capacity within the collaboration network improves the availability of capacity to fulfil customer orders, and hence reduces the chance of being blacklisted by the unhappy customers.

The collaboration utilizing the equal strategy is also able to win slightly more customers than the other two collaboration strategies supported by information sharing. This result supports the previous result in respect to fill-rate performance, suggesting that the equal strategy with no information sharing can, overall, perform just as well in terms of fulfilling the customer demand, which is in line with the fill-rate performance outcomes.

The behaviour pattern in terms of total satisfied orders is more interesting to study due to a number of issues. First, collaborative shippers can gain more customers in the performance-based SC, but this does not guarantee that they could achieve the same level of increase for the orders satisfied due to the dynamic capacity constraints over time. Conversely, for non-collaborative shippers, losing a certain percentage of their customers does not mean they will face the same proportion of decrease in the total amount of satisfied orders since this will be more dependent on dynamic demand supply matching. In addition, unlike in the random SC, the flow of customers in this context is driven by the interactions both between customers and shippers based on performance learning and between collaborative and non-collaborative shippers for their individual order fulfilment. This can affect the ordering decisions and order fulfilment. Hence, the overall system is complex and the system level behaviours are hard to predict given the complex scenario combinations and the mutual interactions between agents.

From the simulation results it is shown that for collaborative shippers, the degree of change (increase) in total satisfied orders is much smaller than the degree of change (increase) in the number of customers. This suggests that under the performance-based SC shippers with horizontal collaboration can only realize a limited level of benefit by having more customers. A sensible explanation would be that more customers result in more orders, which lead to an increasing chance of demand exceeding supply. This behaviour corresponds to the drop in the fill-rate under the performance-based SC.

For non-collaborative shippers, the degree of change (decrease) in total satisfied orders is more in line with the degree of change (decrease) in the number of customers. Overall, therefore, the blacklist policy has a more profound effect on the non-collaborative shippers. The reduction in their total satisfied orders is a direct reflection of the decrease in the number of their customers.

Similar to the base case, information sharing in collaboration under the performance-based SC does not facilitate a higher total throughput of customer orders. This result is interesting for the case of the proportional strategy since the mean capacity utilization of this model is the highest but this does not contribute to increasing the system's overall throughput of customer orders. This suggests that mean utilization performance is not absolutely connected to the order throughput efficiency, when the sharing of capacity is dynamically distributed among partners.

In terms of the results for the total unused capacity under the performance-based

SC, collaborative shippers are seen to reduce their total unused capacity but it is the opposite for the non-collaborative shippers. This result is easy to understand due to the simple fact that the customer preference is increasingly shifted to collaborative shippers, which in the longer term helps them to reduce the underutilized capacity, a key indicator to reflect the operating cost.

On the other hand, changing the ordering preference of customers has a more profound effect on non-collaborative shippers. It is found that the degree of change (increase) in the total unused capacity is even greater than the degree of change (decrease) in the number of customers. This, together with the identical pattern observed in respect to total satisfied orders, suggests that the reduction of customers plays a more dominant role than the increase of customers in terms of the effect on the shipper's total satisfied orders and unused capacity.

Similarly, collaboration with sharing of demand/supply data between horizontal partners does not reduce the unused capacity in the system more than collaboration with no information sharing. In contrast, the total reduction of the unused capacity in the equal strategy is even higher than the other two collaboration strategies under the performance-based SC. This corresponds to the higher system utilization achieved by the equal strategy.

Table 5.18 and Table 5.19 illustrate the results and change percentages for imbalance performance under the performance-based SC.

Table 5.18 Imbalance index for cumulative KPIs under the performance-based SC

CS	Equal	Proportional	Excess
Total order frequency			
Collaborative	1.3%	1.3%	1.3%
Non-collaborative	1.0%	1.0%	0.9%
Synergy	28.1%	34.6%	38.9%
p (C vs NC)	0.0051	0.0008	0.0001
p (IS vs No-IS)		0.9236	0.8533
Total satisfied orders			
Collaborative	2.0%	1.9%	2.0%
Non-collaborative	1.7%	1.7%	1.6%
Synergy	17.9%	11.0%	23.0%

Continued

CS	Equal	Proportional	Excess
p (C vs NC)	0.0099	0.1957	0.0073
p (IS vs No-IS)		0.2232	0.9835
Total unused capacity			
Collaborative	2.8%	5.8%	5.2%
Non-collaborative	2.2%	2.3%	2.1%
Synergy	24.1%	149.9%	147.6%
p (C vs NC)	0.0171	<0.0001	<0.0001
p (IS vs No-IS)		<0.0001	<0.0001

Table 5.19 Change percentages in imbalance index for cumulative KPIs under the performance-based SC

CS	Equal	Proportional	Excess
Total order frequency			
Collaborative	−46.1% (<0.0001)	−51.8% (<0.0001)	−51.3% (<0.0001)
Non-collaborative	−59.7% (<0.0001)	−63.7% (<0.0001)	−62.3% (<0.0001)
Synergy	−746.0%	−2217.3%	−424.1%
Total satisfied orders			
Collaborative	−15.2% (0.0387)	−29.7% (<0.0001)	−15.9% (0.019)
Non-collaborative	−10.8% (0.0941)	−21.0% (0.0039)	−17.2% (0.0363)
Synergy	25.7%	55.5%	-8.8%
Total unused capacity			
Collaborative	−11.1% (0.1015)	7.3% (0.3152)	11.8% (0.1109)
Non-collaborative	−31.6% (<0.0001)	−35.4% (<0.0001)	−36.7% (<0.0001)
Synergy	−644.6%	−196.4%	−267.1%

Comparing the imbalance pattern in total order frequency with the random SC, it is found that the imbalance index decreases for both the collaborative and non-collaborative shippers. This result is interesting in that, with the presence of customers' blacklist behaviours under this supply chain system, imbalance in order frequency for shippers should, from common sense, increase because customers' order preference in respect to shippers should become more differentiated driven by the localized information and decision making, yet the results that have emerged demonstrate the opposite pattern. This is a phenomenon typically seen in complex adaptive systems. The underlying causal mechanisms are sometimes not easy to figure out since such system level behaviours are subject to complex interactions between customers and shippers, as well as between shippers in the collaborative/ non-collaborative system.

In addition, it can be seen that collaborative shippers on average retain a higher imbalance level. This can be a result of the increasing number of customers shifted to them under this supply chain system.

In general, the imbalance index in total satisfied orders is found to be reduced for all shippers under the performance-based SC. This could be due to the presence of customers' blacklist ordering policy which turns out to be beneficial in terms of imbalance reduction for shippers. Also, a bigger imbalance reduction is found in the proportional strategy, indicating that sharing demand information under this supply chain system facilitates a greater reduction of imbalance for the shipper's total satisfied orders. The proportional strategy does not significantly outperform the equal strategy with no information sharing, however.

For the total unused capacity, imbalance is apparently reduced among the non-collaborative shippers but remains statistically unchanged for collaborative shippers. This means the reduced frequency of customer orders due to the blacklist has actually led to a reduction in the imbalance of excess capacity for non-collaborative shippers. On the other hand, the volume of customers shifted to collaborative shippers does not cause a significant increase in imbalance for them. In addition, the equal strategy produces significantly less imbalance than the other two models. This highlights the value of this collaboration strategy for maintaining a good balance in partners' unused capacity. Sharing information in the collaboration from this performance dimension is not really helpful, and even leads to an increase of discrepancies.

5.2.2.4 Customer Profits

Table 5.20 and Table 5.21 present the results regarding customer profits and profit imbalance.

Table 5.20 Customer total profits and imbalance under the performance-based SC

CS	Equal	Proportional	Excess
Total Profits	2,374.8	2,284.6	2,134.5
p (IS vs No-IS)		<0.0001	<0.0001
Imbalance Index	5.4%	5.5%	6.6%
p (IS vs No-IS)		0.8352	0.0001

Table 5.21 Change percentages for customer total profits and imbalance
under the performance-based SC

CS	Equal	Proportional	Excess
Total Profits	−8.5% (<0.0001)	−11.9% (<0.0001)	−11.3% (<0.0001)
Imbalance Index	17.6% (0.0024)	29.9% (<0.0001)	36.6% (<0.0001)

The results show that customers implementing the blacklist policy in their order decisions experience some reduction in their profit performance. Customers blacklist shippers based on whether orders are satisfied or not satisfied. This is a feedback decision reflecting the customer's decreasing confidence for certain shippers, which individually is seen to be rational, but collectively such learning behaviour has contributes to a worse result for their total profits.

To figure out why the profits are decreased, a breakdown analysis of the key elements in the composition of the profits is necessary. First, as analysed previously, the blacklist policy causes customers to order more frequently from the collaborative shippers, resulting in a significant decrease in the total satisfied orders for non-collaborative shippers. Only a smaller portion of this shift in volume is satisfied by the collaborative shippers, however, due to the higher pressure on them to cover the surge in demand. This is reflected by the reduced fill-rate for collaborative shippers under this supply chain system. On the other hand, overall, the total orders satisfied in the supply system are decreased, mainly due to order non-fulfilment. Hence the cost of lost sales is also amplified as it costs more to de-commit an order in the customer's context.

In contrast to information sharing driven collaboration, customers benefit from higher profits when collaborative shippers adopt the equal strategy without information sharing.

In terms of the imbalance in customer profits, the results show a certain increase of imbalance under all collaboration strategies. Unquestionably this is due to the increasing differentiation in the customer's order preference in respect to shippers when the blacklist policy is in existence. Thus, customers not only experience lower profits, but also have to face an increasing imbalance in their profit performance. In addition, customers under the information-driven collaboration strategies do not benefit from less imbalance than under the equal strategy.

5.2.3 Relation-based Supply Chain

This section contains the results for the relation-based SC, under which the supply chain is characterized by adaptive learning and relationship development between upstream shippers and downstream customers. The performance of shippers who collaborate is compared to those who do not in order to determine the value and impact of horizontal collaboration. Further, the results of this supply chain configuration are also compared to the baseline supply chain configuration (the random SC) in order to examine the potential influence of the changing supply chain environment on the logistics supply system.

5.2.3.1 Fill-rate

The simulation results are presented in Table 5.22 and Table 5.23.

Table 5.22 Fill-rate under the relation-based SC

CS	Equal	Proportional	Excess
System			
Collaborative	0.88	0.84	0.88
Non-collaborative	0.89	0.90	0.89
Synergy	−0.02	−0.06	−0.02
p (C vs NC)	0.0369	<0.0001	0.0410
p (IS vs No-IS)		<0.0001	0.6949
Individual			
Collaborative	0.91	0.85	0.91
Non-collaborative	0.91	0.91	0.91
Synergy	0.00	−0.07	0.00

Continued

CS	Equal	Proportional	Excess
p (C vs NC)	0.8205	<0.0001	0.8974
p (IS vs No-IS)		<0.0001	0.8614

Table 5.23 Change percentages for fill-rate under the relation-based SC

CS	Equal	Proportional	Excess
System			
Collaborative	3.1% (0.0003)	−1.1% (0.0842)	4.6% (<0.0001)
Non-collaborative	36.2% (<0.0001)	36.9% (<0.0001)	36.6% (<0.0001)
Synergy	−106.2%	−121.0%	−106.0%
Individual			
Collaborative	2.1% (0.0001)	−1.2% (0.0494)	3.0% (<0.0001)
Non-collaborative	24.2% (<0.0001)	24.6% (<0.0001)	24.4% (<0.0001)
Synergy	−99.4%	−136.9%	−99.7%

A couple of patterns can be identified from Table 5.22 and Table 5.23. First, the fill-rate for non-collaborative shippers is sharply increased. The improvement is profound in that, in all cases, the fill-rate is increased by about 36% at the system level and 24% at the individual level, compared to the random SC. The fill-rate increase is not consistently observed for the collaborative cases, however. The equal and excess strategies generate positive results but the proportional strategy reveals only insignificant changes. In addition, the improvement when shippers are collaborating is far less significant than shippers who are not.

Overall, the results show a noticeable increase in the service fill-rate for the entire supply system. This outcome supports the findings made in the vertical supply chain collaboration literature regarding the benefits of developing a trust-based relationship between suppliers and customers (e.g. Kim 2009). When shippers and customers begin to develop trust on a long-term basis, more stable vertical relationships can be established and their supply and demand transactions can be prioritized. This learning and adapting process, however, is independent from shippers' horizontal collaboration or lack of it.

The relationship-driven supply chain seems particularly to benefit non-collaborative shippers compared to the initial supply chain configuration, with the results consistently showing their fill-rate as sharply increased. This behaviour pattern provides an interesting insight, suggesting that non-collaborative shippers should recognize their limited capability to serve a broader range of customers due to their self-constrained capacity and lack of access to external capacity. Consequently, they should learn to focus on developing their core and strategic customers to ensure quality of service (in this context, the fill-rate) and seek to sustain long-term business with them.

The fill-rate increase for collaborative shippers is limited and in some cases (in the proportional strategy) the fill-rate is reduced. This suggests that creating a more stable demand-supply relationship structure through trust building does not facilitate horizontal collaboration to deliver a significantly higher service level. On the other hand, this might indicate that there is a higher value of horizontal collaboration which lies beyond just serving the narrowly scoped customers, as justified in the random and blacklist mode.

The second pattern lies in the effect of the relationship-driven supply chain structure on the collaboration synergy for shippers. The simulation result shows a big change in respect to synergy gain, namely that in a relationship-driven supply chain network the collaboration synergy is dramatically reduced and becomes negative.

This result demonstrates an interesting pattern. When non-collaborative shippers begin to focus on specific customers, they can maintain the service performance just as well as collaborative shippers who adopt the same relationship-driven approach, and in some cases non-collaborative shippers can even outperform the collaborative shippers. This might suggest that horizontal collaboration could become a less attractive option for shippers if their primary objective for collaboration is to improve the service fill-rate for customers. Participating in horizontal collaboration in a relation-based supply chain network will not be beneficial, as demonstrated by the simulation results. In certain circumstances, the cost of collaboration might even outweigh the benefits from collaboration. Taking the proportional strategy as an example to illustrate the underlying concern, when the vertical relationship with multiple customers starts to become differentiated, shippers need to change the fulfilment strategy and prioritize the available supply for the key customers, rather than putting the capacity into the network for sharing and redistributing it irrespective of the importance of specific customers for each shipper. Independent shippers, however, do not have this coordination problem and can decide how to use their capacity straightaway. Consequently, they can have greater autonomy and flexibility to react to their core customers by providing them with a better logistics supply service.

In terms of the fill-rate difference between the collaboration strategies, again the results are consistent with the initial supply chain configurations. Collaboration strategies with information sharing do not apparently outperform collaboration with no information sharing. This suggests no value to information sharing when partners collaborate primarily in order to improve the service fill-rate.

Table 5.24 and Table 5.25 illustrate the results for imbalance performance in relationship-driven supply chains.

Table 5.24 Imbalance index for fill-rate under the relation-based SC

CS	Equal	Proportional	Excess
Collaborative	4.8%	2.0%	4.5%
Non-collaborative	2.8%	2.3%	2.4%
Synergy	72.1%	−14.3%	85.1%
p (C vs NC)	<0.0001	0.0103	<0.0001
p (IS vs No-IS)		<0.0001	0.5333

Table 5.25 Change percentages for fill-rate imbalance under the relation-based SC

CS	Equal	Proportional	Excess
Collaborative	312.2% (<0.0001)	114.3% (<0.0001)	229.6% (<0.0001)
Non-collaborative	72.0% (<0.0001)	34.4% (<0.0001)	43.4% (<0.0001)
Synergy	−355.9%	−69.1%	−536.6%

Under this supply chain system, the results exhibit two obvious patterns. First, the fill-rate imbalance has been significantly increased in both the collaboration and no collaboration cases. This indicates a negative result, given the development of a long-term supply chain relationship, which causes a larger discrepancy between individual shippers. From an individual perspective, this means someone can have better performance while others do not. This is not an ideal situation, either for individuals or the system, and eventually customers' interests can be affected as well. Second, the long-term adaptive learning and relationship development in the supply chain has a more profound effect on the increase in the fill-rate imbalance for collaborative shippers than non-collaborative ones. In the case of the equal and excess strategies, collaboration generates much higher imbalances than non-collaboration. This observation challenges the value of horizontal collaboration. It is found that not only is the fill-rate no better than under no collaboration case, but the fill-rate imbalance is significantly amplified, leading to a perception of a greater cost of collaboration in service performance under this supply chain system. On the other hand, an exception is made by the adoption of the proportional strategy. It can be seen that the proportional strategy generates the lowest imbalance and consistently outperforms the non-collaboration approaches across all supply chain configurations. This demonstrates that this collaboration strategy is very effective for sustaining good balance of shippers' service performance. The value of sharing demand information is consistently justified to reduce the service imbalance.

5.2.3.2 Capacity Utilization

The simulation results for capacity utilization under the relation-based SC are shown in Table 5.26 and Table 5.27.

Table 5.26 Capacity utilization under the relation-based SC

CS	Equal	Proportional	Excess
System			
Collaborative	0.95	0.94	0.95
Non-collaborative	0.80	0.77	0.81
Synergy	0.19	0.23	0.17
p (C vs NC)	<0.0001	<0.0001	<0.0001
p (IS vs No-IS)		0.0931	0.1391
Individual			
Collaborative	0.92	0.97	0.95
Non-collaborative	0.80	0.77	0.81

Continued

CS	Equal	Proportional	Excess
Synergy	0.16	0.26	0.17
p (C vs NC)	<0.0001	<0.0001	<0.0001
p (IS vs No-IS)		<0.0001	<0.0001

Table 5.27 Change percentages for capacity utilization under the relation-based SC

CS	Equal	Proportional	Excess
System			
Collaborative	16.6% (<0.0001)	16.0% (<0.0001)	17.8% (<0.0001)
Non-collaborative	27.4% (<0.0001)	22.3% (<0.0001)	29.0% (<0.0001)
Synergy	−36.3%	−22.3%	−39.4%
Individual			
Collaborative	31.2% (<0.0001)	4.1% (<0.0001)	18.2% (<0.0001)
Non-collaborative	27.6% (<0.0001)	22.5% (<0.0001)	29.3% (<0.0001)
Synergy	25.4%	−46.3%	−39.6%

A number of key patterns can be identified in the results. First, it can be seen that collaborative shippers considerably improve their utilization performance both at the system and individual levels, compared to what they achieved in the previous supply chain systems, under which they actually have a wider range of customers to serve. Such a result would not be anticipated given the prior understanding of the relation-based SC configurations, where a decrease in the utilization of collaborative shippers would be expected. This is because as the vertical preferential relationship grows, one shipper can have fewer customers to serve, which can lead to a decrease of customer orders to fill the capacity. The results of this study, however, show the opposite of this.

This phenomenon might suggest a theory that the capacity utilization performance is not directly tied to the scale of the available demand sources. Most often, their relationship can be non-linear and complex. This means even one shipper with a vast customer base can still experience low capacity utilization, due to the demand variability, which is sometimes independent of the number of customers. If each customer's variability is significant, having more customers will only contribute to greater variations in demand, which can result in a larger negative result in utilization performance: hence, variability rather than the volume is a key driver that can directly affect the capacity utilization performance. Under this supply chain system, however, the variability is expected to be constantly reduced as long-term relationships are developed, resulting in a more stabilized demand stream from the core customers. This explains why the capacity utilization in the collaboration case shows a clear increase rather than a decrease.

Secondly, it is found that although capacity utilization among collaborative shippers increases, their collaboration synergy is significantly reduced. This is apparently due to the larger improvement in utilization made by non-collaborative shippers. This efficiency increase can be attributed to the mutual learning and preferential relationship development which makes the specific shipper-customer couples become long-term partners. Each shipper, whether he collaborates or not, therefore, will develop their own core customers. This means that non-collaborative shippers can have more stable and structural demands from their strategic customers and that this reduced variability in demand is critical for increasing the utilization rate for non-collaborative shippers since they do not have the option to utilize capacity outside their own organization. Empty running can often occur when the demand is highly unpredictable and, therefore, an increasingly stabilized demand stream as a result of stronger relationship ties with core customers can effectively help non-collaborative shippers to filter the demand dynamics and increase utilization, with the side-effect of making shippers' horizontal collaboration less of an advantage in terms of capacity utilization performance under this supply chain system.

Nevertheless, even given a much lower advantage, the collaboration synergy is still positive. This is because horizontal collaboration facilitates the creation of networked capacity providing an additional buffer for shippers. This buffered capacity helps to filter the demand dynamics better, although the demand is not as volatile as before. In spite of this, the collaborative shippers can manage to optimize the usage of capacity better than in the absence of that collaboration.

Furthermore, it can in fact be seen that all shippers have considerably improved their capacity utilization in a relationship-driven supply chain network. This implies that as shippers and customers rely more on the long-term relationships in their supply and order allocation decisions, the variability in the demand and supply becomes smaller, which ultimately benefits the operational efficiency (i.e. utilization) and effectiveness (i.e. fill-rate).

When comparing the collaboration synergy produced by the three collaboration strategies, two distinct patterns are evident.

At the system level, there is no clear difference identified for the improvement in capacity utilization between the three collaboration strategies. This is consistent with the initial supply chain configurations and it can be concluded that all modes of horizontal collaboration benefit the system's efficiency. The synergy gains are significantly reduced when collaboration takes place, however. This is because the capacity utilization rate of non-collaborative shippers is dramatically increased, making the collaboration net gain smaller. Synergy is found to be higher for the proportional strategy but the difference does not seem to be directly driven by the methods of collaboration and information sharing, but rather as a result of the capacity utilization difference for non-collaborative shippers under each of the cases. This is something that is different from the initial supply chain scenarios: whereas there should be an interaction between collaborative/non-collaborative shippers that makes the non-collaborative shippers end up with different results, they actually behave in the same way as in the past models. In a relationship-driven supply chain network, therefore, whether one shares information or not does not really make a big difference for horizontal collaboration in terms of system level capacity utilization.

At the individual level, the capacity utilization difference between the three collaboration modes is apparently less significant than was the case in the previous supply chain configurations. The proportional strategy still slightly outperforms the other two models, but there is a dramatic efficiency improvement for the equal and excess strategies. This can be attributed to the increasing stabilization of the daily demand, which helps to filter the demand dynamics better, showing that stronger supply-demand relationships can facilitate a very positive environment for horizontal partners to improve the efficiency level. As opposed to the system capacity utilization, at the individual level, information sharing in collaboration consistently makes the utilization clearly better than when there is no information sharing. This also contributes to the higher synergy gains.

In terms of the imbalance performance in capacity utilization, the simulation results are produced in Table 5.28 and Table 5.29.

Table 5.28 Imbalance index for capacity utilization under the relation-based SC

CS	Equal	Proportional	Excess
Collaborative	4.3%	1.2%	3.0%
Non-collaborative	12.7%	14.8%	12.3%
Synergy	−66.4%	−92.0%	−75.6%
p (C vs NC)	<0.0001	<0.0001	<0.0001
p (IS vs No-IS)		<0.0001	0.0025

Table 5.29 Change percentages for utilization imbalance under the relation-based SC

CS	Equal	Proportional	Excess
Collaborative	127.2% (<0.0001)	51.1% (<0.0001)	63.8% (<0.0001)
Non-collaborative	429.0% (<0.0001)	507.0% (<0.0001)	418.9% (<0.0001)
Synergy	204.4%	35.5%	232.1%

As can be seen, the imbalance index is found to be increasingly significant for both the collaborative and non-collaborative shippers. This represents the negative effect of long-term vertical relationship development which can lead to larger capacity utilization discrepancies between individual shippers. It is noticeable that the imbalance index for non-collaborative shippers has been greatly amplified. This means that in the non-collaboration network the logistics production process is concentrated in the hands of a few shippers, while the rest will operate less efficiently. This determines the lower flexibility of non-collaborative logistics system since some shippers will eventually get pushed out of the market. Meanwhile, from another perspective, this could symbolize a system which possesses higher efficiency, as the remaining shippers can consistently operate with higher capacity utilization, and hence a much lower cost, offering customers better cost-efficiency solutions.

In respect to the imbalance performance between collaboration strategies, the result shows that imbalance is apparently increased for the equal and excess strategies, but the degree of increase is not as strong as that observed among non-collaborative shippers. While the proportional strategy is an exception since it generates only a small imbalance, there is still a small utilization difference among the individual partners. It also produces much higher synergy in all supply chain configurations. This result has again demonstrated that sharing the demand information not only helps to improve the individual capacity utilization, but also performs well in terms of balancing the utilization among the collaborative shippers. The rationale for this excellence can be similar to the initial explanation that with the greater transparency of the demand data, the capacity supply among the collaborative partners could be allocated more accurately to enable a closer match with the demand, and hence higher utilization and fewer discrepancies.

5.2.3.3 Cumulative KPIs

This section analyses and compares the cumulative KPIs under the relation-based SC. Table 5.30 and Table 5.31 present the results and change percentages respectively.

Table 5.30 Cumulative KPIs under the relation-based SC

CS	Equal	Proportional	Excess
Total order frequency			
Collaborative	11024.02	11411.78	10922.6
Non-collaborative	8975.98	8588.22	9077.4
Synergy	22.8%	32.9%	20.3%
p (C vs NC)	<0.0001	<0.0001	<0.0001
p (IS vs No-IS)		0.0026	0.4450
Total satisfied orders			
Collaborative	2,373	2,359	2,363
Non-collaborative	1,990	1,911	2,018
Synergy	19.3%	23.4%	17.1%
p (C vs NC)	<0.0001	<0.0001	<0.0001
p (IS vs No-IS)		0.0965	0.1382
Total unused capacity			
Collaborative	128	140	137

Continued

CS	Equal	Proportional	Excess
Non-collaborative	510	589	481
Synergy	−75.0%	−76.2%	−71.6%
p (C vs NC)	<0.0001	<0.0001	<0.0001
p (IS vs No-IS)		0.1367	0.1942

Table 5.31 Change percentages for cumulative KPIs under the relation-based SC

CS	Equal	Proportional	Excess
Total order frequency			
Collaborative	10.2% (<0.0001)	14.2% (<0.0001)	9.4% (<0.0001)
Non-collaborative	−10.2% (<0.0001)	−14.2% (<0.0001)	−9.3% (<0.0001)
Synergy	31403.6%	20872.2%	7868.7%
Total satisfied orders			
Collaborative	16.6% (<0.0001)	16.0% (<0.0001)	17.8% (<0.0001)
Non-collaborative	27.3% (<0.0001)	22.2% (<0.0001)	28.9% (<0.0001)
Synergy	−36.1%	−22.0%	−39.3%
Total unused capacity			
Collaborative	−72.7% (<0.0001)	−69.9% (<0.0001)	−72.3% (<0.0001)
Non-collaborative	−45.6% (<0.0001)	−37.2% (<0.0001)	−48.5% (<0.0001)
Synergy	49.6%	51.5%	52.1%

Note

The large numbers for synergy value under the total order frequency are mathematically correct although they look exaggerated. For example, 31403.6% is obtained by comparing the synergy value in the random SC which is 0.1% (or 0.000724262 when it is not rounded up in the table), with the figure in the relation-based SC which is 22.8% (or 0.228168958). Careful interpretation of these large numbers is needed, therefore.

As can be seen in the results for the total order frequency, compared to the performance-based SC, the total customer order frequency is further increased for collaborative shippers, and decreased for non-collaborative shippers. This means that collaborative shippers obtained more customer order placements under this supply chain network.

Although the characteristics of the relation-based supply chain might be thought to suggest a smaller gap in order frequency between collaborative and non-collaborative shippers, further analysis shows that there can be two underlying causes for the increased difference found here. First, it is reasonable for collaborative shippers to attract and maintain more core customers due to the better availability of capacity supply and greater stability of the service level. Hence, a larger portion of customers are willing to order from collaborative shippers and be permanently tied to them as the positive learnings accumulate. Second, there is also a first-mover advantage for collaborative shippers to lock in more customers at the initial stage of the relationship development. As customers are more likely to develop positive experiences from the collaborative shippers at the early stages, this learning will quickly dominate the customers, forcing them to give up trying alternative shippers. Hence, they will order less and less from the non-collaborative shippers, who will in return rate them down when allocating the supply. The collaborative shippers, therefore, are in a better position to dominate the initial learning of customers and to influence them to decrease their preference for non-collaborative shippers. This will generally increase the order frequency for collaborative shippers, particularly in the initial stage of the interactions.

When comparing the performance of three collaboration strategies, the results show that the proportional strategy with demand information sharing attracts more customers than the other two collaboration modes. The increase in synergy can also be attributed to the significantly lower order frequency of non-collaborative shippers, however. This decreasing order frequency could potentially result from the interactions with collaborative shippers, and the sharing demand information mechanism could also indirectly influence customers to order less from non-collaborative shippers.

In respect to the performance of total satisfied orders, the results under this supply chain system are very positive. Both types of shippers have dramatically increased their total satisfied orders compared to the initial supply chain configurations, meaning more revenue can be generated.

It is not difficult to explain the increasing trend among the collaborative shippers since they have accumulated higher order frequency from customers than under the random and performance-based SCs. Higher order frequency in general increases the number of incoming orders. This increasing order volume can be more or less captured by the collaborative shippers depending on the dynamic fit between the demand and supply. What is surprising in the result, however, is that the magnitude of increase is much stronger than the expectation from the level of increase in order frequency. From the performance-based SC it is learned that increases in the order frequency only facilitate very small increases in the total satisfied orders. The pattern identified under the relation-based SC is just the opposite, however: even though a dramatic increase in the total satisfied orders is observed the relative increase in the order frequency compared to the performance-based SC is not massive. This again suggests that the relationships between these two variables are non-linear and complex. One possible cause for this phenomenon can be attributed to the learning and relationship development between shippers and customers. As the supply/demand relationship goes into stabilization, more stable demand is created by the core customers and conversely more supply is prioritized by the core shippers. Overall, the system variability is much reduced which contributes to more orders being satisfied.

The result for non-collaborative shippers is also surprising and interesting. The total satisfied orders are greatly increased for the non-collaborative shippers in the relationship-driven supply chain, reducing the gap with the collaborative shippers (leading to lower collaboration synergy compared to the random and performance-based SCs). This dramatic increase is actually based on a further decrease in the order frequency from customers, however. This once again reveals the complex relationship between order satisfaction and order frequency. A more important factor to influence the number of satisfied orders could be the adaptive learning behaviour and the long-term relationship development, and this mutual learning and trust benefits non-collaborative shippers more than the collaborative shippers.

When comparing the total order throughput for the three collaboration strategies, no significant difference is evident. In terms of synergy gain, however, the proportional strategy shows slightly better results. This is due to fewer orders satisfied by non-collaborative shippers. Since non-collaborative shippers all adopt the same rule (no collaboration), the cause of the fewer satisfied orders can take account of the interactions with collaborative shippers. Again, collaboration while sharing demand information seems to have a greater influence on the performance of non-collaborative shippers.

In terms of results for the total unused capacity, overall, the pattern is very similar to the result for total satisfied orders: there is a sharp decrease in the total unused capacity for both the collaborative and non-collaborative shippers. This indicates that significant empty running costs can be saved.

Again, the major factor leading to this positive result could be attributed to the long-term preferential relationship between shippers and customers, which considerably reduces the chance of low utilization (as justified in the increase of capacity utilization under this supply chain). But one interesting difference is that collaborative shippers under the relation-based SC can benefit more significantly from reducing the total unused capacity, as opposed to non-collaborative shippers who achieve much greater improvement in the total satisfied orders. This pattern has a practical implication in that if the rates for determining the capacity cost and revenue are very different, there would also be a very different outcome for the ultimate performance (i.e. profitability) between collaborative and non-collaborative shippers, which is necessary to determine the net effect on participants of taking part in horizontal collaboration.

When comparing the total unused capacity of the three collaboration strategies, the results show no significant difference between the equal strategy and the other two collaboration strategies with additional information sharing.

The imbalance results for the cumulative KPIs under this supply chain system are presented in Table 5.32 and Table 5.33.

Table 5.32 Imbalance index for cumulative KPIs under the relation-based SC

CS	Equal	Proportional	Excess
Total order frequency			
Collaborative	17.7%	34.9%	18.9%
Non-collaborative	18.9%	21.8%	16.1%
Synergy	−6.6%	60.3%	16.8%
p (C vs NC)	0.5189	0.0002	0.1749

Continued

CS	Equal	Proportional	Excess
p (IS vs No-IS)		<0.0001	0.6954
Total satisfied orders			
Collaborative	9.7%	32.9%	12.1%
Non-collaborative	19.1%	23.0%	16.5%
Synergy	−49.0%	43.1%	−27.0%
p (C vs NC)	0.0001	0.006	0.0519
p (IS vs No-IS)		<0.0001	0.3065
Total unused capacity			
Collaborative	18.1%	34.4%	41.8%
Non-collaborative	59.8%	66.2%	56.2%
Synergy	−69.7%	−48.0%	−25.8%
p (C vs NC)	<0.0001	<0.0001	0.0043
p (IS vs No-IS)		<0.0001	<0.0001

Table 5.33 Change percentages in the imbalance index for cumulative KPIs under the relation-based SC

CS	Equal	Proportional	Excess
Total order frequency			
Collaborative	633.3% (<0.0001)	1187.5% (<0.0001)	617.3% (<0.0001)
Non-collaborative	651.1% (<0.0001)	715.3% (<0.0001)	559.9% (<0.0001)
Synergy	52.1%	−3939.1%	−126.0%
Total satisfied orders			
Collaborative	310.1% (<0.0001)	1148.1% (<0.0001)	404.3% (<0.0001)
Non-collaborative	897.0% (<0.0001)	988.5% (<0.0001)	737.3% (<0.0001)
Synergy	303.7%	−73.7%	227.5%
Total unused capacity			
Collaborative	478.5% (<0.0001)	532.0% (<0.0001)	791.3% (<0.0001)
Non-collaborative	1727.3% (<0.0001)	1731.0% (<0.0001)	1583.3% (<0.0001)
Synergy	1477.3%	195.0%	164.1%

As can be seen for the total order frequency, the imbalance is dramatically increased for all the shippers. This can result from the customer self-adaptation process for evaluating shippers: individual customers will constantly vary their preference for the different shippers based on their own learning before the preference is locked-in. The high imbalance index means that at any given time some shippers can grab significantly more customers than other ones. This high imbalance is not considered good for shippers as individuals seeking equal and sustainable development. Furthermore, collaborative shippers adopting the proportional strategy have a much higher imbalance than the other collaboration modes. This result highlights that this collaboration strategy has a particularly negative effect, which should be avoided under this supply chain system if the customer order frequency is critical for the operations.

Although shippers' total satisfied orders are increased significantly, the imbalance is also dramatically increased for all shippers. The overall pattern is quite similar to the imbalance in the order frequency, which indicates that the imbalance in the order frequency might have a direct influence on the discrepancies in the total satisfied orders. With such a cause and effect, the proportional strategy having the highest imbalance index is a reasonable outcome. Also, when implementing the proportional strategy, there seems to be an interaction between the collaborative and non-collaborative shippers in that the increase in the imbalance in collaborative shippers also leads to an apparent increase in the imbalance in non-collaborative shippers, although at a more mild level.

A similar imbalance amplification is also found for the total unused capacity. Here, however, the non-collaborative shippers have a much greater imbalance increase than the collaborative shippers. The benefits of collaboration to maintain the lower level of imbalance in unused capacity become more evident compared to the prior supply chain systems. The equal strategy still produces a significantly better result than the other two collaboration strategies, which consistently proves its exceptional value in facilitating the most balanced sharing of unused capacity.

5.2.3.4 Customer Profits

The results for customer's profits and profit imbalance are presented in Table 5.34 and Table 5.35.

Table 5.34 Customer total profits and imbalance under the relation-based SC

CS	Equal	Proportional	Excess
Total Profits	5,270.3	4,944.6	5,285.3
p (IS vs No-IS)		0.0002	0.8698
Imbalance Index	32.7%	31.0%	30.0%
p (IS vs No-IS)		0.6233	0.5111

Table 5.35 Change percentages for customer total profits and imbalance under the relation-based SC

CS	Equal	Proportional	Excess
Total Profits	103.2% (<0.0001)	90.6% (<0.0001)	119.7% (<0.0001)
Imbalance Index	609.6% (<0.0001)	636.5% (<0.0001)	517.8% (<0.0001)

The results show that when adopting adaptive learning, the customer's profits are greatly increased. The rationale behind this should follow the same logic as previously consistently demonstrated. The long-term adaptive learning could eventually facilitate a more stable supply/demand relationship between shippers and customers. As a result, more predictable and structural demands could be created by developing the core customers. Conversely, more prioritized supply is also provided by the core shippers. Overall, the system dynamics are much reduced which contributes to more orders being satisfied, hence more profits.

Consistent with the previous circumstances, customers under the information-driven collaboration strategies do not benefit from the higher profits.

In terms of the imbalance pattern for customer profits, the results show a similar pattern as that identified from the shipper's cumulative KPIs: a sharp increase in the customers' profits also brings a sharp increase in the imbalance. This means that the benefits resulting from the stabilized supply/demand network are not equally distributed among the customers, although they follow exactly the same learning rule. It also indicates the fact that some customers fail to establish their core shippers, or at least their relationships with the shippers are not as strong as the other better performing customers. Also, the time spent in evaluating and growing the mature strategic relationship can vary greatly among the individuals, which can be another cause of high/low performance in respect to the achievement of profits.

Again, customers under the information-driven collaboration strategies do not benefit from a lower imbalance than under the equal strategy.

5.3 Discussion

The various simulation results in the previous sections have shown that horizontal collaboration can significantly influence the performance of the logistics supply system including all relevant stakeholders. This influence is multi-faceted and also mixed across the models. These various effects are closely examined in the different supply chain configurations. This section further compares the results of the different supply chain configurations and identifies a number of key insights from the comparison, which are illustrated as follows.

First, the simulation results strongly support the empirical evidence that horizontal collaboration can help make logistics operations more efficient (i.e. higher capacity utilization), effective (i.e. higher fill-rate) and competitive (i.e. higher satisfied orders/ lower wasted capacity, hence better profitability). Although collaboration might result in sub-optimal decisions and increased costs for participants from time to time (e.g. undertaking additional unused capacity from other partners/de-commit one's own customers due to capacity shared to other partners, as indicated in the different collaboration strategies illustrated in Section 1.1.2), in the longer term, shippers who choose to collaborate significantly outperform their counterparts who maintain the traditional way of self-operating logistics. The positive synergy gains from collaboration are consistently observed across the different collaboration strategies and supply chain systems.

The collaboration synergy can be interpreted from different performance perspectives, however, and the results can vary depending on the types of the supply chain under which the specific collaboration strategy is implemented. In general, it is found that:

(1) Horizontal collaboration benefits shippers most in terms of the service fill-rate in a random marketplace supply chain in which customers have an equal preference for all shippers irrespective of their order delivery performance (as explained in Section 5.2.1.1).

(2) Horizontal collaboration benefits shippers more in respect to the capacity utilization and satisfied orders in a short-term performance-driven supply chain when customers can blacklist shippers subject to their order delivery performance (as explained in Section 5.2.2.2, Section 5.2.2.3).

(3) Horizontal collaboration works best for shippers to reduce the unused capacity and increase the customer order frequency in a long-term relation-based supply chain. But at the same time, the collaboration synergy for other performance metrics is largely decreased due to the dramatic improvement made by non-collaborative shippers in this supply chain (as explained in Section 5.2.3.3).

Second, the results identify that, for the most part, the collaboration strategies driven by the sharing of information do not produce better collaboration results for shippers than the collaboration strategies without any information sharing. Specifically, sharing either the demand or supply information in the horizontal collaboration is not valuable in terms of increasing the collaboration gains. The result is consistent regardless of the system/or individual perspective, and across the different supply chain configurations. The only exception is in the case of the impact on capacity utilization, where sharing extra information does yield improvement in utilization, although only at the individual level, not at the system level.

An underlying explanation for this outcome should be the fact that sharing information can lead to both good and bad collaboration decisions in the course of a collaboration. For example, when adopting the proportional strategy, if at any given time a shipper partner receives a very high demand, he will benefit by having more capacity shared by other partners to fulfil that demand. In another case, however, he will be expected to retain more unused capacity than he would otherwise have done if the total capacity in the community is very high. On the other hand, collaboration without any information sharing but through an equal sharing mechanism can in the longer term neutralize the advantages and disadvantages exhibited in the information-driven collaborations. Since shippers always equally share the capacity for order fulfilment and cost distribution, regardless of the respective supply and demand profile, they avoid encountering the fluctuated/extreme situations in the dynamic collaboration process (for more details and the logic refer back to the model design in Section 5.1.2).

Overall, the observed results provide an interesting comparison concerning the value of information sharing in horizontal versus vertical collaboration in the supply chain network. Crucially, it is found that the more proactive data exchange between the horizontal partners is not beneficial, in contrast to what is commonly sought after in respect to supply chain vertical partners. In the literature on vertical supply chain information sharing, in general, significant benefits are identified for supply chain performance, and information sharing can be especially helpful in matching the supply closer to the demand (i.e. by reducing the bullwhip effect/excess inventory while improving service level) (Lee et al. 1997, Chen et al. 2000, Disney and Towill, 2003, Chatfield et al. 2004, Dejonckheere et al. 2004, Simchi-Levi and Zhao, 2004, Li et al. 2006, Kelepouris et al. 2008, Syuhada, 2014).

In addition, some other arguments have been made in the vertical supply chain literature about the value of information sharing in relation to the different demand variability conditions. Gavirneni et al. (1999) suggested that when the demand variance is high, sharing information is not that beneficial. Chen (1998) demonstrated that demand information sharing is most beneficial when demand variability is low. He concludes that the value of information is a decreasing function of demand variability. Li et al. (2006) further explained that the fill rate drops as the demand variability increases, and hence demand information sharing is only beneficial for stable demand conditions. If these arguments are applied in the context of horizontal collaboration, it could be expected that when the demand stream is better stabilized, partners sharing information would achieve better performance, especially in respect to the service fill-rate. The simulation results do not support this logic, however. Even in a relation-based supply chain network, when the customer demand becomes much more stabilized, the collaborative partners do not obviously benefit from sharing information. The theory about demand variance affecting the value of information sharing is not valid in the context of supply chain horizontal collaboration, therefore.

The lack of value identified for information sharing in horizontal collaboration could imply that partners can achieve equivalent collaboration gains without the need to disclose their sensitive information (e.g. the customer demand/capacity volume) during the course of collaboration, since these are the core competitive assets in the business operations. This is a particular concern when the collaborators are direct competitors. Looked at another way, if a lack of information sharing does not affect the gains from collaboration too markedly, even the most direct rivals in the marketplace could be encouraged to collaborate. Competitors in this case could select the equal capacity sharing strategy without fear of leaking sensitive data, unfair allocation and opportunism during the collaboration.

As an apparent exception, information sharing is found to be helpful for individual shippers to achieve higher capacity utilization. This indicates that sharing demand or supply information can be helpful to increase the shipper's own operational efficiency, since utilization improvement can be considered to be a result of controlling and matching the demand closer to the supply (in this case the logistics capacity). The interpretation of the information sharing benefits from this angle is rarely considered in the vertical supply chain literature where the primary focus for sharing information is to control the supply (i.e. optimize the inventory level, increase the forecast accuracy) in order that it matches more closely with demand. In the context of horizontal collaboration, this insight is, apparently, new. Although an increase in capacity utilization is commonly reported among the empirical studies, the explicit comparison of the utilization level in respect to information sharing or no information sharing during the course of collaboration has never before been possible. This study fills this gap. It also identifies that sharing demand information is more helpful than sharing supply information to filter the effect of demand dynamics and ensure higher efficiency. There is certainly plenty of room for further studies of this new benefit in horizontal collaboration.

Another interesting insight from the results is that horizontal collaboration can help shippers achieve much better logistics performance in a relationship-driven supply chain network where upstream shippers and downstream customers can mutually develop trust towards a long-term trading partnership. This result appears to fit well with the arguments in the empirical studies (Zhu et al. 2014, Jacobs et al. 2014, Verstrepen and Bossche, 2015), which suggest an opinion that horizontal collaboration can be more effective if the collaboration participants develop a stronger vertical relationship with their downstream customers (or upstream suppliers) who are able to support their collaboration, thereby maximizing the collaboration gains. In this model, the vertical support is realized by collaborative shippers' long-term customers, who support them with the more stable and predictable demand which ultimately benefits the collaboration between shippers.

There are negatives as well as benefits in horizontal collaboration in the context of the relationship-driven supply chain, however. The results from the simulation identify two negative impacts with the presence of the long-term vertical relationship development.

First, it is found that with the long-term vertical relationship development, non-collaborative shippers can have an even stronger level of increase in their performance, which in turn, reduces the relative degree of increase in the performance made by collaborative shippers. This means that the collaboration gains in terms of the synergy value become smaller in the relationship-driven supply chain. If the major business objective is to compete for an unfair advantage rather than increase one's own operations performance, horizontal collaboration might be a less attractive option for shippers to consider under this supply chain system.

Second, despite the fact that the relationship-driven supply chain can lead to an increase in performance for horizontal collaboration partners, it can also lead to significant amplification of imbalance in a partner's performance, which can create hurdles for the long-term sustainability of the collaboration community.

The increased imbalance in performance is certainly due to the discrepancies in the individual journey of probing and developing the long-term vertical partners. It can be the case that some shippers fail to establish a strong collaborative relationship with at least one of their downstream customers. It can also be that some shippers' relationships with their customers are not as strong as the other, better performing, shippers, hence they have fewer orders and more variations in orders. Also, the time spent evaluating and growing a mature strategic relationship between a specific shipper and customer can vary greatly among the individual cases, which can be another cause for the high/low performance difference. Apparently, there are strong interactions between all supply chain agents during the transient periods of relationship development. These can lead to different evolutionary paths for any specific shipper and customer in terms of their volume exchanged and trust accumulated over the course of the simulation, thereby creating a big difference in their performance achievement. This phenomenon corresponds to the so called "butterfly effect" or "path dependency"; that very small interactions and state changes early on can cause a dramatic change in the behaviours or outcomes in the later circumstances (Arthur 1994; Shapiro and Kauffman, 1995, Akkermans 2001).

It can also be noticed that, in some key performance indicators, collaborative shippers encounter even a greater imbalance than non-collaborative shippers. This might indicate the creation of an additional imbalance as a result of the mechanisms in horizontal collaboration. To counter this, a fair gain sharing mechanism is crucial to reduce the negative impact of collaboration for partners. This is also highly recommended in many empirical studies (Cruijssen et al. 2007a, Biermasz et al. 2012, Palmer et al. 2012) and seems to be particularly valuable for the collaboration in this supply chain context.

5.4 Conclusion

This chapter has examined what benefits would emerge from participating in logistics horizontal collaboration (LHC) and how such collaboration can affect the supply chain operations for individuals as well as the system as a whole. To quantify the effects of collaboration, the agent-based simulation (ABS) approach was employed in order to explicitly model the behaviours and decision-making in the collaboration and explore their operational consequences.

The results show that LHC can significantly impact the performance of the logistics supply system including all supply chain stakeholders. The impact is multi-faceted and also mixed across the model scenarios. In summary, the simulation model demonstrates that LHC can significantly benefit the logistics efficiency in terms of capacity utilization and customer service in the sense of order fill-rate, and such beneficial effects are consistently observed in different supply chain environments. In particular, LHC can produce better logistics performance in a relationship-based supply chain network where downstream customers can support upstream shippers with more stable and predictable demands. On the other hand, information sharing in the collaboration, for the most part, does not facilitate the higher collaboration gains for partners. Specifically, sharing either the demand or supply information in the horizontal collaboration is not helpful in increasing collaboration gains. Hence there is a difference for the value of information sharing in the context of horizontal collaboration as opposed to vertical collaboration, the latter of which is often justified as providing more beneficial gains.

The research findings contribute to the development of knowledge concerning how to model the LHC in a simulation environment, and to an understanding of its operational impact on partnership performance and supply chain operations.

CHAPTER 6
DISCUSSION

6.1 Findings of Case Studies

This section discusses the main findings from case studies (Chapter 4). The objective of conducting case studies is to develop a fuller understanding regarding to the different types of LHC in practice. Specifically, a typological analysis based on the various empirical evidences was carried out. The typological analysis began by exploring the key elements critical to the development of the LHC project. By comparing and contrasting the different instances and categories of issues among the cases, the study identified that "collaboration structures" "collaboration objectives" "collaboration intensity" and "collaboration modes" are the four key elements that are of great importance to characterize the design and implementation of a LHC project in practice. These elements can assist to form a framework for analysing the types of LHC in a more systematic way. The following part discusses the key outcomes of the typological analysis based on each element.

1) Typology of Collaboration Structure

The first typology describes the possible structure of the connections and relationships between supply chain players in the typical LHC projects. It describes at a high level the types of stakeholders in the supply chain who form horizontal collaborative relationships, and their interactions with other stakeholders outside the horizontal partnership. First, based upon the analysis of a large amount of cases, the typology developed a generalization of supply chain players as three distinctive roles, namely shippers, customers, and logistics service providers, who can represent all active stakeholders in the supply chain network. Then, by analysing the possible collaboration scenarios among these key stakeholders, three generalized and one hybrid LHC structures were identified, as shown in Figure 4.2 and Figure 4.3.

The typology identifies the first collaboration structure as the shipper-centric collaboration network, which describes the horizontal partnership mainly between shippers for outbound logistics. The shipper collaboration community can also actively collaborate with the vertical players such as downstream customers and LSPs. The second collaboration structure (customer-centric collaboration) represents the horizontal partnership mainly between customers for inbound logistics. They also can work with shippers and LSPs to facilitate better performance. The third collaboration structure (LSP-centric collaboration) centres on the collaboration between LSPs to improve their efficiency as the major logistics execution party. They can perform better if they have tighter collaboration with shippers and customers. The typology also identifies a hybrid collaboration structure that can be formed by a combination of at least two of the initial ones, which makes the relationship links and collaboration exchanges more sophisticated but expects higher gains through such high integration.

2) Typology of Collaboration Objectives

The second typology classifies the different objectives driving the LHC. Despite a number of prior studies addressing the objectives of collaboration, their discussions have largely been limited to the theoretical analysis or specific scenarios. There lacks of a concrete analysis of the LHC objectives that can link to the various operational practices. This typology generalized seven unique LHC objectives based upon a rich collection of empirical cases and expert discussions.

Cost reduction is regarded as the most relevant objectives for LHC from case studies.There are various cost reduction opportunities identified based upon a large number of case scenarios. The typology provides a generalization of these cost savings as two main kinds: operational cost and procurement cost. Operational cost reduction is associated with cutting down all kinds of costs of a logistics execution player or a service provider, while procurement cost reduction saves money for players who purchase the logistics service. Besides cost reduction as a monetary measure of logistics efficiency, increasing the logistics capacity utilization and predictability through better integration of logistics resources are the other key objectives to drive LHC. The typology also identifies that LHC is not a mere means to increase partners' own efficiency, but also a key purpose of it is to serve the customer better. This connects to another desire to increase the flexibility of running logistics through LHC, which can lead to more satisfactory customer services while controlling the expense. The typology also identifies a more strategic objective to increase the market share and customer reach through the better consolidation of service networks. Finally, there found to be desires for LHC that could help to reduce the environment pollutions which was rarely discussed in the past but would become an even more important driving force for LHC in the near future.

3) Typology of Collaboration Intensity

The third typology illustrates the LHC practice pertaining to the different intensity of collaboration. It was found from case studies that the collaboration practices were implemented at the various degrees. However, it's hard to draw the boundaries among the different practices. By integrating with the existing literature of collaboration intensity (Lambert et al. 1999, Cruijssen et al. 2007b, Pomponi et al. 2013) with the empirical findings drawn from case studies, a more enhanced typology was developed based on three dimensions: the collaboration relationship for decision making and coordination, the scope of collaborative activities, and the time horizon against which the collaborative activities are planned.

The typology identifies four different levels of collaboration. Starting from the minimum collaboration as autonomy, where there is no strong sense of information exchange and ad hoc collaboration opportunities. Then progressing to the baseline collaboration, where information sharing is increased, and a langer number of coordinated activities are implemented based upon the short-term time window (1—5 days). Then progressing to the strategic collaboration, where the high quality information is shared and the collaboration is planned with the extended time window combining both short-term and middle-term planning (1—3 weeks). Then progressing to the system-wide integration as the highest level, where there is full-scale information transparency between partners, and collaboration can be planned from the short-term strategic window to the long-term one (above 6 weeks).

4) Typology of Collaboration Modes

The fourth typology classifies the different LHC collaboration modes. The existing research on the modes of LHC mainly emphasizes the illustration of potential cost savings through the transport bundling. Analysis of further approaches to improve the performance in horizontal collaboration could not be found, however. This reveals the limited understanding pertaining to the operational aspects of LHC in current contributions. Based on the case studies, a large number of different ways to implement LHC were identified in practice. A typology was developed which generalizes these manifestations into five key LHC modes which have a wide application base.

The typology identifies collaborative distribution as the most common and applicable collaboration mode. Specifically, it classifies three modes of collaborative distribution, namely the shipper mode where shippers collaborate using the milk-run strategy for goods consolidation and distribution; the common LSP mode where the collaboration is operationalized through the use of a common LSP; the LSP mode where LSPs work together to build the milk-run consolidations and distribution trips. An alternative LHC mode was identified as sharing of logistics assets and facilities, which can be further brokendown as empty front/backhauls collaboration and shared warehouse. The typology also identifies a collaboration mode that is rarely discussed in literature-collaboration for freight modal shift. This collaboration mode corresponds to the context of long distance and/or trunk hauls where shippers collaborate to enable the switch to more cost-efficient modes of transport such as railways and waterways. As opposed to collaboration in the downstream distribution operations, the typology also identifies purchasing collaboration which is a more upstream logistics activity. It further classifies the collaborative purchasing into the strategic and operational models which deals with sourcing the service provider and purchasing transport capacity, respectively. Finally, the typology identifies collaborative service as a powerful means for LHC, which can be further classified into strategic and operational models. The collaborative service at the strategic level targets the tendering of the customer service contract while at the operational level it concerns setting up a capacity or service pool to improve the logistics efficiency and flexibility.

The outcome of the typology analysis through the case studies offers some useful insight into the current LHC practice. It systematically identifies several alternative forms of LHC, which facilitates a fuller understanding of the structure and types of such collaborative logistics practice. This typology study can help practitioners to have a more clear idea in relation to the development of a LHC project. There is a strong practical value for the typologies since they are entirely based on the empirical evidence. For researchers, the typologies assist in determining a particular scope for studying LHC, allowing the clearer positioning of different collaboration studies and an easier comparison of results.

6.2 Findings of Simulation Modelling

This section discusses the main findings from simulation modelling (Chapter 5). The objective of simulation modelling is to examine what benefits would emerge from participating in logistics horizontal collaboration (LHC) and how such collaboration can affect the supply chain operations for individuals as well as the system as a whole. To quantify the effects of collaboration, the agent-based simulation (ABS) approach was employed in order to explicitly model the behaviours and decision-making in the collaboration and explore their operational consequences. The horizontal collaboration was operationalized in the form of sharing transport capacity between shippers, which represents the most common and applicable collaboration strategy in practice. The goal of such collaboration is to attain larger economies of scale that would help to cut down the distribution costs and increase the flexibility and availability of supply so as to better serve customers.

In the context of a two-tier supply chain network, the simulation model considered three distinctive horizontal collaboration strategies, i.e. (1) equal strategy (no information sharing); (2) proportional strategy (sharing demand information); (3) excess strategy (sharing supply information), and three supply chain system configurations, i.e. (1) Random marketplace supply chain; (2) Performance-based supply chain; (3) Relation-based supply chain.

The results show that horizontal collaboration can significantly impact the performance of the logistics supply system including all supply chain stakeholders. The impact is multi-faceted and also mixed across the model scenarios. In summary, it can be concluded from the key insights as follows:

(1) In line with the empirical studies, the simulation results show that horizontal collaboration can help to make the logistics operations more efficient (i.e. higher utilization), effective (i.e. higher fill-rate) and competitive (i.e. higher satisfied orders/

lower wasted capacity hence better profitability). The positive synergy gains from the collaboration are consistently observed across the different collaboration strategies and supply chain systems. In addition, the level of synergy can vary depending on which types of the supply chain system are considered and which types of collaboration strategy are implemented.

(2) Collaboration strategies driven by the sharing of information in the most part do not outperform those models without any information sharing. Specifically, sharing either the demand or supply information in horizontal collaboration is not associated with an increase in the gains from collaboration. This could be due to the ways to share information which sometimes can lead to worse decisions and performance. Hence in this LHC setting the value of sharing information is quite different from that in vertical collaboration, which often produces benefits such as the reduction of excess inventory, and the increase of order fill-rate.

(3) Horizontal collaboration can help shippers achieve higher logistics performance with the presence of a stronger vertical collaborative relationship, where shippers and customers develop mutual trust towards a long-term trading partnership. The increased performance is due to the more stable and predictable demand committed to by shippers' long-term customers, who in turn support them to optimize their demand stream from unpredictable spot flows to predictable structural flows, thereby contributing to higher stability and efficiency for the collaborative community.

(4) The benefits of horizontal collaboration in terms of improving the supply chain performance become less significant due to the greater domination of the benefits brought by the vertical collaboration. A long-term shipper-customer trading partnership would help greatly to reduce the uncertainty and variability in both the demand and supply streams in the supply chain network, which are critical and more effective in driving better overall operational performance. As such, the stronger vertical relationships with customers can also benefit shippers who do not participate in horizontal collaboration, potentially allowing them to increase their logistics performance significantly. This in turn leads to a much smaller relative advantage (i.e. synergy) that can be attained from horizontal collaboration.

(5) Participating in horizontal collaboration does not guarantee the achievement

of balanced performance and collaboration gains between partners. In many circumstances, shippers participating in horizontal collaboration can experience much higher imbalance than their counterparts who maintain independent operations. This creation of additional unbalance might be attributed to the various mechanisms set in horizontal collaboration, and can affect the fair gains and sustainability of collaboration.

(6) Customers will be punished for short-sighted behaviours (i.e. through a blacklist policy). Customers blacklist shippers if their orders are not satisfied. This is a feedback decision reflecting the customer's decreasing confidence in the selected shippers. Although, individually, this seems to be a rational decision, collectively, such behaviour will contribute to system-wide higher demand variability, which can cause lower profits due to order non-fulfilment, and particularly worsening the performance of non-collaborative shippers. Conversely, when customers value the long-term relationship with shippers more their profits can go up dramatically, while also benefitting shippers in horizontal collaboration to achieve the higher performance.

The study results have a number of managerial implications for practitioners considering or implementing LHC. First, horizontal collaboration in the form of capacity sharing has a great potential to increase capacity utilization for shipper partners, thereby reducing the empty running cost and increasing the operations profitability. It also benefits customer service in terms of order fill-rate, contributing to higher customer satisfaction and increased revenue for shipper partners. In addition, the value of information sharing seems to be less critical to facilitating these better collaboration results in the investigated collaboration and supply chain settings. This implies that in practical settings close to the configurations of this study, partners can achieve comparable collaboration gains without the need to disclose their sensitive information (e.g. the customer demand/capacity volume) during the course of collaboration, which are the core competitive information in their business operations. Practitioners seeking collaboration can choose to implement a simple collaboration strategy with an equal capacity sharing mechanism to avoid leaking sensitive data, unfair allocation and opportunism. Furthermore, it can be noticed that, in some circumstances, collaborative shippers encounter even greater performance imbalances than non-collaborative shippers. This might indicate the creation of an additional imbalance as a result of the mechanisms in horizontal collaboration. To counter this issue in practice, a fair gain sharing mechanism must be put in place to facilitate the balanced distribution of collaboration gains for partners. This is crucial to maintaining the long-term sustainability of the collaboration community. Lastly, horizontal collaboration can produce higher gains if shippers develop stronger vertical collaborative relations with their downstream customers. In this study, downstream customers can support shippers with more stable and predictable demands, which ultimately benefits the collaboration between shippers. This has wider implications in encouraging practitioners to explore the various vertical collaboration methods in order to facilitate more effective horizontal collaboration. Another typical example noted in the case studies could be asking downstream customers to properly shift the order release date and delivery window so that collaborative shippers could better synchronize their freight flows.

6.3 Contributions

This section discusses the contributions made by the research. First, contributions made to the specific research questions are presented. Second, the contributions made to the general research fields are highlighted.

6.3.1 Answering the Research Questions

There are a number of questions addressed by this study that, to the researcher's knowledge, have not previously been answered in the supply chain management and modelling literature. In answering the research questions posed, the following contributions are made.

1) What are the key elements to be considered for developing logistics horizontal collaboration?

The topic of collaboration in logistics has been thoroughly studied and widely discussed by both scholars and practitioners. Notwithstanding this, among the possible forms of collaboration in logistics, horizontal collaboration remains a neglected area and the related literature is still in its infancy (Cruijssen et al. 2007a, Schulz and Blecken, 2010).

It was concluded that the existing literature lacks a complete understanding of the key elements underpinning the development of LHC. To date, the business concept of LHC is not familiar to most supply chain researchers or practitioners, as indicated by the literature and empirical studies.

From the survey of the previous literature and discussions with logistics and supply chain professionals it was realized that there was no clear definitive model of a successful collaboration because all companies behave differently in different contexts. There are, however, certain elements that have to be in place to make a successful outcome more likely, and it is this that inspired the first research question as a starting point for this research project.

As part of the contribution to this new research field, an empirical study employing the case study approach was carried out to identify and analyse the key elements that are relevant to the critical aspects for developing LHC. Based upon a large number of case examinations and expert discussions, the study identified that "collaboration structures" "collaboration objectives" "collaboration intensity" and "collaboration modes" are the four key elements that are of great importance to characterize the development of LHC. These elements can assist to form a framework for analysing the types of LHC in a more systematic way. As discussed in Section 6.1, each element represents an important aspect of the collaboration development and exhibits many different characteristics and forms.

In contrast to previous studies, the key collaboration elements were derived when the LHC was considered from a broader supply chain perspective. The study focused particularly on the operational aspects of the collaboration elements, taking advantage of the researcher's good industry connections and many first-hand case study materials. By identifying and utilizing the key elements, a promising LHC project or study could be sketched out. Furthermore, with all these elements concluded, it was possible to develop a valuable framework for classifying the different characteristics and forms of LHC that can play a role in more sharply defining the ideal business models for collaboration in specific conditions, and in scoping and designing concrete projects in practice.

2) How can logistics horizontal collaboration networks be classified?

The review of the available literature conducted earlier has revealed several important gaps in the current body of knowledge regarding LHC:

• First of all, due to the infancy of the extant literature in LHC (Cruijssen et al. 2007b, Schulz and Blecken, 2010), the varying characteristics of horizontal collaboration are not well understood and have yet to be explored. LHC within the wider supply chain context often involves more than one type of stakeholder, and horizontal collaboration would be structured and organized in very different ways and with different distinguishing focuses, depending on which part of the supply chain stakeholders participated in, and the specific operational scenarios. So far, however, most studies have neglected such differentiation and implicitly concern themselves with only one form or one fragment of collaborative practice (e.g. LSP-centric collaboration). As a result, the continued development of the understanding of LHC calls for a typological study which can help systematically to classify and illustrate the various properties and forms of collaboration, and consequently support the design and position of LHC in different contexts.

• Secondly, while earlier studies have attempted to identify several important elements such as culture/philosophy (Palmer et al. 2012), conflicts (Wallenburg and Raue, 2011) and profit sharing within the horizontal collaborative initiatives (Krajewska et al. 2008), these have not been linked in a consistent way to support the design of a classification system. It is worth mentioning that some of the elements (e.g. culture/organizational philosophy) are valid in a more general context and hence are not closely linked to the context-specific configurations in the operational aspects of LHC. This is why in this research multiple case studies were employed to derive the key collaboration elements that can explain the different types of LHC, based on the operational practice of companies collaborating horizontally in one form or another.

• Finally, although a number of typological works exist (Cruijssen et al. 2007b, Verstrepen et al. 2009), these approaches do not propose a comprehensive scheme that supports the design and implementation of effective horizontal collaboration. These classification works are either conducted in too narrow a context (e.g. LSP asset sharing), or the proposed elements (e.g. leadership) are not strongly relevant to the operations of LHC. As pointed out by Cruijssen

(2006), more research is needed in order to make the typology of collaboration robust. Hence, it would be very worthwhile to have a single comprehensive typology for LHC in which most of the collaboration scenarios can be positioned and their relevant attributes described.

Based on such findings, an effort has been made here to conduct a comprehensive typological analysis of LHC that takes into account the key collaboration elements when defining and classifying a typical type of horizontal collaboration. It also provides evidence for the interdependencies among such elements. Specifically, the typology study has identified:

• Four possible LHC structures that describe the connections and relationships between supply chain players in the typical LHC projects (namely shipper-centric-, customer-centric-, and LSP-centric collaboration and the hybrid form that combines any two of all).

• Seven unique objectives driving the LHC, which are also the important performance measures to ensure close tracking of the collaboration results and evaluate how well the collaboration meets the expectation (namely the reduction of operational costs, procurement costs, and CO_2 emissions, the improvement of capacity utilization, service levels, predictability/flexibility, and market coverage).

• Four degrees of LHC implementation from autonomy to system-wide integration, characterized by three criteria: the collaboration relationship for decision making and coordination, the scope of collaborative activities, and the time horizon against which the collaborative activities are planned.

• Five alternative modes of LHC which have a wide application base (namely collaborative distributions, sharing of logistics assets and facilities, freight modal shift collaboration, group purchasing and joint-service).

The contribution of making such a systematic typological analysis of LHC in the empirical practices is particularly evident since most prior studies are implicitly concerned with only one form (e.g. transport bundling) or one fragment of LHC (e.g. LSP-centric collaboration) whereas this work systematically identifies several alternative forms of LHC, which paves the way to a fuller understanding of the structure and dynamics of such collaborative practice. According to the typologies arrived at in this study, most collaboration projects can be properly positioned and their relevant attributes described. For practitioners, this will help them understand more systematically how to plan and operate the different types of LHC in the real world business settings. The practical value of this typology study is very strong since they are entirely based on the empirical evidence. For researchers, they can assist in determining a particular scope for studying LHC and for allowing clearer positioning of different studies into collaboration and thence comparison of results.

In addition, the typologies can be used as a useful study framework for developing simulation models that will help to study how the horizontal collaborative activities could be organized and operated in a logistics system.

3) How will partners behave and interact in the logistics collaborative network and how might this have an effect on the individuals, as the well as the logistics system as a whole?

The current literature shows that a lot of attention has been paid to studying the various concepts of LHC, but the explicit impact of implementing LHC on the participating partners, as well as the supply chain system, remains understudied. Very few studies have explored the process of collaboration and how it links to the results in performance. Thus the third research question deals with the investigation of what benefits could emerge from participating in LHC and how such collaboration would affect the supply chain operations for individual companies as well as the system as a whole. To answer this question, the most common type of horizontal collaboration in transport and logistics (i.e. sharing transport capacity between shippers) was analysed in detail. An agent-based simulation (ABS) model was developed to explicitly model a set of behaviours and decision-making in such collaboration and explore their operational consequences. It can be concluded from the key results that:

• LHC can benefit collaborating shippers with the higher utilization, higher fill-rate, more shipped orders, and lower wasted capacity. Such beneficial effects are found consistent across the different collaboration strategies as well as under the different supply chain environments.

• LHC enables higher performance for shippers in a relationship-based supply chain network. This is due to shippers' long-term collaborative customers who could contribute them with more stable and predictable demands, which in turn benefits the horizontal collaboration between shippers.

• Information sharing in LHC does not facilitate higher collaboration gains. More specifically, sharing either the demand or supply information does not help increase the collaboration gains. This could be due to the ways to share information which sometimes can lead to worse decisions and performance. Hence in this LHC setting the value of sharing information is quite different from that in vertical collaboration, which often produces benefits such as the reduction of excess inventory, and the increase of order fill-rate.

• LHC might result in higher imbalanced performance than the absence of collaboration. This is due to the various collaboration mechanisms implemented that can affect the fair gains in the collaboration network.

• When customers value the short-term performance of shippers, they will have worse performance. And this behavior also negatively affects non-collaborative shippers. Conversely, when customers value the long-term relationship with shippers they can increase their performance significantly, and this also benefits more to the collaborative shippers to achieve higher performance.

The new contributions arising from researching this question are twofold. First, the study extends the body of knowledge regarding the behaviours and effects of horizontal collaboration by both investigating the collaboration issues that have not been previously considered and examining issues that have been previously studied in either a conceptual or an empirically based setting but that have not previously been tested through quantitative modelling. The specific new contributions of this part of the research in comparison with prior studies are explained in Table 6.1.

Table 6.1 Summary of new contributions

Focus of Past Studies	New Contributions of This Study
Past studies have generally adopted empirical methods to analyse horizontal collaboration, such as conflict, benefits, barriers, relationship management (Hingley et al. 2011, Wallenburg and Raue, 2011, Schmoltzi and Wallenburg, 2012). The literature, however, has not been clear on what the process of collaboration is. Few studies have explored the process of collaboration and how it links to performance behaviours in the supply chain.	This study has built a simulation model to examine the process of collaboration and has provided a quantitative assessment regarding what benefits would emerge from participating in horizontal collaboration and how such collaboration could influence supply chain operations for individuals as well as the overall system.

Continued

Focus of Past Studies	New Contributions of This Study
Past studies have concentrated on using statistical correlations (Cruijssen et al. 2007a, Schmoltzi and Wallenburg, 2012) or human perceptions (Schulz and Blecken, 2010, Hingley et al. 2011) to explain the benefits and effects of horizontal collaboration, rather than the mechanisms that actually produce them. Hence, there are problems in quantifying the actual effects of horizontal collaboration.	This study has built a model mechanism consisting of the explicit representation of the behaviours and decision making specific to the individual players of the supply chain network, and explored how these individuals can collectively affect the collaboration gains and the operations in the supply chain system as a direct consequence of its built-in mechanisms.
Past studies have mainly analysed horizontal collaboration for players from the supply side (i.e. shippers/LSPs), but few studies have taken into account the impact of collaboration on players from the demand side (i.e. downstream customers).	This study included both the upstream shippers and downstream customers in the same model and examined their interactions and impact on performance behaviours in relation to the collaboration.
Previous studies have tended to model and assess the collaboration synergy in terms of cost reduction only (Cruijssen et al. 2007c).	This model evaluated the collaboration synergy beyond just cost efficiency (utilization), also taking into account the service level (fill-rate) throughput efficiency for customer demand (the number of shipped orders) and the attractiveness for customers (order frequency), all of which facilitated a more comprehensive analysis of the collaboration synergy in key logistics KPIs.
Past studies have emphasized the issue of information sharing between horizontal partners (Palmer et al. 2012, Hingley et al. 2011, Zhu et al. 2014). There are both positive attitudes and negative concerns in respect to such data exchange but the explicit comparison of the collaboration performance as a result of information sharing or the lack of it during the course of collaboration has never before been possible.	This study filled this gap. It has compared three collaboration strategies driven by no information sharing, sharing of demand information, and sharing of supply information. It was found out that information sharing in the collaboration, for the most part, does not facilitate higher collaboration gains for partners, hence the benefits are less evident compared to the value of information sharing in vertical collaboration.
Past studies have predominantly considered sharing demand information in the supply chain collaboration such as POS data or demand forecasting (Lee et al. 1997, Chen, 1998, Zhang and Zhang, 2007). Studies investigating the sharing of supply information are only infrequently considered in the vertical collaboration literature (Sawaya, 2006).	This study modelled the sharing of capacity supply information in a new collaboration context-supply chain horizontal collaboration. It is also the first known study in the horizontal collaboration literature to look at the sharing of both demand and supply information in the same model.

Continued

Focus of Past Studies	New Contributions of This Study
Past studies have mainly focused on studying collaboration between horizontal partners (shippers or LSPs), few have investigated the possibility of connecting horizontal collaboration with vertical collaboration. Only a few studies have made suggestions for developing stronger collaborative relationships with downstream customers in order to facilitate horizontal collaboration (Jacobs et al. 2014, Zhu et al. 2014, Verstrepen and Bossche, 2015). The actual implementation and effects of this have never been explicitly examined, however.	This study incorporated a vertical collaboration mechanism and horizontal collaboration in the same model and conducted a quantitative assessment of their interactive effects. It is the first known study to do so.
Previous studies have examined the benefits and effects of collaboration on the basis of an assumption that all players are collaborative and partners to each other (Cruijssen et al. 2007c). Hence, the collaboration/non-collaboration scenarios have been investigated and compared in a completely separate manner. This is a less realistic assumption given that in any marketplace there are preferences for collaboration or no collaboration.	This study modelled the collaborative and non-collaborative shippers simultaneously in the same model and explored their interactions and mutual influence, as well as the effect on downstream players. This produced new and important management implications as regards to the potential impact of horizontal collaboration on the non-collaborative players in the supply chain network.
Past studies have highlighted the issue of imbalanced performance and fair allocation of gains and costs in horizontal collaboration (Cruijssen et al. 2007a, Hingley et al. 2011, Palmer et al. 2012). But such imbalanced performance between partners has rarely been examined and compared.	The model of this study provided a quantitative measurement of the imbalance level in performance, which is critical for assessing the long-term sustainability of the collaborative partnership. It was found that participating in horizontal collaboration does not guarantee the achievement of the balanced performance and collaboration gains between partners. And partners participating in horizontal collaboration might experience even higher imbalance than their counterparts who maintain operations independently. These sorts of insights are new to the current literature.
Past studies have tended to analyse horizontal collaboration irrespective of the supply chain environment. Most often, the horizontal collaboration is discussed in a general or an implicit supply chain setting.	The model of this study considered three specific yet classic supply chain configurations and examined their links with horizontal collaboration and their interactive effect on the performance change.

Second, this study represents a contribution to the applicability of agent-based simulation to the study of LHC as well as to the broad issues in supply chain management.

To the best of the researcher's knowledge, no other simulation modelling research exists in the field of LHC that aims explicitly to model the behaviours of individual supply chain players and the interactions among them in this context. There are two modelling studies in the literature which have researched profit sharing (Krajewska et al. 2008) and route planning (Cruijssen et al. 2007c). These, however, are primarily based on analytical methods that use static/deterministic configurations and can only cope with small-scale issues in the collaboration (none of them models more than one type of stakeholder in the supply chain, let alone their interactions and adaptability). In fact, in the supply chain modelling literature, supply chain players are generally treated as homogeneous agents who follow the same and simple rules for action, and who do not have the autonomous decision making capability. The individual characteristics and behaviours have thus been neglected and they are collectively represented as the quantity in the supply chain system, which is not ideal for investigating the patterns naturally arising from the micro level dynamics.

This research has directly demonstrated whether the explicit modelling of individual behaviours for the supply chain agents provides any advantages over the use of static and homogenous configurations for modelling the issue of LHC, and, more generally, it has described the agent-based simulation approach that can be thought of as increasingly suitable for modelling supply chain problems. Since the literature on LHC is scarce and primarily qualitative in nature, this study represents the first attempt to use a simulation modelling design to explain the phenomenon of LHC. From a more micro perspective, the agent-based simulation model supports the representation of the explicit elements such as individual behaviours and decisions, and how these dynamics can combine to influence individuals as well as the logistics system as a whole.

In addition, the research has helped to extend the existing agent-based supply chain modelling research to a more realistic level by adding empirical data for the model development that has not been frequently used hitherto. As explained in the model descriptions, the configurations and parameters used in the model are empirically based and hence provide more realistic representations of the modelling elements, making the findings more practically relevant and useful.

Furthermore, by using the ABS modelling paradigm the research has demonstrated that firms are actually part of a supply chain network consisting of complex inter-organizational relationships as opposed to that assumed by analytic models focusing on a dyad or a simple serial supply-chain setting, where the interaction effect within a bigger network of players is often missing, even though these have been shown to be crucially important in this study.

All the new features mentioned above have contributed to the modelling outcomes with new patterns and new insights for LHC, which have not been noted before in the literature and are expected to contribute to a fuller understanding of the dynamic aspects of LHC in theory and practice.

As regards to the use of modelling outcomes in this study, the nature of the contribution can be clarified as follows.

According to Axelrod (1997), computer simulation models can be applied for different purposes, namely prediction, performance, entertainment, training, education, confirmation (theory-testing) and discovery (theory-building).

Due to the fact that LHC is only a recent phenomenon in supply chain management, the relevant research work in this field is still scanty, and the development of suitable theories or explanations of the connection to existing theories are consequently also scarce. This makes the simulation study in this research mainly exploratory in nature; intended to gain new insights into the behaviours and patterns arising from this particular form of supply chain collaboration that have not been widely noted before. The simulation model here, therefore, breaks new ground and should make an important explorative contribution to the theory-building regarding supply chain logistics horizontal collaboration.

This simulation model has also been used, to a lesser extent, for confirmation and prediction. The model developed copes with testing existing theory on the benefits of LHC, and also helps to predict the possible outcomes of this theory in different scenarios.

6.3.2 Contribution to the Research Field

This study investigates LHC, which by its nature is a subset problem of supply chain management and inter-organizational relations. It also employs research methods from computer science to study social science problems. The study therefore generates findings that can contribute to the intersection of three research fields:

1) Horizontal collaboration in the logistics and distribution system

This is the main contribution from this research project. The study utilized both case studies and modelling approaches to derive new understandings about the patterns and issues in this novel research field of the logistics literature. This research was therefore undertaken with a clear position that the primary audience would come from the field of research and practice in logistics. The readers likely to get the most from this thesis are: researchers of LHC, general logistics management, supply chain management, professionals in logistics forecasting and planning, distribution management, fleet management, warehouse management, logistics purchasing, production and operations management, 3PL/carrier management and services.

2) Supply chain collaboration and inter-organizational relationship

More generally, a contribution is also made to the wider research communities in supply chain collaboration and inter-organizational relationships, because the nature and management of the logistics issues are not fundamentally different from the issues in the wider supply chain context, such as manufacturing planning or inventory management. The nature of these questions are similar in respect to how to organize supply that can fit better with demand, or vice versa in the supply chain network. The research outcomes of this study can therefore also apply to the wider context of supply chain issues and management (e.g. horizontal collaboration for sharing manufacturing capacity).

3) The application of simulation modelling (in this case, agent-based simulation) as a useful research tool for researching the issues in a supply chain management context.

This study has demonstrated that simulation modelling, in this case, agent-based simulation, is a useful tool to analyse and explain the behaviour patterns of a supply chain logistics system, by explicitly modelling the individuals of the system. This fills the gap left by empirical approaches that cannot make definitive measurements and predictions.

6.4 Limitations

This section discusses the limitations of this research, as there is no study on this planet that can claim to be perfect.

The limitation for the case studies is mainly regarding the data collection. First, the case studies utilize primary data. The place for collecting the major primary data is China. China by its nature is a developing country experiencing rapid growth, meaning that the logistics infrastructure development and operations might be predominantly focused on business growth and operating efficiency, while neglecting the service quality and environmental sustainability that are often more stressed and well-developed in Western developed economies. Thus, the expert opinions collected might lack a long-term sustainable view towards the development of LHC.

Also, the interviewed companies are typically manufacturing companies or companies that serve the manufacturing supply chain. Hence, the logistics style of these companies typically reflects the service design for the manufacturing industry. Any discussions with the people from these companies can potentially be affected by their habitual mind-set in manufacturing logistics. Logistics features and issues in many other industries might not be properly considered hence restricting the wider validity of the arguments presented here.

In addition, the interviewed logistics professionals were more familiar with B2B contracted logistics. Their input for horizontal collaboration was naturally targeting for the B2B context. They are also usually dealing with dedicated transportation systems applying a FTL rate, meaning that they are less motivated to consider collaboration with outsiders. Professionals from the LTL sector could potentially be more knowledgeable and more innovative in terms of developing horizontal collaboration.

Regarding the secondary data, the potential issues could be associated with a lack of direct control over the original data generation and analysis. For instance, the collected documents about a collaboration project might not describe its full picture and might over-emphasise the successful part of the collaboration while understating the negative outcomes. Hence, the data quality remains less certain for secondary sources.

Limitations also exist in the modelling part. The simulation model applied in this study, only considers a two-tier supply chain system, which is a simplification of an overall supply chain network. In the practical world, a supply chain system can be bigger and more complex, involving multiple tiers of organizations. There are supply chains within supply chains depending on the local or global perspective. Thus, modelling LHC in a multiple-tier supply chain system could possibly exhibit some more interesting and unknown patterns as there are more levels of interactions between players, and logistics plays both an inbound and outbound function at the same time.

Due to time constraints, the study models LHC in the form of sharing transport capacity. There are more collaboration strategies, as indicated by the case studies. Also, the model has focused on collaboration between shippers without considering the involvement of the logistics service provider, who is another key player in the logistics marketplace. Horizontal collaboration between shippers who have the outsourced logistics to LSPs will have many differences in the collaboration configurations. Also, horizontal collaboration directly between LSPs can point to a completely different setting for collaboration, and their connections with shippers, as well as the collaboration impact, are likely to be very different.

Many other factors, such as order criticality and the cost rates of various operations, including capacity positioning, empty running, and lost sales cost rates, are not specified in the model. Without considering these cost rates, the study is unable to assess the explicit financial impact of the various performance indicators, which is necessary to determine the net effect of participating in horizontal collaboration. Future studies can tackle this issue by either collecting the actual cost rates observed in the real business or conducting a sensitivity analysis on a range of cost rates.

6.5 Directions for Future Research

Future research in empirical studies of LHC can consider two directions. First, based upon the typology described by this study, future studies can implement in-depth case studies to concentrate on one specific collaboration form (e.g. collaborative intermodal transport, backhaul collaboration), and explore the operating models and issues at a greater level of detail in order to advance knowledge and, especially, practice. Second, existing studies all consider horizontal collaboration in the context of freight logistics. So far, not a single study has considered the application of horizontal collaboration in the public transportation system. The daily volume transactions in public transport are enormous, and there is great potential to explore the collaboration opportunities here. Moreover, as the freight and public transportation networks are highly overlapped, an even more innovative idea is to explore the possibility of connecting these two networks in some sort of collaboration, which could bring out revolutionary changes in the future.

Suggestions are also given to the future of modelling studies in this area. First, the model developed in this study could be extended to include more than two tiers of supply chain so as to investigate the effects of horizontal collaboration across multiple echelons. It could further explore the differences in outcomes under different supply chain network structures that vary in the size or degree of concentration. The network size is operationalized as the number of supply chain final firms (normally customers). Concentration degree is defined as the ratio of the number of players in two adjacent tiers. Second, configurations for models can consider altering the demand and capacity variability level by changing the coefficient of the variance level. The mixed combinations of these amendments are likely to produce some very different and interesting behaviours and insights. Similarly, the model might also consider the size difference between partners and explore collaboration with an unequal distribution of capacity and demand. Finally, future modelling work should consider modelling the synchronization of issues and policies in horizontal collaboration. This is a key challenge for arriving at more efficient and smarter collaboration for companies. The complexity of developing such a model is further increased, and might require the adoption of a mix of discrete events and agent-based simulations in the same model to allow the behaviours and decisions to be distributed over different levels of time. The latest development of some commercial software such as Anylogic, which promotes multi-methods simulation is reflecting this modelling need and trend.

CHAPTER 7
CONCLUSION

This study has provided an analysis of logistics horizontal collaboration (LHC). This is a relatively new business concept for operating logistics that aims to bring together compatible companies and parallel supply chains to share logistics capacity and capabilities in order to significantly drive down logistics costs and to increase the level of service to customers. This business concept provides some interesting opportunities to transform the traditional logistics marketplace so as to make it more efficient, effective and sustainable. Until now, however, horizontal collaboration has not been particularly evident in logistics practice worldwide. The existing literature lacks a comprehensive understanding of the characteristics and forms of collaboration to guide practitioners in setting up a suitable collaboration project. Undoubtedly, LHC is a big concept and in practice it can be developed into various operating models with different stakeholders and different functions/performance focuses. In addition, the impact of implementing horizontal collaboration on the collaborating partners' logistics operations and the wider supply chain system has rarely been studied and explained in the current body of knowledge in this field. Consequently, the research agenda for this study set out to (1) examine the key elements that can support the design of logistics horizontal collaboration, and make a classification of models for collaboration; (2) model the collaboration process and work out what benefits would emerge from participating in horizontal collaboration and how such collaboration could produce effects on the supply chain operations for individuals and the system as a whole.

The study employs case studies and agent-based simulation. In the first place, the case studies based upon both primary and secondary data are implemented. The result of the case studies is the development of several typologies aiming to understand the various forms and characteristics of LHC between companies.

The development of these typologies is initiated by exploring the key elements which are critical to the start-up of a horizontal collaboration. After analysing interviews with experts and collaboration cases, the study identified that "collaboration structures" "collaboration objectives" "collaboration intensity" and "collaboration strategies" are the four elements critical to the design of a collaboration project. Each element represents an important aspect of the collaboration and exhibits different characteristics and forms. Using the collected data, a typological study was carried out further to define and classify these forms and characteristics within each element, together providing a comprehensive view to explain the different types of horizontal collaboration in practice. Such findings can provide tips for practitioners and scholars about how to design and build a type of collaboration project or study that contributes to knowledge in the design phase of horizontal collaboration for logistics and freight transport.

Secondly, building on the input from the literature review and case studies, an agent-based supply chain configuration was developed to model the various strategies for collaboration and how the relevant behaviours and decision making in the course of collaboration can impact the collaboration gains, as well as the operations in the overall supply chain system. Horizontal collaboration was operationalized in the form of sharing transport capacity between shippers, which represents the most common and applicable collaboration strategy in practice. The goal of such collaboration is to attain larger economies of scale that would help to reduce the distribution costs and increase the flexibility and availability of supply so as to serve customers better.

Specifically, the model considered a two-tier supply chain network with three supply chain system configurations, i.e. (1) a random supply chain, (2) a performance-based supply chain, (3) a relationship-based supply chain, under each of which it implemented three distinct horizontal collaboration strategies, i.e. (1) the equal strategy (no information sharing), (2) the proportional strategy (sharing demand information), (3) the excess strategy (sharing supply information), assessing their operational consequences in respect to collaboration gains and supply chain operations.

The results showed that horizontal collaboration can consistently benefit logistics efficiency in terms of capacity utilization, and customer service in terms of the order fill-rate. Further analysis found that collaboration strategies driven by information sharing do not, in the long-term, outperform those models without information sharing, indicating that the value of information sharing is less critical in facilitating better collaboration results than in the vertical collaboration context. This means that partners do not have to disclose their core competitive information in order to collaborate more efficiently. On the other hand, the results showed that participating in horizontal collaboration does not guarantee balanced performance and collaboration gains between partners. In some circumstances, shippers participating in horizontal collaboration can experience more imbalance than their counterparts who maintain operations independently, which could be a result of the mechanisms in horizontal collaboration. To maintain sustainable collaboration, a fair gain sharing mechanism must be put in place to facilitate the balanced distribution of collaboration gains for partners. Finally, horizontal collaboration can produce greater gains if vertical collaboration is additionally embedded. Stronger vertical collaborative relations between shippers and customers can also benefit shippers who reject horizontal collaboration and downstream customers. This agent-based simulation model contributes to the development of knowledge concerning how to model the various forms of collaboration in action, and to an understanding of their operational impact on partnership performance and supply chain operations. These findings improve the overall knowledge of the operations phase of horizontal collaboration for logistics and freight transport.

LIST OF CASE STUDIES OF LOGISTICS HORIZONTAL COLLABORATION

Case No.	Company Name	Case Description
Case 1	HP & Foxconn & Inventec & Quanta Industry: Manufacturing Region: China Source: The interviewed company	A model shift collaboration between PC manufacturers for their factories located in the hinterland of China. The newly set up factories began full operations in late 2010, replacing factories in coastal regions for the fulfilment of global orders. One of the biggest challenges for inland factories, however, is the management of outbound logistics since 90% of orders are for global exports. The interim workaround was to hire road haulage to connect the factories to the ocean port (Yantian Port located in Shenzhen, China). Road drayage is a very high cost and in this case was particularly inefficient and unreliable during high volume shipping days, creating bottlenecks for the factory throughput. As the high cost and operational constraint continued, factories increasingly realized the need for a modal shift. Cosco (China's major railway service provider) operated an irregular freight lane to the ocean port and could offer an opportunity for more cost-efficient transportation. The threshold for developing a commercial level of train service is very high, however, and it requires high and stable volume commitment. No single shipper could satisfy such high level requirements given the volatility of the PC marketplace. Cosco, therefore, collaborates with all shippers to align their order drop time, manufacturing plan, and pickup window. These collaborative efforts have resulted in the successful establishment of "Five Fixed Train" service with "fixed price" "fixed lead-time" "fixed frequency" "fixed route" "fixed shipping point" entailing a stabilized freight rail service operating twice a week and offering high volume logistics solutions for factories at a much cheaper cost.

Continued

Case No.	Company Name	Case Description
Case 2	HP & Foxconn & Innolux & Quanta Industry: Manufacturing Region: China Source: The interviewed company	A number of Notebook PC/display manufacturers collaborated on a novel logistics project in 2011 called "Trans-Eurasian-Rail (TER)" aimed at developing a rail transport solution for Notebook PCs (NBs) and displays produced in China and requiring shipping to the European marketplace. This project aimed to transfer a great portion of the NB shipments to rail freight since using air freight was very expensive while using ocean freight was too slow. This rail freight lane was first established by one of the manufacturers in collaboration with the service provider (DB Schenker) but encountered several operational problems. The biggest problem was a lack of sufficient and stabilized demand volume to support the weekly running of the train. Hence, horizontal collaboration between shippers was motivated in order to drive more structural freight flows and service stability. This collaboration significantly increased the efficiency and flexibility of train operations, making the rail freight more cost competitive and sustainable.
Case 3	Airbag & Foxconn & Quanta Industry: Manufacturing Region: China Source: The interviewed company	Driven by OBM Manufacture, a packaging materials manufacturer collaborated with two PC ODM manufacturers for an integrated warehousing and packaging process for outbound logistics. The collaborative warehouse operations were supported by intensive information sharing and collaborative decision-making. The ODM manufacturers shared the supply chain data concerned with the monthly and weekly rolling forecast of shipping plans, and the daily operational status and production output for the pick-up schedule. The packaging manufacturer used all received information to plan their own productions in the factory, and shipping plans to ODMs. Once the packaging supply arrived at the ODMs factories, the operational staff from both sides coordinated closely to ensure seamless workflow connections between production lines, packaging stations, and warehouse operations.
Case 4	HP & China-based ODMs Industry: Manufacturing	HP and its various outsourced manufacturing suppliers (ODMs) based in China have experienced high costs for the pre-carriage logistics to the air/ocean port. The company realized that the predominant root cause of this low efficiency was the fragmentation of the outbound logistics operations carried out by these ODMs. Each ODM planned its own independent

Continued

Case No.	Company Name	Case Description
Case 4	Region: China Source: The interviewed company	shipping and connected with its own interfacing logistics service providers (LSPs). Due to the scale limitations and operational volatility, shipping out the cargos in the form of LCL shipments (less than the container load) was the most common outcome of the daily operations. Pressurized by the high costs and low efficiency for the ODM's outbound logistics, HP initiated a programme called "Asian Carrier Hub" aimed at bringing together the small fragmented transport orders to build up, as much as possible, full load containers (FCL). Since HP is paying logistics costs when collaborating with ODMs, it motivated ODMs to align more closely to optimize the outbound logistics. The resulting change process is: (1) ODMs still perform their own order consolidation internally as usual, using their own advanced consolidation engine (ACE) to build up FCLs as much as possible and shipping them out directly, (2) The LCL orders are not shipped immediately but transferred to the Asia Carrier Hub for group consolidation using the HUB consolidation engine. (3) The Hub ships out the HUB FCL shipments and distributes the cost to ODMs.
Case 5	Flextronics & Compal Foxconn & Inventect & Quanta & Wistron & HP Industry: Manufacturing Region: China Source: The interviewed company	A collaborative VMI hub for multiple suppliers and manufacturers in Shanghai, China. The primary aim was for collaboration on the use of a single inventory pooling location in order to simplify the upstream inbound logistics network and reduce the warehousing and transportation cost which was not optimal as a result of fragmentation. Manufacturing suppliers worked together to share the use of the same warehouse for storing and distributing their raw materials. Since this warehouse was geographically near to each of the manufacturers, the components supply for production can be pulled on a JIT basis, which is an additional benefit to the cost savings from inventory pooling. Another major benefit comes from the top quality of the warehousing facilities and services operated by a world-leading warehouse provider, which without collaborative aggregation of demand volume would not have been attainable on a favourable service contract.
Case 6	Everlink & Waimao & DB Schenker Industry: 3PL	This was a collaborative service jointly managed by three LSPs aimed at improving operational efficiency, connectivity and visibility for the pre-carriage logistics from factories to the railway terminal.

Continued

Case No.	Company Name	Case Description
Case 6	Region: China Source: The interviewed company	Everlink and Waimao are customs brokers who managed the customer clearance tasks for freight cargos that factories had shipped for export. The operations included preparing physical shipping paperwork, EDI customs declarations and clearances, and coordination with customs for weighing, commodity inspection, and container sealing. These information flow driven customs procedures managed by brokers were bound in parallel with another physical flow of trucks and shipments managed by a freight forwarder (DB Schenker). For example, the time for freight forwarders to send trucks for queuing at customs check points, and the time for sending trucks to factories for container loading needed to be closely linked to the broker's working procedures to ensure every movement was legally tractable, and not causing disruption in the customs supervised bonded zone. Thus, the seamless integration of information and physical flows between brokers and freight forwarders made the collaborative service cost-efficient for themselves and service-effective for the customers (the factories).
Case 7	HP & Palm Industry: Manufacturing Region: China Source: The interviewed company	This was an integration project aimed at integrating two separate logistics systems into one hybrid system. This integration project involved collaboration by logistics teams from two companies (HP & Palm) after HP acquired Palm in late 2010. Palm still acted as an independent business unit using its own logistics system and ODM factories but there were significant advantages in integrating its operations into HP's global supply chain and logistics system. Hence, joint logistics connection work was planned in 2011 involving two ODM factories (one near Beijing and one near Shanghai) and a wide range of HP appointed freight forwarders serving the global air freight lanes. The collaboration aimed to connect the following systems and operations: √ Setup IT system for shipment consolidation and carrier assignment √ Setup logistics planning (48/24/Pre-ship alerting system, automated shipping docs generation and BOX ID/Pack ID assignment, shipping data SCITS/EDI transaction following HP standards) √ Setup warehouse operations (w/h shop floor system, BOX/ Pallet labels printing, picking report, weighing system, truck

Continued

Case No.	Company Name	Case Description
Case 7		loading/unloading coordination, etc.) so as to connect with the HP outbound logistics system √ Integrating export customs and the pick-up process, forwarder EDI data, and standard operating procedures (SOPs) between ODMs and forwarders √ Ramp up plan for pilot run (UAT/MTP/Golden Transaction/FCS) and mass production
Case 8	Hammerwerk & JSP Industry: Manufacturing Region: Czech Republic Source: CO³ project report by Verstrepen and Jacobs (2012) – Creation of an orchestrated horizontal collaboration for road bundling between two shippers.	Hammerwerk and JSP collaborated for road bundling. The two shippers were neighbours in an industrial park in the Czech Republic and it was found out that they had an overlapping freight flow to Germany, which created a promising opportunity for collaboration to combine the goods shipments together for more efficient logistics. They had hence jointly developed a collaboration plan routinely to bundle their shipments for transport. It was found that just reactively combining the loads of both shippers when they already occurred in the same week (so they could be consolidated without active synchronization or service level flexibility) already contributed to a significant increase of the truck capacity utilization. This helped to reduce the number of transports necessary by more than 20%.
Case 9	Coruyt & Baxter & Ontext & Eternit (shippers) Corneel Geerts & Tri-Vizor & Transfennica (LSPs) Industry: Manufacturing & 3PL & Retail Region: Belgium and Spain	This was about the creation and management of an orchestrated horizontal collaborative community for intermodal transport between four shippers, two logistics service providers and a neutral logistics coordinator. The objective of the collaboration was to set up a dense, stable, balanced and closed-loop shipping corridor between Belgium and Spain, and to reduce empty kilometres and high cost brought by the road haulage. Tri-Vizor acted as the community manager who took care of the transport order collection and processing, proactive FTL load planning and synchronization between shippers in Belgium and Spain, capacity booking with the logistics service providers, incident trouble-shooting and management of the administrative and financial flows. Proactively and optimally combining and synchronizing the pick-up/drop times for shipping cargos enabled the horizontal collaborative community to realize significant synergies in logistics, such as:

Continued

Case No.	Company Name	Case Description
Case 9	Source: CO³ project report by Jacobs et al. (2013) – Creation of an orchestrated intermodal partnership between multiple shippers	√ Reduced transport costs √ Reduced transport kilometres and empty miles √ Enabled "critical mass" for modal shift & inter-modal transport √ Enabled long-term volume stability and predictability √ Reduced CO_2 emissions
Case 10	Mars & United Biscuits & Saupiquet & Wrigley Industry: Food & Grocery Region: France Source: CO³ project report by Guinouet et al. (2012) – Retail collaboration in France	French retailers (e.g. Carrefour) demand full truckload (FTL) deliveries from shippers to their various warehouses throughout France. Vendor Managed Inventory (VMI) makes the shippers responsible for the inventory replenishment at the warehouses. In order to keep logistics costs under control, a group of four shippers led by Mars collaborated to develop consolidated delivery trips and fulfil the full truckload delivery requirement of their common customers. In order to combine the deliveries efficiently, shippers transported their shipments from their factories in France to a shared warehouse in Orleans, which was operated by a logistic service provider (LSP). From this joint warehouse, collaborative deliveries were made by the jointly hired LSP to the various retailer warehouses in France. The collaborative distributions were started in late 2010 and have reached mass production which enables more than 1,200 shared trips per year. The efficiency gains are shared based on the principle of equal profit margins (i.e. each shipper will have a similar saving percentage based on a specific calculation and allocation rule) in order to maintain the stability and sustainability of the collaborative community. This had resulted in an average cost saving of 31% for each participating shipper.
Case 11	PepsiCo & Nestle Industry: Food & Grocery Region: Belgium	This case was about the creation and management of a horizontal collaboration community in fresh and chilled retail distribution between two fast moving consumer goods shippers (Nestle & PepsiCo). In fresh and chilled food products (2–4°C) distribution, goods are often transported under temperature control from producers to retailers in small quantities to avoid expiration. Due to the limited amount of possible combinations within one company's own portfolio, both shippers are faced with the problem of frequent LTL deliveries to the various retail destinations. The logistical cost of fresh and chilled products is hence a key cost driver with great variability.

Continued

Case No.	Company Name	Case Description
Case 11	Source: CO³ project report by Jacobs et al. (2014) – Horizontal collaboration in fresh & chilled retail distribution	Through matchmaking and the help of an industry consortium and LSPs, the two shippers have found to have a high percentage of overlap in their distribution networks in Belgium. The analysis also showed that 90% of the transported volume was transported to only 10 out of 250 delivery locations. This was due to the fact that a small number of common retail customers attracted a major part of the total volume shipped. The common customer destinations were typically the well-known large retailers such as Carrefour. The significant overlap in these destinations indicated a promising collaboration opportunity for bundled deliveries to the common large retailers. The collaboration went live operationally in 2012. From the factories where two shippers transported their products to a shared warehouse, the collaborative deliveries were made to the various common retailers in Belgium. The collaboration has resulted in many improvements in distribution operations, such as: √ Lower transport costs √ Higher fill rate for truck/joint warehouse √ Reduced empty loading meters and transport kilometres √ Reduced CO_2 emissions √ long-term volume stability and "lock-in" of customers
Case 12	Spar & Inbound Suppliers Industry: Retail Region: Belgium Source: CO³ project report by Verstrepen and Bossche (2015) – Retail inbound horizontal collaboration	This was about the detection, creation and management of logistics horizontal collaboration and the inbound transport synergy opportunities in the supply network of the Belgian retail company Spar Retail. Since the population density in Belgium is high and the number of large retail chains are limited, most suppliers have to deliver to a small number of retail distribution centres which are located in the centre of the country. In the case of Spar, the analysis identified clusters of suppliers who were located geographically close to each other and who should therefore have high potential for transport synergies since their outbound network to Spar outlets overlapped. Driven by Spar, a number of inbound suppliers began to collaborate to share the joint logistics service providers and bundle their deliveries. In order to consolidate loads incurred from different suppliers effectively, active synchronization of LTL transport movement towards the retailer was planned on a daily basis.

Continued

Case No.	Company Name	Case Description
Case 12		The collaborative distributions went live operationally in early 2014 and the resulting performance has been exceptionally positive. The horizontal collaboration between inbound suppliers delivered a 50%—66% reduction in transport kilometres without changing order quantities. This collaboration project has shown that suppliers in a retail network can share transport capacity that would otherwise run empty, by engaging in cross-company collaboration. This served to improve the total performance of the retail network and its stakeholders in 3 ways: √ Efficiency: lower transport prices per pallet or per drop, lower reception costs, lower inventories √ Effectiveness: higher service levels or delivery frequency, faster stock replenishment √ Sustainability: lower carbon emissions per pallet or per drop, less wasted vehicle capacity and traffic Another important finding was that horizontal collaboration projects can only be done in collaboration with retailers and LSPs since nobody will have all the necessary data and information, let alone the decision-making power to execute or enforce such a project individually.
Case 13	Nestlé & United Biscuits Industry: Food & Grocery Region: UK Source: Report of Focus Oct. – CILT.UK 2011; A Guide to Transport Collaboration - ECR UK. 2011; Logistics report of IGD. 2008	Nestlé had an empty running issue for its distribution operations in the UK. It delivered over 15 loads per day from its factories in the North of England to its distribution centre in Leicestershire. Only 80% of these loads could be tied to a return journey, however, so every day 2 or 3 trucks would return to the North empty. United Biscuits delivered loads on a daily basis to Yorkshire from its distribution centre close to Nestlé's in the Midlands, and some of these loads presented opportunities for round tripping vehicles. Both shippers wanted to save money, reduce CO_2 emissions and stop wasting scarce resources. By sharing the use of trucks, they created round trips and reduced empty backhauls, which saved one million km of road usage over a period of four years. The basic collaboration procedures were: (1) Nestlé traffic called UB on day 1 to offer loads for shipping on day 3; (2) UB then planned the deliveries to collect; (3) UB transport provided a spreadsheet showing its delivery location and time and collection time to Nestlé's dispatch warehouse; (4) Standard trailers were provided enabling operational flexibility;

Continued

Case No.	Company Name	Case Description
Case 13		(5) Vehicle collected and delivered and drivers telephoned confirmation; (6) UB collated POD's and returned to Nestle. The basic collaboration procedures were: (1) Nestlé traffic called UB on day 1 to offer loads for shipping on day 3; (2) UB then planned the deliveries to collect; (3) UB transport provided a spreadsheet showing its delivery location and time and collection time to Nestlé's dispatch warehouse; (4) Standard trailers were provided enabling operational flexibility; (5) Vehicle collected and delivered and drivers telephoned confirmation; (6) UB collated POD's and returned to Nestle.
Case.14	Nestlé & Mars & Tesco Industry: Food & Grocery & Retail Region: UK Source: Logistics Manager Dec. 2009	In 2009, Nestlé and Mars formed a horizontal partnership to work together to reduce the environmental impact of their deliveries of Christmas and Easter confectionery to Tesco. They shared trucks to deliver combined loads of chocolates including Mars' Celebrations and Nestlé's Quality Street. The logistics collaboration also involved their major downstream customer—Tesco, who made significant changes to its own systems to synchronize the order patterns, lead-times and delivery bookings in a way that would enable orders from Nestlé and Mars to be combined into single loads. The initiative was first trialled at Christmas 2009, and then repeated the following Easter. By summer 2010, more than 70 combined deliveries had been made to Tesco, resulting in fewer vehicles arriving at the retailer's regional distribution centres and removing more than 16,000 km worth of duplicate truck movements from the roads. Results from this initiative suggested that upscaling the operation for other seasonal volumes could eliminate more than 100,000 km worth of duplicate truck journeys every year. The companies are now in the process of extending the number of Tesco regional distribution centres that receive combined deliveries during key seasonal periods.
Case 15	Sainsbury & Nestle Industry: Food & Grocery & Retail Region: UK	Nestlé and Sainsbury's collaborated with each other to identify and implement a number of standard backhauls in 2007. The Sainsbury's fleet based in Maidstone found a further opportunity to collect bottled water from the Nestlé warehouse in Dunkirk and deliver to Nestlé in Bardon. This indicates a regular freight flow that is ideal for transport sharing.

Continued

Case No.	Company Name	Case Description
Case 15	Source: ECR UK – Transport Collaboration Guide, 2011 and IGD, 2011	In order to make use of the spare capacity, the timings for shipment were adjusted to match the spare tractor capacity in the off peak times at Maidstone. The collaboration resulted in considerable annual kilometres savings, with 21,000 km for Nestlé and 43,200 for Sainsbury.
Case 16	Unilever & Tesco Industry: FMCG & Retail Region: UK Source: ECR UK—Transport Collaboration Guide, 2011 and IGD, 2011	By sharing the full picture of their transportation network in the UK. Tesco and Unilever identified the possibility of creating a backhaul picking up the stock from Unilever's distribution centre in Doncaster and delivering to Tesco's distribution centre in Goole utilising the empty transport capacity. This collaboration on backhauls has created an annual saving of more than 11,000 km with potential now for more lanes to be introduced across the network.
Case 17	Wincanton & Sainsbury & Panasonic Industry: FMCG & Retail Region: UK Source: Wincanton annual report 2012	Wincanton logistics was in intensive talks about collaborative transport and using their network and customer base to identify opportunities for collaboration, supported by technology to provide shared fleet. Specifically, Wincanton identified the opportunity for collaborative working with existing customers Sainsbury and Panasonic; delivering value through greater flexibility, cost savings and a lower carbon footprint. In March 2012, Wincanton, Sainsbury's and Panasonic began a collaborative transport contract in the Midlands, moving to a centrally planned solution where Wincanton's shared user fleet was used to smooth out the peaks and troughs of the customers' weekly distribution patterns and help to downsize the dedicated fleet capacity to both shippers (31% and 44% respectively). This is an unusual example of horizontal transport collaboration between two shippers from completely different sectors (one for electronic products, another for grocery).
Case 18	ASDA & Unilever Industry: FMCG & Retail Region: UK	Both Unilever and ASDA experienced an issue of empty running within their trucking operations. Unilever delivers goods into ASD0'sA Washington Depot each day, but with 50% of legs running empty from Washington to Doncaster. ASDA also delivered trunk stock into the North West Midlands each day, returning empty to the North East. Unilever and ASDA opened up a partnership to share

Continued

Case No.	Company Name	Case Description
Case 18	Source: ECR UK—Transport Collaboration Guide, 2011 and IGD, 2011	opportunities in their network to help reduce empty food miles. Through this partnership Unilever and ASDA have been able to reduce over 80,000 road kms each year.
Case 19	The Pallet Network Industry: 3PL Region: UK Source: Robert Mason et al 2007; thepalletnetworkltd.co.uk	The "Pallet Network" is a partnership community with over 100 of the largest independent road hauliers in UK. It concentrates on jointly planning the supply and delivery of pallets through a more responsive and cost efficient way of logistics operations. The key feature of this networked operation is the exploitation of a single point of control for all the operations, with a modular pallet system which allows a high level of customization and service whilst efficiencies are managed through economies of scale. Haulage companies who join a network mutually benefit from collaborating in the consortium but have no need to integrate their business with other hauliers other than through the pallet network coordinator. Pallets are picked up from local suppliers, consolidated for a region, shipped to a central distribution hub, before being re-allocated to their end destinations where the reverse process of trucking, deconsolidation and final delivery is followed. This network has realized considerable efficiency gains. It allows LSPs to handle the small but frequent loads required by customers who implement JIT operations efficiently, thus supporting reduced inventory levels especially at customers.
Case 20	Tetley (Tata Global Beverages) & Kellogg's & Kimberly-Clark Industry: FMCG & Food: Region: UK Source: Case report of North	Facilitated by Norbert Dentressangle (LSP), Tetley has formed a collaboration with other two major FMCG manufacturing customers (Kellogg's and Kimberly-Clark) who also appoint the same LSP. Under the new collaboration arrangement, Norbert Dentressangle relocated the warehousing from the current Tetley warehouse at Newton Aycliffe, to its own Merlin warehousing facility in Manchester, which is shared with the existing occupant, Kellogg's. In addition to products from Tetley and Kellogg's, Norbert Dentressangle's Manchester site also consolidated products from Kimberly-Clark's northern distribution centre in nearby Chorley, prior to delivery to retail and wholesale customers throughout the UK, delivering significant efficiency, cost and environmental benefits to all parties.

Continued

Case No.	Company Name	Case Description
Case 20	American horizontal collaboration in the supply chain summit, Atlanta 2011. Logistics Manager, Oct 2011	Before this, Kellogg's and Kimberly-Clark's were already in an active collaboration that reported 7% savings in transportation costs and 30,000 gallons of diesel and 380 tonnes of CO_2 per year.
Case 21	Cainiao Network (Alibaba Group) & SF Express & STO Express & YTO Express & ZTO Express & Yundaex Express Industry: E-commerce & 3PL Region: China Source: Industry research reports by HeadSCM Research 2014, Logistics Digest Jun. 15th 2015, China E-commerce Research Centre July. 2015	Cainiao Network is a logistics technology company under the Alibaba Group. It has the most advanced technologies in the mobile internet, GIS, cloud computing, big data, and the internet of things. In 2013 the retired Alibaba CEO Jack Ma launched this new company with the aim of using "Internet Thinking" and "Internet Technology" to transform the traditional logistics industry. The company soon launched a project called "China Smart Logistics Network" relying on horizontal collaboration with China's top five logistics companies to meet a target of delivering online shopping orders to any place in China within 24 hours in about 7—8 years. Specifically, this mega collaborative logistics network is made up of two parts— "Skynet" and "Groundnet". Cainiao Network is focused on developing the Skynet using data technology (DT) to analyse the frontend sales data, consumer behaviours, browsing/order history, etc., and visualize/transform these data into logistics forecasts and pre-alerts shared to the collaborating LSPs. The collaborating traditional LSPs who constitute the Groundnet then utilized these data to proactively plan their logistics capacity/anticipatory shipping across regions to react more effectively to the demand from buyers and sellers in the Pan Alibaba E-commerce ecology. At the same time, the Groundnet at the backend shares the dynamic capacity supply and the delivery status to the Skynet in real time to guide Alibaba in planning the online business with sellers fully considering the logistics capability and constraints. By relying on this magnificent collaborative logistics system, Alibaba has achieved an incredibly huge sales record in China's "Double Eleven" shopping day (Single's day) since 2014. The latest report from fortune.com reported that this collaborative logistics system in 2015 Single's day delivered order values of $14.3bn that is more than the total sales value made in "Thanksgiving" "Black Friday" and "Cyber Monday" in USA.

Continued

Case No.	Company Name	Case Description
Case 22	Cainiao Network (Alibaba Group) & Best Express & TTK Express & Deppon & GT Express & Kuaiditu Industry: E-commerce & 3PL Region: China Source: Industry research reports by TechSina	Cainiao Network innovated a B2B crowdsourcing model for logistics services in late 2015. By collaborating with several logistics companies, it consolidated the logistics supply power of more than 200,000 couriers across the major cities in China. Cainiao developed an APP platform based on the mobile internet and GIS technology to quickly connect users who had the logistics demand and the couriers of the collaborating companies who were dynamically moving in that city. In the traditional approach, couriers had to finish the task of parcel delivery to receivers, return to the local service station, get new orders and then be assigned to go to the sender's home to get the new goods for a subsequent delivery. This is a very inefficient operational process, mainly due to the fact that the sender's locations are widely scattered, often resulting in long waiting times for senders to have their goods collected by couriers. Relying on this APP platform, the sender's location can be instantly matched to a courier's current location and the new order can be directly assigned to this courier, meaning that couriers can perform collection and dispatch at the same time without frequently returning back to the service station to check for new orders and take on new tasks. The collaboration also enables traditional logistics companies to obtain more orders than through their own sales channels as Cainiao Network possesses and shares millions of logistics orders per day through.
Case 23	Cainiao Network (Alibaba Group) & RRS (Haier Group) Industry: E-commerce & Household Appliances Region: China Source: China E-commerce Research Centre July. 2014; HeadSCM Research 2014	In late 2013, Cainiao Network launched a collaboration with RRS, a logistics company under Haier Group responsible for large item logistics. The main reason Cainiao Network wanted to collaborate with RRS was because of its powerful logistics network coverage and capability for large item logistics. In China, RRS has operated distribution centres in 2,800 cities, and over 17,000 logistics service stations in communities. By connecting with the RRS network, Cainiao would be able to help Alibaba to expand the online shopping and logistics deliveries to the 3rd and 4th tier cities, and vast rural areas in China, accounting for a population of some 700 million. RRS would also help Alibaba to ship the large item products quicker than the other LSPs which would help Alibaba in marketing the large items online. For RRS, managing such a large item logistics network is a big cost and only the scaled economy could support the

Continued

Case No.	Company Name	Case Description
Case 23		sustainable running of this mega network. Relying on internal orders only, it would not be possible to generate sufficient demand volume to keep assets running. The company therefore had to open its network for social use in order to attract more orders. Cainiao as the logistics control tower of Alibaba's various E-commerce sites would be the best partner to collaborate with. In addition, Cainiao's advanced data technology in logistics would help to maximize the potential of RRS's ground logistics network.
Case 24	JD logistics (JD.com Group) & China Post Industry: E-commerce & 3PL Region: China Source: Industry research reports by Tech163, TechSina, chinapost.com	JD.com, an E-commerce company and a major opponent of Alibaba, has been eating away at Alibaba's market share. Its magic weapon is the heavy asset-driven self-built logistics system operated by JD logistics, which offers consumers significantly quicker home deliveries than all other E-commerce companies (in big cities like Beijing/Shanghai, customers can even receive orders within 2 hours after clicking "buy"). With the ambition of "buying globally", a cross border e-commerce service linking global sellers to Chinese consumers, in 2015 JD logistics launched a horizontal collaboration with China Post. With this collaborative agreement, JD logistics domestics distribution network would be better connected to China Post's global shipping network and resources, and would thus rely on China Post to perform efficient customs clearance. This collaboration would help to bring more foreign sellers to JD.com and enable Chinese customers to more easily buy global products.
Case 25	RRKD.cn Industry: Internet Region: China Source: Industry research reports by China E-commerce Research Centre Aug. 2015; RRKD.cn	RRKD.cn is an internet company in China that applies the C2C crowdsourcing model for logistics services. It developed an APP platform based on the mobile internet and GIS technology to connect individual people directly for creating logistics demand and supplying logistics capacity. This business model is innovative and disruptive in that it creates a platform for horizontal collaboration directly between individual people to timely and cost-efficiently deliver small parcels in the complex urban distribution networks that would often be a higher cost/lower speed if a logistics company were hired to fulfil the delivery task. This mobile APP platform takes full advantage of the "Shared Economy" concept to reduce the logistics cost and increase the delivery speed. Users of this platform can be both the source

Continued

Case No.	Company Name	Case Description
Case 25		of "demand" and "supply". When one user incurs a delivery demand, the APP can quickly identify several people who are geographically near to him and who have the spare capacity to help transport the parcels or who are coincidentally going to the same destination and willing to offer a hand. The cost of the delivery is significantly lower because the logistics is fulfilled by using the power of the social network as opposed to the heavy asset-driven logistics companies with high fixed costs, and much slower responses and delivery times. Conversely, when one user has the spare capacity during his off-working time, he can grab orders from the APP to help other users to deliver the goods. Such a mutual collaborative model is squeezing out the traditional logistics companies in segments such as urban and last mile distribution.
Case 26	PepsiCo & Main Suppliers Industry: Food & Grocery Region: UK Source: ECR UK – Transport Collaboration Guide, 2011 and IGD, 2011	PepsiCo collected raw materials from its main suppliers to meet the requirements of six of its seven plants through daily communication between the two parties in order to ensure "cost effective collection and continuity of supply to the production plants", equating to 180–190 collections in a week from 14 collection points. "Due to rising costs and service issues over potato supply to its plants in Leicester, Pepsi Co. undertook a benchmarking exercise to evaluate whether to invest in fleet and resources to integrate deliveries as front haul on the way to the farms and stores rather than run empty to the collection point."
Case 27	Kimberly Clark & Unilever Industry: FMCG Region: Netherland Source: case report of North American horizontal collaboration in the supply chain summit, Atlanta 2011; Supply chain quarterly – Quarter 2. 2011; Logistics Manager, Oct. 2011	Kimberly-Clark and Unilever collaborated to enable combined truck-loads deliveries which enhance their customer service levels resulting in a shortened replenishment cycle more frequent deliveries to align to point-of-sale data of their customers. Specifically, a 57% increase in weekly deliveries and a 31% decrease in weekly drops. The collaboration also produces other benefits besides transportation savings (i.e. by shortening the cycle time for deliveries, collaborative distribution could reduce store inventories while increasing on-shelf availability of products for customers). The collaboration is also expanded to engage with a third-party logistics company who operate a shared distribution centre for them and handle transportation on their behalf.

Continued

Case No.	Company Name	Case Description
Case 28	Baxter & Donaldson Industry: Manufacturing Region: Belgium and Ireland Source: Eye for Transport March. 2013	This is about the horizontal collaboration for orchestrated co-loading of transports between Belgium and Ireland. Baxter, a global healthcare company, and Donaldson, a global manufacturer of filtration systems, have found that within their respective logistics networks there are compatible freight flows that are promising for bundling. A particular case is between Belgium and Ireland, where both shippers have adelivery destinations in the same enterprise park in Ireland. Facilitated by a LSP (Tri-Visor) who actively help to manage and synchronize the shipments of both companies in real-time, the two shippers are able to routinely build up the consolidated journeys for this freight lane. They have successfully been co-loading their transports between Belgium and Ireland since August 2012. The result of the shipment synchronization is that every week the containers from Belgium to Ireland are being filled to their maximum volumetric capacity with a mix of Baxter and Donaldson products. The benefits for the companies involved in co-loading are manifold, but mainly include substantial savings in transportation costs in combination with the use of fewer containers, and with higher capacity utilization. Besides, important sustainability gains are being realized through the synchronized co-loading (i.e. CO_2 reductions of more than 15% compared to individual operations).

LIST OF ABM PAPERS PER SUPPLY CHAIN FIELDS

Article	SS	CP	SC	RU	IVP	PP	RA	PS	RP	BSR	OG	CS
Caridi et al. (2005)			√									
Bhattacharyya and Zhang (2010)			√									
Sinha et al. (2011)							√					
Fu et al. (2000)					√							
Lin et al. (2002)			√									
Zhang and Bhattacharyya (2010)					√							
Kim et al. (2006)							√					
Kwon et al. (2007)			√									
Zarandi et al. (2008)					√							
Moyaux et al. (2010)								√				
Groves et al. (2014)		√										
Amini et al. (2012)						√						
Li and Chan (2013)					√							
Zhang and Geng (2012)			√									
Wu et al. (2011)				√								
Jeong and Khouja (2013)				√								
Giannoccaro (2011)											√	
Jiang and Sheng (2009)					√							
Ehlen et al. (2014)				√								
Chan and Chan (2010)			√									

Article	SS	CP	SC	RU	IVP	PP	RA	PS	RP	BSR	OG	CS
Nikolopoulou and Ierapetritou (2012a)	√											
Sun et al. (2012)												√
Mizgier et al. (2012)			√									
Chang et al. (2014)	√											
Giannoccaro and Pontrandolfo (2009)			√									
Hua et al. (2011)				√								
Behdani et al. (2010)					√							
Kim (2009)					√							
Albino et al. (2007)			√									
Arunachalam and Sadeh (2005)		√										
Chan and Chan (2004)			√									
Cid Yanez et al. (2009)						√						
Ibrahim and Deghedi (2012)			√									
Fu-ren et al. (2005)	√											
Lau et al. (2004)			√									
Datta and Christopher (2011)				√								
Lu et al. (2005)			√									
Nair and Vidal (2011)				√								
Allwood and Lee (2005)		√										
Hilletofth and Lättilä (2012)					√							
Ilie-Zudor and László (2009)	√											
Zhang and Bhattacharyya (2010)	√											
Kim et al. (2008)					√							
Li and Zhang (2003)	√											

Article	SS	CP	SC	RU	IVP	PP	RA	PS	RP	BSR	OG	CS
Ferreira and Borenstein (2011)									√			
Pino et al. (2010)			√									
Huang and Liu (2008)					√							
Wang et al. (2008)					√							
Wu et al. (2013)				√								
Yang et al. (2004)	√											
Chatfield et al. (2004)			√									
Guang-Feng and Woo-Tsong (2011)								√				
Huiting et al. (2008)					√							
Chinh et al. (2013)					√							
Chan and Chan (2005)			√									
Sirivunnabood and Kumara (2009)				√								
Hing Kai and Chan (2006)				√								
Hing Kai (2009)			√									
Hou et al. (2008)										√		
Xu and Zhu (2013)			√									
Yang et al. (2009)		√										
Yuan et al. (2011)				√								
Xie and Chen (2005)			√									
Xie and Chen (2004)		√										
Du et al. (2008)				√								
Meng et al. (2011)												√
Luin et al. (2006)					√							
Mujaj (2008)								√				
Sawaya (2006)			√									
Moyaux et al. (2004)					√							
Yu and Wong (2015)	√											
Liu et al. (2014)	√											

Article	SS	CP	SC	RU	IVP	PP	RA	PS	RP	BSR	OG	CS
Schieritz and Grobler (2003)	√											
Allwood and Lee (2005)		√										

Annotation

SS = supplier selection

CP = supply chain competition

SC = supply chain collaboration

RU = risk and uncertainty management

IVE = inventory control and management

PP = production policy

RA = resource allocation

PS = pricing strategy

RP = regulation policy

BSR= buyer-supplier relationship

OG = organization governance

CS = contract scheme

REFERENCE

ABDUR RAZZAQUE M, CHEN SHENG C, 1998. Outsourcing of logistics functions: a literature survey [J]. International journal of physical distribution & logistics management, 28(2): 89-107.

AFRICK J, MARKESET E, 1996. Making contract logistics work [J]. Transportation & distribution, 37(1): 58-60.

AHN H J, LEE H, 2004. An agent-based dynamic information network for supply chain management [J]. BT technology journal, 22(2):18-27.

AKKERMANS H, 2001. Emergent supply networks: system dynamics simulation of adaptive supply agents: proceedings of the 34th annual Hawaii international conference on system sciences[C]. Piscataway: IEEE Press: 11

AKKERMANS H, DELLAERT N, 2005. The rediscovery of industrial dynamics: the contribution of system dynamics to supply chain management in a dynamic and fragmented world [J]. System dynamics review, 21(3): 173-186.

ALBINO V, CARBONARA N, GIANNOCCARO I, 2007. Supply chain cooperation in industrial districts: a simulation analysis [J]. European journal of operational research, 177(1): 261-280.

ALLWOOD J, LEE J H, 2005. The design of an agent for modelling supply chain network dynamics [J]. International journal of production research, 43(22): 4875-4898.

ALTIOK T, MELAMED B, 2010. Simulation modeling and analysis with arena [M], Pittsburgh: Academic Press.

ANGERHOFER B J, ANGELIDES M C, 2000. System dynamics modelling in supply chain management: research review: proceedings of 2000 winter simulation conference [C]. Piscataway: IEEE Press: 342-351.

ARUNACHALAM R, SADEH N M, 2005. The supply chain trading agent competition [J]. Electronic commerce research and applications, 4(1): 66-84.

AUDY J F, D'AMOURS S, ROUSSEAU, L M, 2010. Cost allocation in the establishment of a collaborative transportation agreement—an application in the furniture industry [J]. Journal of the operational research society, 61(10): 1559.

AUDY J F, D'AMOURS S, LEHOUX N, et al. 2010. Coordination in collaborative logistics [R]. Brussels: International workshop on supply chain models for shared resource management.

AUDY J F, LEHOUX N, D'AMOURS S, et al. 2010. A framework for an efficient implementation of logistics collaborations [J]. International transactions in operational research, 19(5): 633-657.

AXELROD R, 1997. Advancing the art of simulation in the social sciences [M]// Simulating social phenomena. Berlin: Springer:21-40.

BAHRAMI K, 2002. Improving supply chain productivity through horizontal cooperation—the case of consumer goods manufacturers[M]//Cost management in supply chains. Berlin: Springer: 213-232.

BARRATT M, 2004. Understanding the meaning of collaboration in the supply chain [J]. Supply chain management, 9(1):30-42.

BEHDANI B, 2012. Evaluation of paradigms for modeling supply chains as complex socio-technical systems: proceedings of the 2012 winter simulation conference (WSC) [C]. Piscataway: IEEE Press.

BERGER T, SCHREINEMACHERS P, 2006. Creating agents and landscapes for multiagent systems from random samples [J]. Ecology and society, 11(2): 19.

BHATTACHARYYA S, ZHANG Y, 2010. Information sharing strategies in business-to-business e-hubs: an agent-based study [J]. International journal of intelligent information technologies, 6(2): 1-20.

BIERMASZ J, KNEPPELHOUT N V K, 2012. CO^3 project report: report on the legal framework for horizontal collabration in the supply chain.

BRAILSFORD S, HILTON N, 2001. A comparison of discrete event simulation and system dynamics for modelling health care systems[R]. Southampton: Operational research applied to health services.

BRITTEN N, 1995. Qualitative interviews in medical research [J]. The British medical journal (The BMJ) clinical research, 311(6999): 251-253.

BRYMAN A, 2012. Social research methods[M], Oxford: Oxford University Press.

CAPUTO M, MININNO V, 1996. Internal, vertical and horizontal logistics integration in Italian grocery distribution [J]. International journal of physical distribution & logistics management, 26 (9):64-90.

CARIDI M, CIGOLINI R, DE MARCO D, 2005. Improving supply-chain collaboration by linking intelligent agents to CPFR [J]. International journal of production research, 43(20):4191-4218.

CHAN H K, CHAN F T S, 2004. A coordination framework for distributed supply chains: 2004 IEEE international conference on systems, man and cybernetics[C]. Piscataway: IEEE Press:4535-4540.

CHAN H K, CHAN F T S, 2010. Comparative study of adaptability and flexibility in distributed manufacturing supply chains[J]. Decision support systems, 48(2):331-341.

CHAN H K, CHAN F T S, 2005. Comparative analysis of negotiation based information sharing in agent-based supply chains: 2005 3rd IEEE international conference on industrial informatics(INDIN) [C]. Piscataway: IEEE Press: 813-818.

CHANG L, OUZROUT Y, NONGAILLARD A, et al. 2014. Multi-criteria decision making based on trust and reputation in supply chain[J]. International journal of production economics, 147(b): 362-372.

CHANG O K, KWON I H, BAEK J G, 2008. Asynchronous action-reward learning for nonstationary serial supply chain inventory control[J]. Applied intelligence, 28(1): 1-16.

CHARMAZ K, 2006. Constructing grounded theory: a practical guide through qualitative analysis [M], London: Sage Publications.

CHATFIELD D C, HAYYA J C, HARRISON T P, 2006. A multi-formalism architecture for agent-based, order-centric supply chain simulation[J]. Simulation modelling practice and theory, 15(2):153-174.

CHATFIELD D C, KIM J G, HARRISON T P, et al. 2004. The bullwhip effect—impact of stochastic lead time, information quality, and information sharing: a simulation study[J]. Production and operations management, 13(4):340-353.

CHEN F, 1998. Echelon reorder points, installation reorder points, and the value of centralized demand information[J]. Management science, 44(12): 221-234.

CHEN F, DREZNER Z, RYAN J K, et al, 2000. Quantifying the bullwhip effect in a simple supply chain: the impact of forecasting, lead times, and information[J]. Management science, 46(3):436-443.

CHOPRA S, MEINDL P, 2007. Supply chain management: strategy, planning & operation [M]. 3rd ed. Upper Saddle River, New Jersey: Pearson Education.

CHRISTOPHER M, 1992. Logistics and supply chain management: strategies for reducing costs and improving services[M]. London: Prentice Hall.

CHRISTOPHER M, 2011. Logistics and supply chain management[M]. 4th ed. London: Prentice Hall.

COMMISSION E, 2011. White paper on transport—roadmap to a single European transport area: towards a competitive and resource efficient transport system[M]. Luxembourg: Publications Office of the European Union.

COMMISSION OF THE EUROPEAN COMMUNITIES, 2001. White Paper: European transport policy for 2010: time to decide[R]. Brussels: CEC.

COYLE J J, EDWARD J B, LANGLEY C J, 2002. The Management of Business Logistics: A Supply Chain Perspective[M]. 7th ed. Mason, Ohio: South-Western/Thomason Learning.

CRAIGHEAD C W, HANNA J B, GIBSON B J, et al. 2007. Research approaches in logistics: trends and alternative future directions[J]. The international journal of logistics management, 18(1):22-40.

CRESWELL J W, CLARK V L P, 2007. Designing and conducting mixed methods research[M]. Thousand Oaks: Sage Publications.

CRUIJSSEN F C A M, 2006. Horizontal cooperation in transport and logistics[M]. Tilburg: Tilburg University.

CRUIJSSEN F, COOLS M, DULLAERT W, 2007a. Horizontal cooperation in logistics: Opportunities and impediments[J]. Transportation research part e-logistics and transportation review, 43(2):129-142.

CRUIJSSEN F, DULLAERT W, FLEUREN H, 2007b. Horizontal cooperation in transport and logistics: a literature review[J]. Transportation journal, 46(3): 22-39.

CRUIJSSEN F, DULLAERT W, JORO T, 2010. Freight transportation efficiency through horizontal cooperation in Flanders[J]. International journal of logistics, 13(3):161-178.

CRUIJSSEN F, OLLI B, DULLAERT W, FLEUREN H, et al. 2006. Joint route planning under varying market conditions[J]. SSRN electronic journal, 1:49.

CURRY L A, NEMBHARD I M, RADLEY E H, 2009. Qualitative and mixed methods provide unique contributions to outcomes research[J]. Circulation, 119(10):1442-1452.

DATTA P P, CHRISTOPHER M G, 2011. Information sharing and coordination mechanisms for managing uncertainty in supply chains: a simulation study[J]. International journal of production research, 49(3):765-803.

DEJONCKHEERE J, DISNEY S M, LAMBRECHT M R, et. al, 2004. The impact of information enrichment on the Bullwhip effect in supply chains: a control engineering perspective[J]. European journal of operational research, 153(3): 727-750.

DICICCO-BLOOM B, CRABTREE B F, 2006. The qualitative research interview[J]. Medical education, 40(4): 314-321.

DISNEY S M, TOWILL D R, 2003. The effect of vendor managed inventory (VMI) dynamics on the Bullwhip Effect in supply chains[J]. International journal of production economics, 85(2003): 199-215.

DONG F G, LIU H M, LU B D, 2012. Agent-based simulation model of single point inventory system[J]. Systems engineering procedia, 4: 298-304.

EUROPEAN COMMISSION, 2010. EU Energy and Transport in Figures[M]. Luxembourg: Publications Office of the European Union.

EHLEN M A, SUN A C, PEPPLE M A, et al. 2014. Chemical supply chain modeling for analysis of homeland security events[J]. Computers & Chemical Engineering, 60(10): 102-111.

ELDABI T, BALABAN M, BRAILSFORD S, et al. 2016. Hybrid simulation: historical lessons, present challenges and futures[R]. Washington, DC: 2016 Winter Simulation Conference (WSC).

ELLRAM L M, 1991. Supply-chain management: the industrial organisation perspective[J]. International journal of physical distribution & logistics management, 21(1):13-22.

EPPSTEIN M J, GROVER D K, MARSHALL J S, et al. 2011. An agent-based model to study market penetration of plug-in hybrid electric vehicles[J]. Energy policy, 39(2011): 3789-3802.

ESPER T L, WILLIAMS L R, 2003. The value of collaborative transportation management (CTM): its relationship to CPFR and information technology[J]. Transportation journal, 42(4): 55-65.

EVANS T P, KELLEY H, 2004. Multi-scale analysis of a household level agent-based model of landcover change[J]. Journal of Environmental Management, 72(1/2): 57-72.

EYEFORTRANSPORT, 2011. North American horizontal collaboration in the supply chain report—a brief analysis of eyefortransport's recent survey[R]. Eyefortranport.

FORRESTER J W, 1961. Industrial Dynamics[M], Cambidge: MIT Press.

FOSTER T, 1999. 4PLs: The next generation for supply chain outsourcing[J]. Logistics management & distribution report, 4: 35.

FOSTER T A,1994. What to tell your boss about logistics[J]. Distribution, 4.

FREY J H, FONTANA A, 1991. The group interview in social research[J]. The social science journal, 28(2): 175-187.

GAVIRNENI S, KAPUSCINSKI R, TAYUR S, 1999. Value of information in capacitated supply chains[J]. Management science, 45(1): 16-24.

GIANNAKIS M, LOUIS M, 2011. A multi-agent based framework for supply chain risk management[J]. Journal of purchasing and supply management, 17(1): 23-31.

GIANNOCCARO I, PONTRANDOLFO P, 2009. Negotiation of the revenue sharing contract: An agent-based systems approach[J]. International journal of production economics, 122(2009): 558-566.

GIGERENZER G, SELTEN R, 2002. Bounded rationality: the adaptive toolbox[M], Cambidge: MIT Press.

GILLHAM B, 2000. Case study research methods[M], London: Continuum.

GOKHALE S S, TRIVEDI K S, 1998. Analytical modeling[M]//In encyclopedia of distributed systems. The Netherlands: Kluwer Academic Publishers.

GOLICIC S L, DAVIS D F, 2012. Implementing mixed methods research in supply chain management[J]. International journal of physical distribution & logistics management, 42(8/9):726-741.

GRIMM V, REVILLA E, BERGER U, et al. 2005. Pattern-oriented modeling of agent-based complex systems: lessons from ecology[J]. Science, 310(5750):987-991.

GUINOUET A, JORDANS M, CRUIJSSEN F, 2012. CO^3 project report: retail collaboration in France.

HAGEBACK C, SEGERSTEDT A, HAGEBACK C, et al. 2004. The need for co-distribution in rural areas—a study of Pajala in Sweden[J]. International journal of production economics, 89(2):153-163.

HARRISON A, 2002. Case study research[M]//Partington D. Essential skills for management research. London: Sage Publications:158-180.

HERNANDEZ S H, 2010. Modeling of collaborative less-than-truckload carrier freight networks[D]. West Lafayette: Purdue University.

HINDESS B, 1988. Choice, Rationality, and Social Theory[M]. London: Unwin Hyman.

HINDLEY P, 2013. The value of assessing the carbon impact of the supply chain as part of your business strategy. Total Logistics.

HING KAI C, CHAN F T S, 2006. Early order completion contract approach to minimize the impact of demand uncertainty on supply chains[J]. IEEE transactions on industrial informatics, 2(1): 48-58.

HINGLEY M, LINDGREEN A, GRANT D B, 2011. Using fourth-party logistics management to improve horizontal collaboration among grocery retailers[J]. Supply chain management: an international journal, 16(5): 316-327.

IBRAHIM Y, DEGHEDI G, 2012. Sharing breakdown information in supply chain systems: an agent-based modelling approach[J]. International journal of management and decision making, 2(4):19-30.

JACOBS K, LENT C V, VERSTREPEN S, et al. 2014. CO³ test case report: horizontal collaboration in fresh & chilled retail distribution.

JACOBS K, VERCAMMEN S, VERSTREPEN S, 2013. CO³ test case report: creation of an orchestrated intermodal partnership between multiple shippers.

JIANG C, SHENG Z, 2009. Case-based reinforcement learning for dynamic inventory control in a multi-agent supply-chain system[J]. Expert systems with applications, 36(3): 6520-6526.

JOHNSON R B, ONWUEGBUZIE A J, TURNER L A, 2007. Toward a definition of mixed methods research[J]. Journal of mixed methods research, 1(2): 112-133.

KAROLEFSKY J, 2001. Collaborating across the supply chain[J]. Collaboration in practice: a supplement to food logistics and retailtech magazines: 24-34.

KELEPOURIS T, MILIOTIS P, PRAMATARI K, 2008. The impact of replenishment parameters and information sharing on the bullwhip effect: a computational study[J]. Computers & operations research, 35(11):3657-3670.

KIM W S, 2009. Effects of a trust mechanism on complex adaptive supply networks: An agent-based social simulation study[J]. Journal of artificial societies and social simulation, 12(3):4.

KING N, HORROCKS C, 2011. Interviews in Qualitative Research[J]. The modern language journal, 95(4):670-671.

KNEMEYER A M, CORSI T M, MURPHY P R, 2003. Logistics outsourcing relationships: customer perspectives[J]. Journal of business logistics, 24(1): 77-109.

KRAJEWSKA M A, KOPFER H, LAPORTE G, et al. 2008. Horizontal cooperation among freight carriers: request allocation and profit sharing[J]. Journal of the operational research society, 59(11):1483-1491.

KRUEGER R A, CASEY M A, 2000. Focus groups: a practical guide for applied research[M]. 3rd ed. Thousand Oaks: Sage Publications.

LAMBERT D M, EMMELHAINZ M A, GARDNER J T, 1999. Building successful logistics partnerships[J]. Journal of business logistics, 20(1): 165-181.

LANE D C, Forrester J W, 1997. Invited review and reappraisal: industrial dynamics[J]. Journal of the operational research society, 48(10): 1037-1042.

LANE D C, 2000. You just don't understand me: modes of failure and success in the discourse between system dynamics and discrete event simulation[D]. London: London School of Economics and Political Science, LSEOR 00.34: 26.

LARSSON R, 1993. Case survey methodology: quantitative analysis of patterns across case studies[J]. Academy of management journal, 36(6):1515-1546.

LAU J S K, HUANG G Q, MAK K L, 2004. Impact of information sharing on inventory replenishment in divergent supply chains[J]. International journal of production research, 42(5): 919-941.

LAW A M, KELTON W D, 2000. Simulation modeling and analysis[M]. 3rd ed. New York: McGraw-Hill.

LE BLANC H, CRUIJSSEN F, FLEUREN H A, et al. 2006. Factory gate pricing: an analysis of the dutch retail distribution[J]. European journal of operational research, 174(3):1950-1967.

LEE H L, PADMANABHAN V, WHANG S, 1997. The bullwhip effect in supply chains. Sloan management review, 38(3): 93-102.

LEE J H, KIM C O, 2008. Multi-agent systems applications in manufacturing systems and supply chain management: a review paper[J]. International journal of production research, 46(1):233-265.

LEITNER R, MEIZER F, PROCHAZKA M, et al. 2011. Structural concepts for horizontal cooperation to increase efficiency in logistics[J]. CIRP journal of manufacturing science and technology, 4(2): 332-337.

LEWIS M W, 1998. Iterative triangulation: a theory development process using existing case studies[J]. Journal of operations management, 16(4): 455-469.

LI J, SIKORA R, SHAW M J, et al. 2006. A strategic analysis of inter organizational information sharing[J]. Decision support systems, 42(1): 251-266.

LIN F-R., HUANG S-H, LIN S-C, 2002. Effects of information sharing on supply chain performance in electronic commerce[J]. IEEE transactions on engineering management, 49(3): 258-268.

LIN F-R, SUNG Y-W, LO Y-P, 2005. Effects of trust mechanisms on supply-chain performance: a multi-agent simulation study[J]. International journal of electronic commerce, 9(4): 91-112.

MACAL C M, 2004. Emergent structures from trust relationships in supply chains: Proceedings of agent 2004 conference[C].

MACAL C M, NORTH M J, 2006. Tutorial on agent-based modeling and simulation PART 2: how to model with agents: proceedings of the 2006 Winter Simulation conference[C]. Piscataway: IEEE Press: 73-83.

MACAL C M, NORTH M J, 2010. Tutorial on agent-based modelling and simulation[J]. Journal of simulation, 4(3):151-162.

MORGAN D L, KRUEGER R A, 1997. The Focus Group Kit. 6 volums[M]. Thousand Oaks: Sage Publications.

MANGAN J, LALWANI C, BUTCHER T, et al. 2008. Global logistics and supply chain management[M]. 2nd ed. Hoboken: John Wiley & Sons.

MASON R, LALWANI C, BOUGHTON R, et al. 2007. Combining vertical and horizontal collaboration for transport optimisation[J]. Supply chain management: an international journal, 12(3):187-199.

MCCUTCHEON D M, MEREDITH J R,1993. Conducting case study research in operations management[J]. Journal of operations management, 11(3):239-256.

MOORE K R, 1998. Trust and relationship commitment in logistics alliances: a buyer perspective[J]. The journal of supply chain management, 34(1):24-37.

MORASH E A, CLINTON S, 1997. The role of transportation capabilities in international supply chain management[J]. Transportation journal, 36(3): x-17.

MOUTAOUKIL A, DERROUICHE R, NEUBERT G, 2012. Pooling Supply Chain: literature review of collaborative strategies[M]// IFIP advances in information and communication technology: collaborative networks in the internet of services, Berlin: Springer:513-525.

MOYAUX T, CHAIB-DRAA B, D'AMOURS S, 2004. Multi-agent simulation of collaborative strategies in a supply chain: proceedings of the third international joint conference on autonomous agents and multiagent systems: volume 1[C]. Piscataway: IEEE Press:52-59.

NAESENS K, GELDERS L, PINTELON L, 2009. A swift response framework for measuring the strategic fit for a horizontal collaborative initiative[J]. International journal of production economics, 121(2):550-561.

NAIM M M, POTTER A T, MASON R J, et al. 2006. The role of transport flexibility in logistics provision[J]. The international journal of logistics management, 17(3):297-311.

NIAZI M, HUSSAIN A, 2011. Agent-based computing from multi-agent systems to agent-based models: a visual survey[J]. Scientometrics, 89(2): 479-499.

NIKOLOPOULOU A, IERAPETRITOU M G, 2012. Hybrid simulation based optimization approach for supply chain management[J]. Computers & chemical engineering, 47(20): 183-193.

OHNO T, 1988. Toyota production system: beyond large-scale production[M]. Cambridge: Productivity press.

PALMER A, SAENZ M J, WOENSEL T V, et al. 2012. CO^3 project report: characteristics of collaborative business models.

PATTON M Q, 2002. Qualitative research and evaluation methods[M].3rd ed. Thousand Oaks: Sage Publications.

PECK S L, 2004. Simulation as experiment: a philosophical reassessment for biological modeling[J]. Trends in Ecology & Evolution, 19(10):530-534.

PIDD M, 2004. Computer Simulation in Management Science[M]. 5th ed. Hoboken, New Jersey: John Wiley & Sons.

POLER R, MULA J, DíAZ-MADROñERO M, 2013. Operations research problems: statements and solutions[M]. London: Springer.

POMPONI F, FRATOCCHI L, ROSSI TAFURI S, 2015. Trust development and horizontal collaboration in logistics: a theory based evolutionary framework[J]. Supply chain management: an international journal, 20(1): 83-97.

POMPONI F, FRATOCCHI L, TAFURI S R, et al. 2013. Horizontal collaboration in logistics: a comprehensive framework[J]. Research in logistics & production, 3(4):243-254.

POTTER A, MASON R, LALWANI C, 2007. Analysis of factory gate pricing in the UK grocery supply chain[J]. International journal of retail & distribution management, 35(10): 821-834.

RAVINDRAN A R, 2009. Operations Research Methodologies[M]. London: CRC Press, Taylor & Francis Group.

ROBSON C, 2002. Real world research: a resource for social scientists and practitioner-researchers[M]. Hoboken: John Wiley & Sons.

ROORDA M J, CAVALCANTE R, MCCABE S, et al. 2010. A conceptual framework for agent-based modelling of logistics services[J]. Transportation research Part E: logistics and transportation review, 46(1): 18-31.

SABATH R, 1998. Volatile demand calls for quick response: The integrated supply chain[J]. International journal of physical distribution & logistics management, 28(9/10): 698-703.

SALZARULO P A, 2006. Vendor-managed inventory programs and their effect on supply chain performance[D]. Bloomington: Indiana University.

SAWAYA W J, 2006. The performance impact of the extent of inter-organizational information sharing: an investigation using a complex adaptive system paradigm and agent-based simulation[D]. Minnesota Twin Cities: University of Minnesota.

SAWAYA W J, 2007. Using empirical demand data and common random numbers in an agent-based simulation of a distribution network: proceedings of the 39th conference on Winter simulation: 40 years! The best is yet to come[C]. Piscataway: IEEE Press: 1947-1952.

SCHIERITZ N, GROBLER A, 2003. Emergent structures in supply chains—a study integrating agent-based and system dynamics modeling: proceedings of the 36th annual Hawaii international conference on system science[C]. Piscataway: IEEE Press: 94.1.

SCHMOLTZI C, WALLENBURG C M, 2012. Operational governance in horizontal cooperations of logistics service providers: performance effects and the moderating role of cooperation complexity[J]. Journal of supply chain management, 48(2):53-74.

SCHULZ S F, BLECKEN A, 2010. Horizontal cooperation in disaster relief logistics: benefits and impediments[J]. International journal of physical distribution & logistics management, 40 (8/9): 636-656.

SIEBERS P O, AICKELIN U, CELIA H, et al. 2007. A multi-agent simulation of retail management practices: proceedings of the 2007 summer computer simulation conference[C].

SIEBERS P O, MACAL C M, GARNETT J, et al. 2010. Discrete-event simulation is dead, long live agent-based simulation[J]. Journal of simulation, 4(3): 204-210.

SIMATUPANG T M, SRIDHARAN R, 2002. The collaborative supply chain[J]. International journal of logistics management, 13(1): 15-30.

SIMCHI-LEVI D, ZHAO Y, 2004. The value of information sharing in a two-stage supply chain with production capacity constraints: the infinite horizon case[J]. Probability in the engineering and informational sciences, 18(2): 247-274.

SIRIVUNNABOOD S, KUMARA S, 2009. Comparison of mitigation strategies for supplier risks: a multi agent-based simulation approach: 2009 IEEE/INFORMS international conference on service operations, logistics and informatics[C]. Piscataway: IEEE Press: 388-393.

SLACK N, CHAMBERS S, BETTS A, et al. 2006. Operations and process management: principles and practice for strategic impact[M]. Harlow: Prentice Hall.

SLIKKER M, FRANSOO J, WOUTERS M, 2005. Cooperation between multiple news-vendors with transshipments[J]. European journal of operational research, 167(2): 370-380.

STANK T P, GOLDSBY T J, VICKERY S K, et al. 2003. Logistics service performance: estimating its influence on market share[J]. Journal of business logistics, 24(1): 27-55.

STEFANSSON G, 2006. Collaborative logistics management and the role of third-party service providers[J]. International journal of physical distribution & logistics management, 36(2): 76-92.

SUTHERLAND J, 2003. Collaborative transportation management–creating value through increased transportation efficiencies. Business Briefing: Pharmagenerics:1-4.

SWEETSER A, 1999. A comparison of system dynamics (SD) and discrete event simulation (DES): proceedings of 17th international conference of the system dynamics society [C].

SYUHADA M M, 2014. The benefit of information sharing in a multi-echelon supply chain: EurOMA Conference 2014[C].

TAKO A A, ROBINSON S, 2012. The application of discrete event simulation and system dynamics in the logistics and supply chain context[J]. Decision support systems, 52(4): 802-815.

TATE K, 1996. The elements of a successful logistics partnership[J]. International journal of physical distribution & logistics management, 26(3):7-13.

TAYLOR K, LANE D, 1998. Simulation applied to health services: opportunities for applying the system dynamics approach[J]. Journal of health services research & policy, 3(4): 226-232.

THIERRY C, BEL G, THOMAS A, 2010. The role of modeling and simulation in supply chain management[J]. SCS M&S magazine, 1:1-8.

TYAN J C, WANG F K, DU T, 2003. Applying collaborative transportation management models in global third-party logistics[J]. International journal of computer integrated manufacturing, 16(4/5):283-291.

VERSTREPEN S, BOSSCHE L V D, 2015. CO^3 test case report: retail inbound horizontal collaboration.

VERSTREPEN S, COOLS M, CRUIJSSEN F, et al. 2009. A dynamic framework for managing horizontal cooperation in logistics[J]. International journal of logistics systems and management, 5(3/4): 228-248.

VERSTREPEN S, JACOBS K, 2012. CO^3 test case report: creation of an orchestrated horizontal collaboration for road bundling between 2 shippers.

VICS, 2004. VICS CPFR: an overview. Voluntary interindustry commerce standard, May, available at: www.cpfr.org.

WALLENBURG C M, RAUE J S, 2011. Conflict and its governance in horizontal cooperations of logistics service providers[J]. International journal of physical distribution & logistics management, 41(4):385-400.

WALLER M, JOHNSON M E, DAVIS T, 1999. Vendor-managed inventory in the retail supply chain[J]. Journal of business logistics, 20(1):183-204.

WINSBERG E, 2003. Simulated experiments: methodology for a virtual world[J]. Philosophy of science, 70(1):105-125.

WOMACK J P, JONES D T, ROOS D, 1990. The machine that changed the world: the story of lean production—Toyota's secret weapon in the global car wars that is now revolutionizing world industry[M]. New York: Simon & Schuster Ltd.

XIE M, CHEN J, 2005. Studies on horizontal cooperation among homogenous retailers based on multi-agent simulation: 2005 3rd IEEE international conference on industrial informatics[C]. Piscataway: IEEE Press: 181-186.

XU Y, ZHU X, 2013. Research on information sharing problem in retailer-dominant supply chain based on the MAS: proceedings of the 25th Chinese Control and decision conference (2013 CCDC) [C]. Shenyang: Northeastern University Press.

YIN R K, 2003. Case study research: design and methods[M]. 3rd ed. Thousand

Oaks: Sage Publications.

YIN R K, 2009. Case study research: design and methods [M]. 4th ed. Thousand Oaks: Sage Publications.

YU C, WONG T N, 2015. An agent-based negotiation model for supplier selection of multiple products with synergy effect[J]. Expert systems with applications, 42(1): 223-237.

ZHANG C, ZHANG C, 2007. Design and simulation of demand information sharing in a supply chain[J]. Simulation modelling practice and theory, 15(1):32-46.

ZHANG Y, BHATTACHARYYA S, 2010. Analysis of B2B e-marketplaces: an operations perspective[J]. Information systems and eBusiness management, 8(3):235-256.

ZHU J, ONGGO B S S, SPRING M, 2014. Horizontal collaboration in logistics: a typology of collaboration modes: EurOMA conference 2014 [C].